AMERICA'S CORPORATE BRAIN DRAIN

AMERICA'S CORPORATE BRAIN DRAIN

Why we leave
Where we go
How we can reverse the flow

Babs Ryan

Sparks Worldwide LLC
Chicago

Sparks Worldwide LLC, PO BOX 10527, Chicago, IL 60610-0527

Limit of Liability/Disclaimer of Warranty: Although extensive efforts have been made in preparing this book, the author/publisher makes no representations or warranties with respect to the accuracy or completeness of the contents of this book and concedes that there may be mistakes. Web site references in the end notes may no longer be available at the time of publication. Names and details of companies and/or individuals may have been altered to conceal their identities.

The author/publisher specifically disclaims any implied warranties of suitability for a particular purpose or for a particular situation. This book is designed to provide information on the subject matter covered and is sold with the understanding that the author/publisher is not engaged in offering legal, psychological, employment, political, or management services. If legal, employment, or other expert assistance is required, the services of a competent professional should be sought.

Neither the publisher nor author shall be liable for any loss or damage caused, or alleged to have been caused, directly or indirectly, by the information contained in this book, including but not limited to special, incidental, consequential, or other damages.

If you do not wish to be bound by the above, return this book to the publisher within 10 days of purchase for a full refund.

Publisher's Cataloging-in-Publication Data

Ryan, Babs.
    America's corporate brain drain : why we leave, where we go, how we can reverse the flow / Babs Ryan. -- 1st ed.
      p. cm.
    Includes bibliographical references and index.
    LCCN 2008902871
    ISBN-13: 978-0-9814947-0-8 (cloth)
    ISBN-10: 0-9814947-0-6 (cloth)

    1. Organizational change. 2. Job satisfaction-- United States. 3. Employee retention--United States. 4. Corporations--United States. I. Title.

HD58.8.R93 2008   658.4'06
                    QBI08-600126

Printed in the United States of America

10 9 8 7 6 5 4 3 2 1

Available in bulk at discount prices and online. For more information, go to http://www.braindrain.biz.

To Dad
In your footsteps, again.

Contents

Preface

Sixty-seven percent of American workers dream of starting their own companies. I wasn't one of them. Early in my career in the corporate world, I tasted success. I was a marketing director by age 26, living in London, driving a company BMW, and merrily globetrotting.

Identified by my company's executive board as a high-potential business leader, I was one of the few chosen for its career development program, or programming, depending on your point of view. In my first programming session, the trainer asked: "What do you want to be doing in five years?"

Without hesitation, I replied, "Global division leader in a huge company." Five years later, I was self-employed.

I boomeranged several times between corporate America and the American dream, entrepreneurship. When I vented frustration about corporate politics, innovation atrophy, and roadblocks, friends reminded me how I was happiest when running the show. During annual performance reviews, several of my bosses secretly coaxed me to "think about" starting my own business. I suspected they were doing the same and was proven correct on many occasions.

I can pinpoint the moment I realized my friends, mentors, and coaches were right. When I announced my plans to quit one job, my brusque boss surprised me by begging me stay. He promised: "I'll reorganize the department." I declined, explaining that my level of responsibility was blocked since he was unlikely to move up or change jobs and appeared in good health—although not quite in those words.

"The p-p-problem is," he stuttered, "that you want *my* job."

No, I didn't. I wanted his boss's, boss's, boss's job. I wasn't suffering from a bout of narcissism or egomania. Quite simply, I was not afraid.

What are *they* afraid of? Alas, we can think of many corporate executives who would fail to prove that their companies earned a dime more because of their unique contributions. In fact, companies realize losses by paying their salaries. Lacking the ability to make a difference running a department, they certainly couldn't run a company, not even their own. Change jobs by going to another conglomerate, and they might be found out. So they do anything to prevent change.

According to the workers who can make a difference, the most oft-mentioned tactics employed to prevent changes were:

1. Maintaining decision-making empires by ensuring competent workers were channeled into a myriad of ambiguous, powerless departments and positions

2. Preventing products from changing to block new hires or innovators from having greater expertise

3. Bullying or endorsing bullies to weed out threats

4. Hiding behind the veneer of teamwork to mask their lack of individual contributions

Because the majority of us really do want to make a difference in our livelihoods, we started to hate big businesses. So the best and brightest, who were not afraid, changed. They left to run companies, because they can.

Business-book readers have sought magic bullets for instilling leadership, innovation, and ethics in their companies—but they haven't found them. Prescriptive books recommended changes that readers had little influence over. Workers want solutions they can control, such as quitting.

Despite economic fluctuations, there will be a devastating talent shortage within the next seven years. Guess who'll be banging down the deserters' doors. Should you give them a high five or just one finger? Now the corporate leavers and those left behind (still in big companies) have all the control.

What prompted the research and writing of *America's Corporate Brain Drain* was the passion, anger, and frustration of so many people I spoke with who had worked in big companies. I had no trouble getting examples of corporate malfeasance. I was flooded, yes, nearly drowned by horror stories. Personal stories or those of a best friend overflowed with descriptors matching divorce: disillusioned, cheated, stunned. I thank those people for their candor and trust for this tapestry of what it's like to work in America. Their stories are true, but in many cases, I've changed names or details to protect the innocent from the wrath of the not-so-innocent.

Along the way, I discovered a few Goliath companies that everyone said were great places to work. We need more. In every big company where I worked, there was something wonderful I found that I took with me when I left—a group of brilliant, inspiring, lifelong friends. To those bosses, peers, staff, clients—you are the sparks! With all my heart, thank you for your contributions to the book, my business success, and personal happiness.

CHAPTER

1

The Funnel

August 17, 1985. Relief. My last Civil Aviation Administration of China (CAAC) flight. The national airline of People's Republic of China didn't have the best safety rating. As I rationalized my chances of survival by applying the law of averages, my desire to land in Hong Kong became more urgent.

I needed to use the restroom. On my last four-hour CAAC flight, the lavatory's light didn't work nor did the toilet flush. The stench was so horrendous, the woman behind me sprayed her entire bottle of Eau de Something to counterbalance the effect. Was that why the flight attendants handed out fans?

Mao had been dead less than 10 years. Only six years had passed since the trans-China Silk Road had been opened to American tourists. The Great Wall Hotel was still the only large Western-style hotel in the country, and it was not on my itinerary. Besides our small group, we saw no big-nose-round-eyes (or "Foreign Devils" as Westerners were better known) throughout west China. The 62-year-old Irish woman, who tripped, tumbled, and broke her arm because her camera was plastered to her eye, had to ride to the hospital sidesaddle on a bicycle rack because there were no privately owned motor vehicles except the single-seat tractors.

The plane touched down in Hong Kong. I'd arrived; my luggage had not. Fifteen roles of exposed film, a pair of cloisonné vases, a terra-cotta warrior tchotchke, two Mao suits (different colors, of course), a silk jacket, an airplane fan, clean underwear: I'd miss them. I'd also miss dodging the sea of bicycles to cross Main Street, grannies pushing bamboo strollers, morning tai chi on the sidewalks, knowing that I was eating the best food the country had to offer, eight-inch acupuncture needles hooked to electric currents, and Mao's imposing gaze over Tiananmen Square and his own mausoleum.

Hong Kong—a bastion of capitalism—just a hop, skip, and jump through passport control from "Communist" China. I watched the hustle and bustle of commerce from a friend's modern high-rise flat at the tip of Kowloon Peninsula. As well as having an unobstructed view of Victoria Harbour (water views bestow positive feng shui and are therefore more expensive), this apartment had maid's quarters. Cars, not bicycles, swarmed a dense network of roads. To prevent traffic gridlocks, exorbitant fines charged by the minute were imposed for breaking down in the tunnels linking Hong Kong Island.

Public toilets had marble walls and floors, and running water to wash hands. Ahhh.

The Hong Kong brain drain had already started; "brain drain" meaning the emigration of highly educated, skilled, or trained people. A few months before I arrived, the Sino-British Joint Declaration was finalized. The British government agreed to return Hong Kong to China on July 1, 1997. The brief agreement also stated that for 50 years hence, "The current social and economic systems in Hong Kong will remain unchanged, and so will the lifestyle. Rights and freedoms, including those of the person, of speech...of choice of occupation...will be ensured by law in the Hong Kong Special Administrative Region. Private property, ownership of enterprises, legitimate right of inheritance and foreign investment will be protected by law.... There will be free flow of capital."

Yet uncertainty about the future, particularly after the strong-arming during the Tiananmen Square uprising in 1989, fueled the exodus of Hong Kong's brightest. The brain drain peaked in 1992, lowering the unemployment rate to 2 percent.

It could be uncertainty about the future or politics: The peak of America's *corporate* brain drain has yet to be realized. During 2000, the young, the daring, the frustrated, the optimists, and the bored flocked to dot-com start-ups, causing the U.S. unemployment rate to dip below 4 percent, the lowest since the 1960s.

Alas, by 2001, the party was breaking up. Nevertheless, the dot-comers had tasted creative juices and entrepreneurial nectar, and were unlikely to feel satiated returning to "stable" Fortune 500 environments.

The next wave of the brain drain in America's biggest corporations has started. It's not the dot-com crew bailing out. This time, it's the leaders of innovation.

Here are the facts:

1. In *48 Days to the Work You Love*, author Dan Miller says 70 percent of white-collar workers are unhappy at their jobs. The Bureau of Labor Statistics found 67 percent unhappy workers. Salary.com's survey confirms that 2 out of 3 employees are looking for work elsewhere.[1] "Job hatred," the *Chicago Tribune* headlined, is "a crisis in corporate America."[2]

2. Half the workforce is comprised of baby boomers: the oldest boomers hit the national retirement age less than three years from now.[3] But they aren't willing to wait until age 65 to bolt from corporate America. Experienced boomers are packing their bags now, often negotiating for early retirement. Will they boomerang back to big business as consultants? Unlikely. An AARP study revealed that about half of those who do plan to work in their retirement years plan to put their energy into a new interest.[4] By 2010, the Bureau of Labor Statistics predicts a labor shortage of 5 to 10 million, primarily in the "knowledge" industries (aerospace, energy, health care, teaching, and high tech) that have an older-than-average workforce.

3. Wake up, big business. Today's American dream is entrepreneurship. Sixty-seven percent of employees dream of starting their own businesses.[5] Each year, 6 million of the best and brightest will embrace entrepreneurship.[6] According to the Kauffman Center for Entrepreneurial Leadership, today's 27 million small-business owners didn't get the boot—89.7 percent of entrepreneurs *quit* their former positions,[7] and the majority are getting even by competing head on, by producing successful

products related to their previous field that big brother squashed or ignored.[8] *Business 2.0* adds: "The number of workers who are delivering take-this-job-and-shove-it speeches and bailing for more rewarding, less spirit-crushing work is at a five-year high.... The Bureau of Labor Statistics' so-called quit rate, a measure of, as the name implies, people who have quit, has swelled by a third since 2003. There are now about 2.6 million people leaving their jobs each month, the same level as in the pre-9/11 economy." [9]

4. A 2006 collegegrad.com survey found that 70 percent of new college graduates say they would prefer working for a medium or small employer compared to a large company.[10] Fifty-six percent of college students say they're likely to start their own businesses or work for themselves someday. Twice as many students say they'd rather be a founder of a start-up company than CEO of a Fortune 1000 company.[11] Twenty-somethings are opting to live with Dad or Uncle Joe rather than earn enough to live alone while working for Uncle Sam or another big organization loaded with politics.

5. Big companies, unable to compete using the human resources they have and unable to attract outstanding leaders and producers, are looking elsewhere. *Christian Science Monitor* says, "No longer is it just Disney toys and Nike shoes made in Haiti and Indonesia. It is software engineering, accounting, and product development being outsourced to India, the Philippines, Russia, and China."[12] By 2015, 3.3 million U.S. white collar jobs will be overseas, according to Forrester Research.[13]

Every generation is coming to the realization that the majority of the brightest sparks aren't in big companies. Big business has lost its minds.

What the statistics don't convey is the resentment, and yes, anger, toward big business. The leavers and the left behinds (those still in big companies) are pissed off.

At my Entrepreneur Club meeting last week, I met a new member who talked excitedly about a product he developed at a company I'd worked for. "Have you heard about it?" Jake begged to know.

I called my friend Carol, still working for Jake's former employer. "Hey, Carol, what ever happened to Jake's product?"

"It was a great idea, but it never went anywhere."

If I had a dime for every time... In large companies, most employees can rattle off a list of great ideas that never went anywhere. And for each great idea, they can come up with some dog ideas also called "new" products that were launched, and failed.

The innovation leaders, surrounded by dogs, are deciding to leave the pack. Coincidentally, they are leaving to search for the same thing as the consumers they aim to please. Alf Nucifora, a national business reporter and host of the *Power Lunch* business radio program in Atlanta, remarks on the results of the Yankelovich *Monitor* annual trends and lifestyle survey:

> Unquestionably, novelty in today's marketplace is conspicuous by its absence. Hence, the boom in boredom.... Eighty-four percent believe that today's TV programs are boring. Seventy-one percent believe the same about big-budget movies. The retail vista is crowded with sameness for as far as the eye can see.... The fast-food parity of McDonald's, Wendy's and Taco Bell is matched by the mundane experience of category killers like Home Depot and big boxes like Wal-Mart...already 88 percent of Americans say they're bored with the Internet.

The answer, says Yankelovich's David M. Bersoff, is to "build surprise, novelty and interest not just in products but in the consumer's experience with products."[14]

Top talent are thinking like shoppers. McKinsey's study, *The War for Talent*, concluded that employment seekers and employees see jobs as "products." For smart executives who thrive on staying ahead of the competition, the "product" positions available today from large corporations are uncompetitive, me-too, boring, lacking novelty, or, the most common descriptor, frustrating. Where are these top guns going when they can't find the right "product"?

The big companies' mantra is: "Don't build ideas, buy them." The entrepreneur thinks: "If you can't buy it (because it doesn't exist), build it." Fed up with unfulfilled promises of opportunities to build and market new products, the brightest are starting their own companies—and competing head-on with the large corporations they've deserted.

Despite the relatively diminutive resources of small companies, the U.S. Small Business Administration reports that they produce 55 percent of innovations, twice as many per employee as large companies. The National Commission on Entrepreneurship reiterates that more than half of innovations come from small firms and adds that 67 percent of inventions and 95 percent of all radical innovations since World War II have come out of small businesses. It provides examples: Air-conditioning, airplanes, frozen food, and high-capacity computers are among the innovations brought to you by pint-size companies. New women-owned firms grew by 13.9 percent between 1997 and 2000, while overall the new business rate was 9.1 percent.

Overall, the 27 million small businesses in the U.S. provide between two-thirds and three-quarters of net *new* jobs and represent more than 99 percent of all employers. These companies employ almost half of the U.S. workforce. Most started as one- or two-man bands.

America's corporate brain drain. You'd think that Goliath companies would be anxiously sandbagging the funnel to stop the exodus. You'd be wrong. Korn/Ferry International's executive survey reported that only 21 percent of companies were taking action now to prevent future talent shortages.

Should they be worried? Since the beginning of 2002, the number of self-employed has been slowly, but steadily, increasing, according to the U.S. Department of Labor. The U.S. Bureau of Labor Statistics cites that the gap between the number of jobs and available workers is closing, and the available workers won't necessarily be qualified to fill the open jobs. In *Employment Management Today*, Rebecca Theim says, "Talented workers are showing greater willingness to go it on their own, rather than work for less-than-stellar employers."[15] *BusinessWeek Online* confirmed that, stating that the labor report is showing "a record rise in self-employed workers."[16]

Cynics claim that the increase in self-employment is due to layoffs and an unstable economy. They believe the situation will reverse soon after the big firms start to hire again. As the layoffs dive deeper into the work pool, and some of the high-salaried high performers are swept away in the cost cutting, they figure, the cream of the crop will inevitably market their own talents. Acclaimed business consultant and author Peter Drucker stated that 30 percent of laid-off managers start working as consultants.

The cynics' view is shortsighted. The young and the restless (and the older restless) aren't returning to big companies just because they start hiring again. According to a nationwide survey by Challenger, Gray & Christmas, jobless execs younger than 40 who started businesses increased by 36 percent in the first three months of 2002 although national unemployment was falling.[17]

Although the percentage of laid-off workers who started their own businesses is rising (to 11.4 percent), the vast majority of consultants and self-employed earned that status through choice. Remember that the Kauffman Center found that among people who launched their own businesses, 89.7 percent chose to quit their current positions. Furthermore, the Center claims that entrepreneurship rises during recessions since innovative businesspeople perceive that start-up costs are lower, and they want to spend more time with their families. Just ask laborers remaining at Dow Chemical, Eastman Kodak, Cigna, AT&T, Motorola, WorldCom, Coca-Cola, or Circuit City. Not only are many doing the work of two, three, or four people, but every day they worry that they'll get called into the manager's office to join their former colleagues who are receiving unemployment checks. Job security is ancient history. In a study of 3,600 workers by economists Charles E. Manski of Northwestern University and John D. Straub of University of Wisconsin-Madison, those who work for others experienced less job security than the self-employed. There's never been a better time to go it alone.

What's next? Havoc. Talent-starved HR recruiters and corporate senior "leaders" will be hunting entrepreneurs, small-company employees (now half the workforce), and deserters. What will they use as bait for workers who have tasted freedom? Can they delay retirees from enjoying second careers and second homes? What happens if the government steps up patrolling the *fronteras*, preventing pools of hard-working immigrants from taking high-demand service positions?

The most likely employees to abandon the supertankers will continue to be the best and the brightest: the "change agents," the mavericks, the visionaries. In *Leaders Talk Leadership*, top executives say that the capacity to lead change will be the most sought-after skill for top management due to intensifying competition. They believe the corporations that will survive will do so by putting the best people, who can lead change, in charge of opportunities, not problems.[18] That would be a significant about-face.

Corporate America never thought it would come to this. With its larger resources and promises, top talent poured in. But large corporations have become funnels. One by one, the most flexible and heavy hitters have found their way through the passage to a better deal. Getting through the narrow passage to make the break and start one's own business seems daunting, but once one is through the passage, the world is wider and there are far more opportunities. The force of gravity is powerful. Seeing others successfully make the transition makes it easier for those left behind to leave. There's nothing blocking the funnel, and soon all the finest talent will be gone. The rough stuff that can't cut it will be all that's left inside.

In Hong Kong, many émigrés returned to their homeland, due to growing opportunities—as entrepreneurs. How can you benefit from America's corporate plight? Whether you're among the 27 million who are already divorced from corporate life or still toughing it out, you'll now discover how you can boomerang—bounce back and end up on top by capitalizing on America's corporate brain drain.

CHAPTER

2

Process Jobs That Cut the Cheese

November 25, 1989. The end of my trip to the U.S.S.R. was drawing near. A few weeks earlier, I'd arrived in Moscow just in time for the November 7 celebration of the Russian Revolution, marked by a parade in Red Square. Snow was gently falling as thousands of citizens carrying pictures of Lenin, colorful streamers, and red balloons marched toward St. Basil's Cathedral. Like a Disneyland snow globe.

Last stop, Leningrad. The city was beautiful but horribly cold. I'd always wanted to travel to the U.S.S.R. I marveled at the historical royal treasures and architecture; buildings that looked like Wedgewood china.

I had just finished another bland dinner. The highlight of the meal was a small dish of low-grade caviar. Tourists always wanted to say they'd had Russian caviar. As I left, the busboys hurriedly cleared the plates from the first seating to prepare for the soon-to-arrive onslaught of noisy foreigners for the second dinner seating. Donna and Mark stopped to share their misery at the doorway of the dining hall.

"They stole my chocolate bar, right out of my suitcase," said Donna.

"The room cleaners took my cigarettes," sniped Mark.

Donna would not be outdone: "They stole my underwear!"

In 1989, shortages of everything were a problem. It wasn't about money: It was about access. There was little opportunity for Russians to get well-constructed underwear, Marlboro cigarettes, or Cadbury chocolate, unless they worked in a hotel with foreign guests.

"Margaret said they took her perfume and toothpaste." I wasn't sure if Donna was more upset losing about the chocolate she'd been rationing or the disappearance of her last bits of clean underwear. The rationale of the housekeeping staff was that it was simple and inexpensive for tourists to acquire more English chocolate, American cigarettes, or French underwear, so one shouldn't mind losing easily replaceable items. Their rationale conveniently disregarded the fact that it was impossible to replace clean underwear during your two-week trip.

I was about to excuse myself to tend to my travelers'-tummy issue when, out of the corner of my eye, I spotted the busboys doing something that would permanently diminish my appetite. Most tourists didn't really like caviar (particularly this caviar) and, after a spoonful, left the remains. The busboys scooped the remaining caviar from each little dish into a communal bowl, reset the tables for the second seating, and distributed the communal contents into the clean dishes for the next horde of hungry tourists.

I remembered all the times I stood on my virtual, pro-travel podium, adamant that people have a greater chance of getting hepatitis A in New York City or London than in Asia. Wrong. Suddenly, I had a flashback of Tuesday's beef stew. It looked suspiciously like Monday's leftover beef medallions.

Soviets obviously believed in sharing—underwear, food, and much more. A typical vending machine, for example, had a single glass in the dispenser rather than wasteful, disposable paper cups or bottles. Drop in a few kopeks, and your beverage dispensed into the glass. Enjoy your drink, and return the used glass to the receptacle for the next thirsty passerby.

Eating was always a highly rated activity on my travel itinerary. The summation of my trip to the Soviet Union in 1989 was "fabulous place, bring your own food."

Supermarkets were anything but "super" in Russia, where food seemed scarce. The grocery store was a warehouse of empty shelves with no more than six choices of "food," but massive quantities of those few items. Jars of tomatoes, bottles of cooking oil, some type of spice in plastic bags, and a pile of pigs' heads in a freezer were today's specials. According to the Russians, anything advertised or available in quantity was not worth having.

Here was the paradox. In Tashkent, Uzbekistan (another Soviet republic), I saw mountains of fresh fruit, vegetables, rice, pasta, breads, and pastries. Stacks of watermelons that could fill a football field, pyramids of pomegranates, apricots, grapes, and pears.

A trip out of town revealed why none of Uzbekistan's healthy choices made it to Russian grocery stores. By the side of the road was a delivery truck with its hatch down. There was a crowd of people clamoring at the back where the driver was gleefully passing the cargo to the highest bidders. Guess he got "held up" during his delivery.

The Russians weren't starving. If the food wasn't in the supermarkets, where was it? As I wandered through the neighborhoods of Moscow, I saw small, specialized stores—one selling milk, another displaying chicken, a bakery with an assortment of bread, a small cheese store, a cake shop. Hmmm, bread and cheese for lunch sounded appealing. Not much chance of getting the runs from that!

When I entered the cheese shop, there were three long queues and I wasn't sure which line I should wait in. Noting my confusion, a woman directed me to queue up directly behind her. Whispering, she complained about how it took all day to shop for food. There were three lines in each shop, she explained. One to place your order, the second to pay, the third to pick up the order.

The only people who looked more miserable than the shoppers were the workers behind the counters. Talk about emotionally crippling jobs. I suppose it's because a person who is competent at taking orders isn't necessarily competent enough to operate a cash register. Of course, a person who operates a cash register wouldn't be able to hand the right piece of cheese to the right customer. The person who cuts and wraps the cheese must be incapable of doing anything service related. It *must* be more efficient if each employee only does one thing. He or she becomes an expert order taker or cheese cutter and can do it much faster. Building employee expertise must create phenomenal job satisfaction. Just think: If each employee fully serviced one customer at a time, instead of doing just one task for all people, there would be one extremely long queue instead of three long ones—right? There must be fewer mistakes because the order takers and cheese cutters are specialists. With only one person handling the cash, employee honesty wouldn't be an issue. This type of thing would never happen in *our* country.

Don't laugh too loudly. As new General Motors CEO, Rick Wagoner gained superstar status by reducing the design-to-market cycle time of new vehicles from four years to 20 months. All he did was modify the organizational structure of design decision making to create one queue instead of three. Wagoner deserves applause because, unlike at most large companies, he's not only made progress at building walkways between the departmental empires, but he's done it in such a way that the results are impressive. Not quite as impressive though, as at Kawasaki. In 1986, when I was head of the marketing department for Kawasaki in the U.K., Japan's design-to-market cycle time (pun intended) was eight months for their motorcycles. Granted, the average superbike had only 3,000 parts, but Japanese suspension damping systems and engine performance enhancements were so light, small, and advanced that the car industry used to imitate them. Eight months. Blank sheet to street.

If you've worked for a large corporation, no doubt you've been through lots of reorganizations, or to use the more politically correct euphemism, restructurings. In more than a decade working for large companies, I never had the same manager for more than two years. The average tenure was about a year. One of my staff, rated a top performer, had 14 managers in four years doing the same tasks with the same type of products. The statistics on changes in management are consistent with my experience. The proportion of managers who change jobs each year has risen from 10 percent in 1980 to 30 percent. Restructuring is an increasing reason; promotion is a decreasing factor.[1]

Ever watch a magician do the trick with the ball under the walnut shells? After showing a red ball under one of the shells, the trickster shuffles the shells and you're supposed to guess which shell the red ball is under. The trick is that the magician removes the ball before shuffling the shells. No win. This typifies large-company restructuring. The jobs and people rarely change; they've just been shuffled around a little. And no matter where you end up, no one's a winner.

When no one's winning, you shuffle the shells again and again.

What about the company with 700 employees that divided its marketing department into three separate marketing groups, declaring that the new structure would serve its clients better (or was there another reason)? The products of all three departments were structured the same, and they all shared the same client contacts. Upon restructuring, marketing support functions couldn't report to any single marketing leader, since that group might get preferential service over other marketing teams. So marketing support areas reported to various other departments. Hence, three employees needed to be present at each client debriefing. There were three times as many support function meetings. New committee meetings were required to coordinate the output of the three departments. Weeks were spent redoing CEO presentations because the three marketing heads didn't agree on the format or information in presentations for bigwigs, since each department would want to include only the data that would emphasize its successes. You can imagine the impact on customer service and sales. Clients moved to competitors who didn't make them wait in the three queues.

When I was in that Russian cheese shop, U.S. auto production lines weren't much different. Little more than a decade ago, the union employee who put handles in doors all-the-live-long-day began to insert the lock cylinders too. He or she began to rotate jobs with colleagues on a daily or bi-hourly basis and could participate in decisions on budgeting. It took this long to realize that it's more lucrative to have five door experts than one handle expert, one window expert, one lock expert, etc. Maybe someday, they'll have all *car* experts.

Former Toyota CEO Fujio Cho revealed that formal standardization of work processes did not exist in the Japan plant. Instead, "work procedures in Japan are taught by experienced workers."[2] In the U.S., it takes 13.5 months for employees to reach maximum efficiency in a new job.[3] Will the cheese order takers last 13.5 months to train up-and-coming cheese order takers? Or will they leave to open their own cheese shops? (Fear not, this is not another business book all about moving cheese.)

Welcome to the 21st century. Now the store doesn't just have cheese. According to *Fortune* magazine, most automakers believed that having separate plants for each model line was the key to greater productivity. Honda changed the game by modifying its production lines to handle every model, with minimal changeover requirements.[4] Watch to see who wins.

I met Joanne on my first day of work in 1989. She was friendly and feisty and, above all, a smart businessperson. A division of retail operations wasn't profitable. Joanne's professionalism, dedication, efficiency, and honesty had won her many friends in the local stores. Now her job was to close the stores—all of them. The company was going to focus on selling direct to the public through direct mail. As usual, Joanne was successful not only at completing the task, but at salvaging friendships.

Joanne's performance was about to be rewarded with a sidestep to the service quality department.

Just as Six Sigma has been all the rage in the past 10 years, in the late 1980s "service quality" was the buzz word. Big companies rapidly played follow the leader to construct service quality departments whose mission was to improve the quality of products and customer service. The methodology was to create quantifiable benchmarks and measure performance against those targets.

Prior to Joanne's transfer, telephone complaints were near the top of the list of quality issues. In 1989, most companies had not yet adopted voice mail, which required expensive new hardware and software. (By the way, Gordon Matthews, an entrepreneur who held 35 patents, invented Voice Mail.[5]) Open-plan offices sounded like carolers' bells at Christmas—ring, ring, ring.

So a service quality rule was passed that no phone could be left ringing more than three times (quantifiable). If your colleague was away from his or her desk, or you were walking by on your way to a meeting, you were required to answer that ringing phone and take a message.

With employees scrambling to answer phones, the focus shifted, not surprisingly, to the switchboard operators. Direct dialing was in our future, so all calls still went through the main switchboard and were then transferred, or switched, to the employee's or department's extension. Now that the extensions were being answered, employees claimed that customers and clients were complaining that switchboard operators took too long to answer phones.

After analyzing the call volumes, current performance, and caller expectations, and quantifying the "defect rate" (sounds a lot like Six Sigma to me), someone had decided that the switchboard operators would have to answer all external calls within five rings (quantifiable).

Since the operators' jobs and bonuses were dependent upon answering within five rings, they were not going to fail. To meet the hurdle, they had to get rid of the customers who were already on the lines more quickly. In the past, callers were allowed to spend more than a few seconds explaining their needs so they were transferred to the best people to solve their problems or sell them the right product. Helping people, after all, was the most enjoyable part of the operator's job.

To gain companywide support for the new service quality department (coming to your department soon!), the company newsletter publicized the telephone study findings and decisions. There was incredible pressure to beat that five-ring goal. And beat it they did. Customers and clients heard "hello" before five rings. Then, they were cut off mid-sentence to be transferred, often to the wrong department, so that the next call could be answered. The "nicest" employees (read "those who would complain the least and worked the hardest") received most of the misdirected calls. They took and delivered dozens of messages for colleagues on other floors who were away or busy, because you could only transfer the call if the extension picked up to prevent more ringing. (When's the last time you heard a human being answer the phone at a big company?)

Enter Joanne. Joanne tried to solve the problems without creating new ones by using all the business and people skills she used in her former assignments. She spent hours listening to the operators and tried to preserve the most enjoyable part of their workday—the part that kept them at the retailer—interacting with customers and clients. She provided the operators with information, including new data, so *they* could solve the problem, presented several viable alternatives, and developed a motivational plan to promote the best operators to other service departments. Ultimately, the decisions were not

Joanne's. Daniel had authority over switchboard operations, and any changes, or lack thereof, would be his decision. Perhaps Daniel should have listened to the operators and collected new data.

Joanne stayed in service quality long enough to pass her 10-year mark in the company. Then she left to start her own. Today, Joanne owns a leading interior design firm, with many of the firm's managers as her clients.

Joanne is typical of top performers in large companies. Businesspeople with outstanding leadership and change management abilities usually leave soon after being "rewarded" with a "process" role. **A process role is one where the person didn't cause the existing problems but has to fix them without having responsibility for or authority over the products involved or the people who will have to implement the changes.** In process roles, you do not own decision making for the company's products or services. Process roles are created because:

1. The organization needs to address a companywide issue (e.g., product quality),

2. The company lacks employees who have specialist skills (e.g., e-business),

3. Other big companies are creating those process departments,

4. Managers are incompetent,

5. Management will not fire incompetent staff (see 4 above),

6. There is no current job role available for a favorite and/or high-performing employee, or unpopular and/or incompetent person, and/or

7. A competent line manager is moved from managing products to coordinating a process because he/she threatens a mediocre boss's reputation.

In the bank, a few vice presidents ended up with the title "special projects." Obtaining this inauspicious title ensured the VP would be making lots of phone calls with the office door closed. On the flip side, you could be "director of" anything (or nothing), meaning you'd be around awhile.

As Joanne proved, she was capable of running an entire cheese shop or large division of a cheese producer. Instead, her new role was only to fix cheese shop problems created by those incapable of running an entire cheese shop or large division.

There's a simple litmus test to reveal if your company has too many process roles. How many people attend meetings with external parties? How many are present in business pitches? If you have more than four, you're probably representing an acidic company with incompetents in the key roles masking their lack of skills with an army of pissed-off process workers with no authority or responsibility.

How many times has your "team" outnumbered the client's? How many attendees bring nothing except their egos, including the sales or account manager? (Yes, gatekeepers are process managers.) Who are the puff daddies in the room who only spent a few hours (or minutes) reviewing presentation materials? Who generated the ideas and put together the pitch for a prospective partner? Why would you believe other companies hire people who are so stupid they can't see the differences? Why would you want to do business with a company full of stupid people? Why would a potential client want to do business with people who assume they are stupid?

You don't see small companies bringing six or eight people to business meetings with external vendors or clients. It's not because they can't get that many people to pose for a couple hours. It's because the few small-business attendees who participate are empowered to make decisions, understand the client's needs, developed the strategy and tactics for fulfilling the client's needs, have the knowledge and expertise to answer the client's questions on the spot, *and* are going to implement the decisions made. **They are producers, not processors.**

Process roles drive the best and brightest out of companies. Not only do great employees who become process owners leave; so do the forward-thinking others who have to deal with the growing bureaucracy.

There's countless process roles. Here's a list of the top eight silliest process roles in corporations today, and why, if your company has these, it really cuts the cheese.

Silly Process Role #1
Quality Guru

Recently, the most popular process roles are "master black belt" and "black belt." These are the titles for the so-called champions of Six Sigma methodology. Six Sigma is the new millennium moniker for service quality, and to be "in," you have to say you're doing it. As someone who has earned Six Sigma Green Belt Certification, I'm happy to inform those who have not been baptized (or never took a statistics course) that Six Sigma translates to 3.4 defects per million for each product or service transaction. In other words, if your company manufactures screws, fewer than four out of every million produced should be defective to ensure customer satisfaction. In a service industry role, such as answering switchboard calls, the theory is that you would determine through market research which level of performance customers would find acceptable (e.g., five rings) and attempt to ensure that there are six or more rings only 3.4 times for every million callers.

OK, I may have inaccurately described what the defect rate should be, or did I? Because 10 people doing the same project wouldn't define the problem the same way, leading every one of them to a different solution after filling out all the same charts and going to all the meetings.

As early as January 2001, *Fortune* magazine published an article titled "Why You Can Safely Ignore Six Sigma," which highlighted how Six Sigma made no difference in rate of new product success, nor would it improve sales of outdated bow-wow products, despite improvements in quality. In that article, David Fitzpatrick, the worldwide leader of Deloitte Consulting's Lean Enterprise Practice stated: "...I would say fewer than 10 percent of companies are doing [Six Sigma] to the point where it's going to significantly affect the balance sheet and the share price in any meaningful period of time."[6] He states that it's easy to track defects if you're manufacturing pills. But identifying and quantifying errors or mistakes in the customer service center is subjective and vague. In short, it depends on who's counting.

It may sound as if I'm bashing Six Sigma *methodology*. Untrue. Improving quality and making people's lives better is the driving force behind every inventor and dynamic businessperson. A lot of Six Sigma methodology makes sense, but creation of more process roles to integrate Six Sigma into organizations is causing more problems than it solves. Remember, Six Sigma is just another reincarnation of service quality, and the literal meaning of "service quality" is each employee doing the job right.

Concisely, **Six Sigma process roles, like other process roles, exist because of incompetence of the existing employees who should be doing those jobs.** Six Sigma departments exist because people simply aren't doing their jobs right.

If 10 percent of all the screws your company produces are defective or customers constantly complain about your crummy service, you need to do something about the *people* who have been managing or doing those jobs. Many times, the product stinks and should be replaced or significantly improved. If the people who work in your company are not capable of replacing or improving the products they sell, replace the people with others whose capabilities *include* product development.

The worst thing you can do to fix quality issues in a company is to hire people whose sole job is to try to get others to do their jobs right. If an existing employee lacks the training or experience to do the job right, fix *that*. If the employee can't or won't integrate new skills or product improvements, remove him or her. The solution is to increase the breadth of knowledge, experience, and expertise of existing, capable employees, thereby improving employee satisfaction. Creating a labyrinth organization of niche "experts," form fillers, and rubber stampers will never reduce problems and increases office politics.

Read this discussion-string rebuttal by a Six Sigma advocate on an e-bulletin board:

Sorry…but Six Sigma is a whole lot more than the conventional quality tools, haphazardly applied. You are correct in stating that none of the tools are [sic] NEW. Six Sigma however provides a roadmap, on how/when to use each tool. Conventional methods don't do that. Furthermore (and most importantly), Six Sigma REQUIRES that projects actually affect the bottom line a significant amount. Conventional methods don't require that. And in addition, Six Sigma requires accountability from the project leader....[7]

Give me a break. Do we really need Six Sigma so that competent screw manufacturing experts know how and when to talk to their customers and prospects, and to investigate all alternatives before changing the screw production? Is it only since Six Sigma that well-managed companies require that projects impact the bottom line? The last sentence of this e-entry is fascinating. The advocate thinks Six Sigma methodology *improves* quality because the "project leader" (read process role) is accountable.

What about the operations manager in charge of the manufacturing. Isn't he/she accountable? If the product is defective, isn't the engineer or profit and loss (P&L) leader accountable? Shouldn't the operations manager and engineers or P&L leader have the competency to fix the problem, or involve the resources to design and manufacture a better screw? Can't *they* assemble the temporary expertise, hire *and* manage people who can, or obtain the knowledge required to make things better? Why are they called "managers"?

The five steps of Six Sigma methodology (although there are several permutations so that it can cover everything from new product creation to changing the toilet paper in the men's room) are Define (the problem), Measure, Analyze, Improve, Control. Do you know any great business leader who hasn't always followed these steps in decision making? If you provide the set of Six Sigma tools and a reasonable amount of training or retraining to a competent employee, surely he or she is capable of choosing and applying any relevant tools. Undoubtedly it can be done without adding new departments, testing, months of training, mountains of meetings to discuss which and how many forms to fill in, and "special" meetings to present the forms.

Companies are crediting cost savings and quality improvements (that are taking longer to achieve) to implementing Six Sigma. Many of the accredited improvements happened in spite of, not because of, Six Sigma. **Let's put "quality people" in all roles throughout the company, instead of creating a few "quality roles."**

This just in (insert ticker tape noise here). Six Stigma, er, Sigma, has been updated by adding an new exciting process called "Lean" to be called, you guessed it, "Lean Six Sigma." This has as much potential as a diet on a cruise ship. (Insert SNL's Debbie Downer noise here.)

Today I called the main switchboard of Gap, Inc. It took 2:38 minutes for a polite operator to answer the phone. Everything is relative. I have waited 38 minutes on the American Express Membership Rewards points redemption line even though it costs $395 annually to have "the privileges" of Platinum Card membership. (Yes, I am aware that "Membership Has Its Privileges" is no longer Amex's tagline. But I can't "Do More" in "My Life" while waiting half an hour for them to answer the phone.) These waiting times may not represent costs or lost business for these companies (I haven't seen the data). In fact, if I do wait on the phone long enough to redeem my 80,000 points for an airline ticket to go scuba diving in Palau, Micronesia, it will cost Amex hundreds of dollars. If I'm not willing to wait on hold with doo-be-doo-be-doo music for 38 minutes, they've avoided a large expense. I finally hung up, called the general Platinum Card toll-free number, and was transferred immediately to the redemption department. They still tell Platinum Card members to call the same points redemption line as the people who pay $110 per year for 38 "rewarding" minutes of waiting. Guess they didn't adopt Six Sigma. Only kidding; they did!

What if the company knows that slow response times are damaging its business? Perhaps the problem is someone cut too many staff or the wrong staff so that the cost of lost business exceeds the payroll savings. Maybe the system was down? There could be any number of reasons. **The worst way to handle problems is to assign a separate department to identifying what's wrong and fixing it.** This is a clear sign that your functional managers aren't doing or can't do their own jobs. Functional managers should have accountability, authority, and responsibility for identifying and fixing issues and growing the business. If they can't do it, find someone who can. Don't hire a Six Sigma babysitter.

Companies that had quality issues before Six Sigma will continue to have issues, because the process is subjective. Management can decide that some solutions are "out of scope," i.e., cannot be considered, such as exiting certain employees. Research questions are limited to suppositions by the authors. Often, the solution to the problem is limited to options collected via internal brainstorming or selected employee opinions. Would anyone ever recommend a solution that would eliminate his or her job? What if the contributors of the hypotheses are not aware of new technology, aren't skilled at generating original ideas, or wouldn't abandon a current product in lieu of one they have no expertise with? Suppose the cause of defects is corrupt executive managers. (We've seen that recently.) Finally, the weighting of how good and how important each potential solution is on the Six Sigma Pugh Matrix is arbitrary. With a functional manager and a process manager now involved, who will make those subjective decisions that will influence the action taken? Will any action make a difference if functional managers simply aren't doing their jobs? Why believe that they'll do their jobs in the future?

If you want your top-performing business experts and future leaders who have the potential to captain your company to go to your competitor someday, sic a Six Sigma champion on them. Now, instead of spending time growing the company, they can spend time deciding how many and which charts to fill in, and have tons of meetings to present charts.

Six Sigma methodology is becoming passé in the corporate world, and the number of job descriptions requesting Six Sigma training has dwindled to a trickle. No doubt, another euphemism for "people doing their jobs correctly" will rise from the ashes to replace "Six Sigma" and "service quality," because the same "boys' club" members (who are not necessarily boys) will still be in the top jobs.

If you've found reading about Six Sigma long-winded, imagine how competent managers feel about having to deal with this hype every day because of their "unqualified" colleagues. Makes you want to leave and start your own business. But it's certainly not the only process role that makes working in big companies a big nightmare. And you'll learn why this and other process roles have opened the door of opportunity for those smart enough to avoid them.

3

The Cheesiest Job in America Today: Project Manager

November 19, 2007. As I skated on skis to the lift, I faced Kofi Annan, former UN Secretary-General, who was carefully stepping through the man-made snow with a group of suited followers.

"*Sabaah al-khayr*," ("good morning" in Arabic) I said instinctively, trying to remember where I'd seen him before. I'd studied Arabic for six months and was delighted when mistaken by locals as Lebanese. Although everyone spoke English, I was going to use every one of the 500 Arabic words I could remember on this trip.

"Thank you," he kindly replied.

I sat on the ski lift, quickly placed the face with the name, then returned to wondering why it felt so bloody cold in a 30° domed ski resort when it was only 95° outside.

All the world was in Dubai. In another year, the world's tallest building, largest shopping mall, and grandest passenger and cargo airport would be here. I wanted to be a permanent fixture here, too. I yearned to contribute to 9 percent annual population growth. I missed living in an international community.

More than 80 percent of the population is expatriates. Although a minority in their own country, most Emiratis are intentionally and proudly distinctive—men impeccably groomed in blinding white, starched *kandouras* (robes) with nary a wrinkle; women made up like movie stars in bejeweled or embroidered silk *abayas* (robes) and matching *hijabs* (head scarves).

The land of opportunity. "What do you like most about living here, and what do you dislike most?" I asked everyone. Disney World is a great place to visit, but you probably wouldn't want to live there. I'd lived abroad for 11 years, so I knew the difference between being a tourist and an expat.

Without hesitation, expats boasted how this is one of the safest places in the world.

Dina, a former client, is Palestinian. In return for treating me to some of Dubai's hippest restaurants, I brought Dina a gift box filled with almond-stuffed dates. "Don't leave it on your car seat," I warned her. "Someone will smash your window."

"Huh?" She didn't understand.

Imagine never expecting your car to be vandalized or stolen. Or not having to worry about your house being burgled, getting raped or mugged, or your kids being abducted or abused by a pedophile. Wouldn't it be nice if you didn't have to think about being accidentally shot in a gang drive-by shooting in the mall parking lot or being intentionally driven off the road by debt-ridden Mr. Road Rage, in his gas-guzzling SUV, who had a bad day at work (surprise—every day for him is a bad day at work)? How nice to eat in a restaurant and not watch over your shoulder for some loser who will try to steal your handbag and identity.

I'm miffed by the ignorance of people whose first comment about Dubai is about how unsafe the Middle East is. I live in a "nice" neighborhood in Chicago. In the past two years, I've witnessed the aftermath of four separate crimes within 100 feet of my front door: a purse snatching, beating, pistol-whipping of a frail 70-year-old dry cleaning store owner, and property theft. The Bureau of Justice Statistics shows that America now leads in the world in imprisoned citizens per capita—one in 100. And that's just Yanks who got caught and couldn't afford a connected lawyer. Why would you think that the people you work with are any more law-abiding? One in 17 Americans currently use illegal drugs; imagine the number of dopers if we include prescription painkillers. And America is such a happy place to be that the *Scientific American Mind* reports that one in nine American women and one in 20 men are on antidepressants. Add another chunk of sleeping pill junkies, anti-anxiety pill poppers, plus the drama addicted, attention seeking, self-centered friends, family, coworkers, guys in the supermarket, gals in SUVs you're surrounded by every day, and it all adds up to America being "the greatest nation in the world." Please ensure you've checked your bigotry at the door before making a *bon voyage* wish to "be safe" or commenting "aren't you afraid" to those traveling abroad.

Oh, the big downside of Dubai—traffic sucks.

Almost 4,000 people move to Dubai each week from other countries, mainly from the Indian subcontinent, so traffic sucks more each week. And, as you would guess, a lot of them go there to build that airport, tallest building, mall, housing, roads, and metro (so that people stop whining about the traffic). In fact, 24 percent of all the construction cranes in the world are in this city.[1] The architecture is stunning. The speed and quality of construction are staggering.

Why does it take less than half the time to build everything, with equal or superior quality? Survey says…"money." It may be the most popular answer, but it's not necessarily the best answer. The answer is because of the quality of people who plan, engineer, manage, and construct. And if you think employee quality is a given with lots of money, look how some CEOs' salaries equate with their performance and ethics.

One person you'll find on a construction site is the project manager. The project manager title is an ambiguous one. Sometimes it's a "real" job with line or P&L responsibility and authority, for example, in the construction industry. Most often, it's not. So, to continue our list of silly process roles that cut the cheese in big companies, here's a sample of job descriptions for project managers (Silly Process Role #2) in the U.S. As you read, look at what is common to all, and what is missing from all of them:

Honda: Coordinate user requirements…. Develop flexible, real-time systems to improve communications and efficiency…. Serve as Purchasing liaison… Lead and participate in project team meetings. Daily communication with other Honda companies, departments and affiliates. Confirm and communicate status of project process…. Required Skills: …Cross-functional interaction and ability to negotiate and build consensus…. Desired skill: Strategy development with emphasis/consideration given to reflection, current influences, and corporate vision/direction. [Huh?]

Comcast: Gathering user experience related business requirements from a variety of internal and third-party sources and helping to translate those requirements into actionable design tasks.... Tracking and reporting of design projects.... Drive the critical decisions necessary to manage unit programs/projects to an on-time completion.... Own the responsibility for managing the on-time, within budget, beyond expectation delivery of assigned user experience projects.... Participate (and lead) in the development of project objectives and requirements.... Manage internal and partner activities in support of projects.... Track project issues and manage issue resolution.... Contribute to ideation, development and execution of user experience projects.

UnitedHealth Group: Work closely with Leadership.... Consult all Business partners to plan for their development needs and strategic plans. Develop project proposals and determine time frame, funding needs, procedures for accomplishing project.... Establish work plan.... Review status reports.... Direct the production of requirement documents which communicate process workflows.... Prepare project reports for senior management.... Ability to communicate internally and externally with all levels of employees, including senior management.

Coors: ...lead communication efforts...partnering with key stakeholders from the ideation stage through the development stage.... Contribute to the innovation process...documenting and communication [sic] key project milestones and earnings.... This position requires the ability to relate with others building credibility and rapport: giving personal and reassurance [sic]; and building cooperative, collaborative relationships. The ability to deal with ambiguity, have a sense of team, decision making.... Excellent communication, interpersonal and facilitation skills are required.

Nike: Lead the development and execution of plans focused on integrating the voice of the customer into Nike business processes.... Work with the regions to document current processes, identify gaps and develop new process maps.... Communicating Integrated Customer Management (ICM) strategies and providing implementation progress reports to regional directors and process sponsors.... Participate in the development of 3-year strategic plans and annual ICM roadmaps and work with our ICM Director to establish priorities and business objectives.

It's easy to see what these job descriptions have in common. All of them have responsibility for "driving" functional teams to communicate and collaborate, who appear to be unable to do this on their own or under the supervision of their "leaders." All of them have responsibility for collecting and producing documentation on who does what and who won't do what, and reporting this to senior management.

Noticeably absent is any mention of directly managing *people*. Instead of leading and people and products, they get to lead plans. And they get to work with the person who establishes priorities and manages the people. Whoopee. This project manager can develop plans until the cows come home. They'll all be barbecued. What, by the way, does an ICM team do?

A process role project manager is one who has no management authority over the people whose activities or work he or she is to coordinate. Even more baffling than project managers who aren't allowed to manage the people who do the work is why the people managers aren't capable of managing their own projects.

This is the Association of Project Management's definition of "project management": "Planning, monitoring and control [sic] of all aspects of a project and the motivation of all those involved in it to achieve the project objectives on time and to the specified cost, quality and performance." (Alternative definition: "The controlled implementation of defined change.")

No mention of managing *people*. Let's say you were a fantastic businessperson with the ability to manage people *and* projects. Which job would you choose: A. Manage people but not projects, or B. Manage projects but not people (although you do get to try to "motivate" someone else's people)? If you pick A., you manage people but not their goals or what they do. You get to decide which of your staff works on each of the project teams. If you pick B., the exciting project manager role, you don't determine the project scope, final deliverable product or service, timelines, budgets, or resources. The answer is probably C. None of the above. Leave and start your own business.

I asked a project manager why she thought her job was essential: "I'm a translator. I understand IT staff's technical language and structure and explain it so that the users in the company can understand it and get what they need."

Fascinating. Here's an alternative: Perhaps the company should hire IT people who can understand users and are willing to speak their language, or users who understand IT people, or both! I've never understood why companies hire dozens of couriers and messengers (aka project managers) when the senders and recipients are in the same building.

For the sake of providing job spec examples, I singled out a few large companies. Nonetheless, almost all the other companies' project manager process role positions are the same. There were 3,982 positions with this title on just one job search Web site. Reading between the lines, it's apparent that the project manager process role was created because of internal *interpersonal* issues, lack of communication and coordination, or lack of performance and accountability among the managers of people.

For fun, do a search on an Internet dating service and see how singles (well, some of them are single) profiled their ideal mate:

- "He is not afraid to share his feelings."
- "Must be faithful"
- "Doesn't mind his partner keeping in touch with her family and friends"
- "Abbsolutelly no fat ladyes" [sic]
- "We should be great friends together."
- "I'm not TOO PICKY when it comes to women. All I ask is that she's very pretty with a nice body. I despise women who are controlling, spoiled, stuck-up, insensitive, who are selfish, who use

people and complain about everything, especially men! And please, don't expect me to call you everyday."
- "A good cook would be a total bonus."
- "Even though your [sic] considered a real 'traffic stopper', you prefer a guy who has character depth, not GQ appearance."
- "I like female equivalents of myself."
- "If you are on parole or belong to a motorcycle gang, no thanks. Extra bonus points: sensuous voice, witty sense of humor and don't put ketchup on hot dogs."
- "No bad drivers, bad grammar, bad hair days, being late, boy bands, chain restaurants, chocolate milk, clutter, control freaks, malls, pbj sandwiches and snobs"
- "Good personal hygiene"
- "Looking for honesty"
- "You own a set of tools and your house is very organized. Dancing is not a sacrifice for you. You are taller than me."
- "Prefer a doctor"
- "I want a woman who knows when it is the right time to give it up."

You can tell exactly what type of relationship issues or positive experiences these daters have had in the past. The woman who is looking for a partner who won't mind her conversations with family and friends obviously dated a man who did. The unfaithfulness of a former mate haunts one hopeful. Someone who "prefers" doctors has compared.

Job descriptions have numerous similarities to personal ads. They are both advertisements seeking to attract the most compatible candidate. In a job description, however, the most compatible candidate will have to appeal to a party of interviewers, each of whom has a different history and list of must-haves and must-not-haves. What is the chance that the best candidate to do the job will be chosen?

I can't recall seeing a recruitment ad that listed "good personal hygiene" as a job requirement. That's because it's a given that any employable candidate would have good hygiene. If you did see this requirement, you could safely assume that Pigpen had worked for the company. What should you assume when you see a company advertising for people with "good interpersonal and communication skills?" Isn't that a given?

Communication is a two-way process. "Inter"personal means between two people. You can buy the best phone in the world, but if the phone at the other end is broken, nobody's listening. Corporations keep replacing the phone that's working. Why isn't the broken telephone replaced? Is it a favorite color? Does it have sentimental value to the CEO? Is it because somebody important brought it in and can't admit it's not working? Or is it because the last person who tried to fix the dysfunctional phone got a nasty shock?

Typically, the dead phone hasn't been working for some time, despite numerous complaints. Obviously, the telephone company is a mess. Where there's one duff phone, you'll find more that have been out of order for quite some time. Eventually, people with working phones get tired of screaming at dead receivers. They go to another phone company where they test the lines before they switch. The smartest operators start their own network. Bigger phones aren't always better.

Read this revealing project manager job description from H&R Block:

> **H&R Block:** Responsible for coordinating the analysis, construction, and implementation of software projects.... Responsible for the management and development of project milestones. Responsible for complete project documentation within functional area. Responsible for managing the day-to-day relationships with clients and project team managers.... Effective oral, written and interpersonal communication skills. Proven ability to work with technical members of a team.

You could ascertain that at least one former employee had trouble getting along with a named group—the technical members of a team. The specificity of this part of the job description would lead one to believe that several people have failed at this role in the past because of the inability to collaborate with the techies. Where do you think the problem lies? Could the techies be the reason the projects are not successfully completed? Since project managers are responsible for timely completion of project (while having no authority), they'll either quit or be asked to leave the company if the techies refuse to collaborate. Instead of the diagnosis reading that there were problem techies, each project manager was probably labeled with a case of "lack of interpersonal skills." Looks as if the company doctor keeps amputating the wrong limb!

It's interesting that companies will keep feeding the revolving door with project managers with "excellent interpersonal skills" being their most sought-after area of expertise. Project managers wouldn't be necessary if the people they are supposed to motivate, monitor, and liaise with had excellent interpersonal skills. Even in a soft economy with high unemployment, companies continue to hire additional employees with great interpersonal skills rather than replace those who never had them.

Catherine, a former project manager, had outstanding interpersonal skills. Her company mailed catalogs selling merchandise. She called regular meetings (a top project manager responsibility) to check off that each department was ready to handle customer orders before mailing the new catalogs. Catherine was being diligent: Senior managers were aware that on two previous, recent occasions, customers received the catalogs but were unable order because of telephone issues. The teleoperations "techies" were responsible for getting the phone lines up and running before catalogs went out to receive orders.

On July 10 and again on July 28, the teleoperations department confirmed it had completed each task on Catherine's list, including testing the phone lines. On August 16, the catalogs were mailed. On August 20, it was discovered that the telephones numbers for customer ordering were not working and never had been. It would take three more days to do the tasks to get the phone lines set up properly. Too late, since most customers place orders within three days after receiving the catalog. The teleoperations techies knowingly gave false information (that means they lied) to the project manager, costing the company $560,000 in lost revenue.

Why did the techies give false information? Were they sick of all the project meetings, where most of the discussions were irrelevant to their area? With all the meetings, were they behind in their work? Hell, no. The project manager was just being "anal" requiring that the lines had to be working and tested weeks before the mailings. They don't need her to tell them when to do it! After the July 28 meeting, they had intended to set up the phone lines, but a major hardware problem arose, diverting their attention. If they'd been honest with the project manager, the mailing could have been delayed a few days with negligible financial damage.

Shortly after Catherine sent out a report (another responsibility of project managers) to all the project team participants and senior management informing them that the $560,000 loss was due to the teleoperations project team members not setting up the phone lines and reporting (lying) to the contrary, she lost her job. Before she was dismissed, the senior vice president of sales sent an e-mail to all the project report recipients saying, "The problem is not people who make *mistakes*, but rather those who are fingerpointing."

Who cut the cheese?

After Catherine left, the teleoperations manager continued to misinform (lie to) project managers intentionally. In total, five catalogs were sent with disrupted order taking, costing the company more than $2 million in lost revenue, in addition to the cost of the catalogs and morale, as profits plummeted. The teleoperations manager and the Tony Soprano of sales prospered at the company, no doubt seeking new project managers with "the ability to have excellent communication skills with teleoperations techies and sales." All the king's project managers and all the king's Six Sigma black belt men will never put that dumpy system in order again.

Due to her excellent reputation (and interpersonal skills), Catherine quickly found another job, at another large company. She's still young.

The managing director of the catalog company had set up the project management department because sales were down. The solution is to have competent teleoperations staff and sales managers who are accountable, who are able to work well with others. Would a competent sales manager want to prevent people from identifying the source of corporate failures and roadblocks—particularly if they were his direct reports?

Project management is Six Sigma thinly disguised. Go back to the Quality Guru Silly Process Role and replace "Six Sigma" with "project management." See. You have the same incompetent people who deliver poor service and don't communicate. You don't want to fire the incompetent people so you add a new department full of people with checklists. What comes next—certification? Well, since you mentioned it... Yes, now that the popularity of Six Sigma has waned and is quietly disappearing from companies like Motorola and Chase, the gold star in project management is the new must-have certificate. The Project Management Institute rubber stamp (PMI) or Project Management Professional (PMP) certification means you're fully qualified to beg people who are incapable of managing a project to do their jobs. Imagine that—I can actually get a certificate for knowing how to manage a project. Where do I sign up? A dual Six Sigma black belt certificate combined with a PMI or PMP certificate is now more prized than increasing net income or creating and introducing a profitable new product. Forget the companies' line managers getting PMP certification and training (instead of the project managers). I'm flummoxed about why line managers have been sitting behind those desks for years without knowing how to manage projects.

Do you know any small-business owners who hire a project manager as one of the first 10 employees? Perhaps it's because they and their employees are capable of managing projects by themselves, and managing their lives and careers too. Perhaps that's why they don't work in big companies anymore.

Welcome to the land of fast-paced, creative ingenuity where every client's wish is your command. That's whether it's 4 p.m. or 3 a.m. In the advertising agency world, the project manager is called "traffic manager."

Let's say you're working on a print ad for a magazine. The magazine has a deadline for the films of your advertisement to go to the magazine printer. There's a chain of people who have to do things (e.g., typeset, proof, flight check, get approvals) in a particular order. Miss the deadline, no ad this month. No ad, no client sales. No sales, client dumps agency. Agency dumped, agency dumps you. That's pretty much how the world turns in the *Bewitched* land of Darrin Stevens.

Enter the traffic manager, or traffic cop as they're often fondly referred to. There are several other names for them too, not all of them nice, since they're the folks who make sure the chain gang keeps moving.

If each person in the team turns around his or her chunk of work within the specified period, you don't need someone whose primary function is to burst a blood vessel cajoling slackers to do their work, so the next person in the chain can do his.

As group account director at an integrated advertising/marketing agency, I eliminated the traffic cop role and put a sign in/out sheet on the job jacket. When you completed your work and passed the jacket to the next dude, you documented your "to whom and when." The roadblocks were clear, and management acted. Having management manage was far better than paying some screaming traffic cop whom the slackers would ignore anyway (in the same manner the slacker ignored his work responsibilities).

When big companies hand project managers' checklists and process manuals back to their line managers and make them accountable for doing things right, the up-and-coming future CEOs of America might stick around. In fact, with the opportunity to manage people *and* the projects they work on, a few who left might even come back.

CHAPTER

4
Even More Silly Jobs

April 1, 2001. April Fool's Day. I'd like to be in any other country right now. I'd like to be in any other place than the office on a Sunday. Tomorrow I'll be surrounded by all the process people. None of them is in the office today.

Yes, there's more. Lots more. You couldn't possibly find space to sideline all the competent workers in corporations into just two process departments. Here are a few other silly jobs that were created especially for people who might have moved up the corporate ladder, and why they really cut the cheese. At the end, see if you can name 20 other silly jobs you've seen in big companies.

Silly Process Role #3
Chief Strategy Officer (CSO)

An additional senior-level position is gaining popularity: chief strategy officer. If the president or CEO of your company is not also its chief strategy officer, you ought to be very, very frightened.

Well-managed companies don't have a separate chief strategy officer or anyone with "strategy" or "strategic" in his title because it sends a clear signal that:

1. The CEO is not strategic.

2. No one else in the company is strategic.

3. Any manager who tries to collaborate with other departments will be stepping on the CSO's toes.

4. Being strategic in that company is an exclusive quality (e.g., tactical people are unable to also be strategic).

5. The company does not have an agreed and communicated strategy.

The strategy officer title warns shareholders and employees to run for their lives.

One of the lucky few selected for an executive leadership course was Morgan. The course consisted of problem solving during challenging, outdoor team activities. The participants had never tried scuba diving, caving, or rock climbing. A brief training exercise preceded the scavenger hunt. To choose the top leaders, course work included aptitude and psychological tests. One test rated one's tactical and strategic skills on a two-dimensional scale—strategic on one end, tactical on the other.

At the end of the course, team members plotted where each of their associates ranked on the scale. Some members were correctly pinpointed by how strongly strategic or how strongly tactical they were. With Morgan, there was a paradox. Half the participants saw Morgan as strongly strategic, the others as strongly tactical. Examples were cited: Morgan's meticulous map reading, prioritizing, checking scuba equipment, choosing the best person for each part of the hunt, watching the timer, clarifying the goal, communicating with team members.

Rather than notice the similarities, members honed in on the differences. Predominantly strategic members saw Morgan as tactical; more tactical members thought he was strategic. We judge people by their differences rather than their similarities. Travelers who have been to London recall the "elevator" is called the "lift." On a trip to Syria, tourists notice the women in burqas, ignoring those in business suits.

Morgan was strategic *and* tactical. He was dead center on the scale, and only one of his peers predicted correctly. That peer also scored in the middle of the scale. The majority of team members read

Morgan's chart as determining that he had *neither* strong strategic nor strong tactical qualities, believing they are mutually exclusive. In fact, Morgan was practically off the scale on both characteristics.

Using scales to pigeonhole people is dangerous. The Myers-Briggs type indicator scales people as making decisions by *either* "judging" or "perceiving." Another scale is "thinking" or "feeling." Someone who is in the middle of that scale could be either weak at both or exceptionally strong at both. The cream of the crop are all of the above.

Either-or scales are used on many Internet dating sites to match people, and you've seen the blissful results of that—daters who have been on the site longer than they've been in a relationship.

It's time we stopped believing that tactical workers make good subordinates and strategic workers make good managers. The best people at any level are those who are both strategic and tactical. Those who believe these are mutually exclusive clearly aren't strategic and tactical. The majority of people who are both strategic and tactical appear to have left the nest to start their own companies where they can use all their strengths. Strategic thinking should be universal, not a title that belongs to an individual or a department.

Creating a new position of chief strategy officer verifies that top brass don't have to have both strategic and tactical ability stay at the top. Due to the lack of opportunity to use his spectrum of skills and managerial pigeonholing, Morgan left to start his own manufacturing business.

"Customer insights director" is a real title of the same ilk (and often in the same companies) as chief strategy officer. You may recognize the job description as having another similarly silly title in your company.

Surely more than one person has insight into what customers want than a single director. Does creating this title mean that other staff lack insight (because it certainly sends this message), or is it because you need to attract or retain better research staff? I guess research folks don't like being called "planning directors" anymore, or "research folks." Or perhaps the title has nothing to do with creating or translating research at all. Exactly what did you say are the qualifications required for this position—qualifications that no one in your company currently has? Exactly why is it OK that you've hired a ton of people, none of whom has insight?

With a title as ambiguous as this one, you're certain to have a mess on your hands as this new "position" fights for a piece of power in your crumbling pie. Will he steal pieces from research, marketing, CRM, new product development, sales, or customer service? Alas, the existing staff greedily hoarded the entire pie when they heard you thought they weren't good enough to handle serving it. Even if a few crumbs are left, you can be sure no one will lend the insights director a fork. All will have their knives out. Those who create this position are lacking foresight, not just insight.

Silly Process Role #4
Any Title Containing "Support" or "Services"

Sales support, technical support, user support, customer support, operations support, administrative support, product support, field support. Are they titles you'd like on your résumé? If not, why would anyone believe that these titles would attract or retain top talent?

The human resources director and the SVP of Sales aren't known as "CEO support managers." The word "support" translates as "nonthinking order taker" to those with the title and those who work around them. A "support" title is insulting and signifies that the employee's key role is to wipe the floor behind someone else, or wipe something else. If the job is important enough to get a human being to do it, give the person a title that describes what his or her contribution is. Better still, have people clean up after themselves.

The same goes for people's titles that include "services" such as "marketing services." Employees' titles should not indicate that they are subservient to other employees. It's very easy to remove the word "services" to attract an intelligent doer rather than a dumb waiter. To keep them, remove the attitude that put the title there in the first place.

A company's political underwear is showing when it creates "support" titles. The group these people "support" has the political power. With nowhere to move up, they'll move out, preferably where they're wearing the pants.

Remember: It's better to be an athlete than an athletic supporter.

Silly Process Role #5
Niche Specialist (Subject Matter Expert)

If you watched the TV game show *Who Wants To Be A Millionaire*, you'll recognize its similarity to the career ladder of executives. How high up the ladder can you go?

When hiring entry-level staff for information technology (IT) positions, interviewers are equally interested in candidates with degrees in engineering, computer science, or information systems and seek general aptitude. For the new employee, the knowledge required to make decisions is lower, and so is the payback. On *Millionaire*, most contestants can answer the $200 question. Most of us know that Madison Square Garden is in New York, without being a travel agent or having an advanced educational degree.

Junior staff acquire expertise when specializing in certain areas or on a few products. By making correlations to other products or processes, they increase their value. In the hot seat, you may not remember which planet is fifth from the sun. However, with four multiple-choice answers, if you remember Earth is third, Pluto is way out there, and Venus relatively close to Earth, by deduction, your final answer would be Jupiter. Or, you might remember the mnemonic "my very easy-going mother just served us nine pies" to associate the first letters with the order of the planets. Through correlation, we become experts on a variety of subjects. Relational thinking is the way we learn.

The best managers (or presidents) don't have all the answers, but they know what "lifelines" they have and when to use them. When duped, they first "ask the audience" of staff they have. Next they use "50/50" to discard the weakest solutions. Finally, they "phone a friend" if they can't find the expertise in-house.

Can you answer this $250,000 *Millionaire* question? "Which of the following is not a type of snake: A. Mamba, B. Chuckwalla, C. Fer-de-Lance, D. Krait?" In business, it's not a game. The financial stakes are often just as high.

There are 2,700 species of snakes. You'll notice that "hire a herpetologist" (reptile expert), is not one of the *Millionaire* lifelines. Nor should you *hire* an expert every time you *need* an expert. Whether you correctly chose "Chuckwalla" (a lizard) or not, if

$250,000 were really at risk, you wouldn't forget the answer. Train, teach, ask, rent, but don't hire.

The parallel between *Millionaire* contestants and business leaders doesn't end there. Why isn't the phoned friend the contestant? It's because the winner is the person who has acquired a wide scope of general and specific information, assembles the best team, *and* knows when and how to use all resources, internal and external.

Hire a specialist and you'll lose a great worker. According to *Harvard Business Review*, the top five reasons why people leave their jobs (in order) are the following:

1. Job content
2. Level of responsibility
3. Company culture
4. Caliber of colleagues
5. Salary[1]

Add interest and responsibility to existing employees' jobs by acquiring, not hiring, knowledge. Provide opportunity for existing employees to increase their sphere of learning and you'll cultivate a better future manager. One reason why there are so many inept, insecure managers in big companies is that they were niche specialists. Employees who are great all-arounders are the first to leave to start their own companies, because they have what it takes to manage an entire company. Aren't they the people who should be running big companies?

When companies feel they are missing the bus on the way to the future, they create special knowledge positions, such as e-business manager. Unfortunately, by the time these positions are created and filled by experts whom the interviewees can agree on, the bus has almost completed its route.

In the late 1990s, dot.com trailblazers were paid big bucks to return to corporate America and head up e-business departments. The pioneers moved from an environment where e-business was the business to one where the existing managers didn't understand the basics of using the Web as a medium. Line managers directed e-business managers to stick their existing products on the Web, while e-business managers argued to make changes to the product and ordering/billing processes for it to be successful. Turf battles ensued.

Some of the biggest retailers, such as Wal-Mart, spun e-business into an autonomous company. In 2001, it reversed this strategy. Wal-Mart, described as an e-commerce "midget" in January 2000, is now in the top three. eBay and amazon.com are the leaders. How did their management teams do it? They didn't treat e-business as a process role. John Fleming, Wal-Mart.com's CEO and former head of merchandising for the stores, used his broad expertise to find ways for each of the two empires to complement each other. He utilized the parent company's distribution system and offered products on walmart.com that leveraged "the company's in-store offerings such as higher-end consumer electronics and appliances and additional book and movie titles."[2]

Specialist process roles usually become settings for political battles. Greg arrived as a vice president of marketing for a retail product line for kids' outdoor play equipment (OPE). Out of a large marketing department with 60 people, he was one of only 20 who had held marketing jobs in other companies, and one of four who had held a marketing position in a non-toy industry. (Greg's boss, the marketing director, was not one of the 20. He'd come from the finance department.) Greg knew how and when to use e-marketing as a business strategy. He also knew how and when to use PR, direct mail, telemarketing, event marketing, promotion. Greg lasted 18 months and left to start his own marketing services agency.

His reason for leaving was that he was unable to implement any strategy with underpinning tactics for his product line, because turf battles broke out regarding who owned the promotional in-store strategy, e-business strategy, etc. The in-store promotions manager determined that a storewide discount, advertised in a preprint, otherwise known as a free-standing-insert (FSI), should be inserted into Sunday newspapers delivered near each store. The discount strategy worked for all products from dolls to OPE.

Greg agreed that the promotion should be advertised in FSIs but disagreed about blanket discounting, because that was what the competitors had always done. Furthermore, Greg's philosophy was that discounts denigrated the perceived quality and value of the product line. Parents chose a brand of OPE because it was the safest, sturdiest, and most fun for kids, not because it was slightly cheaper. Engendering brand loyalty was essential, he believed, because parents would add units onto the play equipment: adjoining swings, slides, forts, rope ladders, and bridges.

Instead, Greg wanted to set up a traveling road show to enable sampling of his product line. Each weekend, a gated playground with mulch could be set up in front of a different store. Children coming to the toy store or department store could actually try out and play on the outdoor play equipment. Parents would see their children enjoying the equipment and feel secure while checking out the construction of the entire set assembled. Different displays of forts, swings, and ladders would show several combinations of units assembled. Finally, instead of a discount, Greg wanted to hire small delivery trucks. If a customer purchased the play equipment, it could be loaded into a truck, delivered, and assembled in the backyard of the customer within three hours of purchase. The stores usually charged for delivery and would not do assembly. Research indicated that moms and dads would be willing to pay for assembly and saw free delivery as a huge benefit. The discount the in-store promo manager wanted was equivalent to the delivery costs. The assembly option would be a revenue generator.

Greg showed research that indicated that many more customers would purchase, but also customers would buy more connective units (higher average sale) and make more subsequent unit purchases due to the store outdoor play event, free delivery, and assembly option. The research also indicated that customers would buy related products at the time of OPE purchase, such as mulch and play guides, further increasing store revenues.

Greg knew how to make outdoor events successful; he'd done them in a previous job for a home improvement warehouse. Correlation. The in-store product specialist had never participated in this type of event—he wouldn't be the expert if the event came to fruition. Greg would get the credit if it worked. And if Greg was successful, an in-store promotions manager wasn't necessary.

After a year of similar battles with refusal to even test Greg's ideas, he resigned, the outdoor events never took place, and OPE sales have remained stagnant. Often it's the other way around. The cross-functional specialist has the idea that hasn't been done before, and the long-standing product "specialist" blocks it. Whichever way you swing it, creating cross-functional expert positions (which are in effect process jobs) never works and leads to talented specialists or multitalented businesspeople leaving. The blockers and tacklers, eager to maintain the status quo, are the winners, while the company is the loser.

What does work? Train the existing managers how to e-market, do direct mail, and implement original sales promotions. Hire departmental managers with these skills. Best yet, hire a small-business owner running a competitive business. If the existing managers can't or won't implement new ways of doing things, remove them. By hiring specialist "experts," you are giving incompetent managers permission to stay incompetent. When they are successful at blocking specialists from integrating new ideas on their turf, they know the expert will soon disappear. Make innovation and best business practices part of managers' jobs and responsibilities— not someone else's.

Niche specialists are happy and successful in businesses that focus singularly on their niche. They often make great consultants. Hire their wisdom, not them.

Jeff Goodwin, executive vice president of Citibank's Financial Services Division in the U.K., was my boss. Initially, I transferred to his group to salvage the suffering personal loan business. The finance team members were among my favorite colleagues, not just because of their intelligence, but also because of their sharp sense of humor, which I absorbed from the other side of the partition. My strategy to bolster personal loans profitability would need to consist of short-term and long-term gains for the product. Together the finance team and I dissected the product, running sensitivity analyses to find which part of the product made the biggest, or quickest, net income impact.

Our personal loan product offered an optional insurance product whereby loan payments would be made on behalf of the customer if he/she was involuntarily laid off, severely ill, or died. An affiliated company provided the insurance product. Although the consumer paid a few extra dollars on each loan payment for coverage that went to the affiliate, Citibank's spiff or commission for selling the insurance on each loan at that time was $556, paid up front by our insurance partner. This cash flow benefit was a valuable source of revenue. Our insurance penetration was 17 percent when I arrived; that is, 17 percent of customers selected the insurance option.

We did consider removing the option and automatically including the insurance benefit with each loan. After all, it was only a few dollars per payment. We examined the break-even point of fewer, more profitable loan sales. Making the insurance an integral part of the product was abandoned because national insurance laws dictated that if it were mandatory, the cost of the insurance would have to be included in the APR (annual percentage rate). In the early 1990s, APRs for unsecured loans in England averaged 29 percent! We'd be uncompetitive with APRs in the high 30s or even 40s. How could we get customers to request the insurance coverage voluntarily?

After a few months, innovative changes to direct mail offers had boosted penetration to 40 percent. We thought we could do better. Although today it seems as if telemarketing calls have been around forever, in 1990, the practice was in its early stages with most companies in the U.S. and in its infancy in the U.K. Citibank U.K. hadn't done telemarketing because a few anti-change agents claimed, "It won't work over here." That's often the same cry heard about innovation at U.S. companies.

I approached Jeff. "I just know if we talk to our customers and tell them the benefits, they'll buy the insurance product. Can I test it?"

Jeff looked at my proposal. "OK," he said. "Here's the deal. You can pick one person from anywhere in the company to work with you for three months to prove whether or not it works." Great leaders love testing!

There were no telemarketing experts in the company, but there were some great customer service folks. Dawn had some product knowledge and seemed the most enthusiastic about learning something new. I downloaded everything I knew about telemarketing; she tried every approach she could dream up to see which worked best.

Penetration soared on some days to 83 percent. The average was 65 percent. Jeff kept his word. He didn't create a separate telemarketing department; we expanded the personal loan division.

Within two months, I had 17 people calling personal loan applicants, adding insurance to personal loans. Since there was a shortage of experienced telemarketers in London at that time, we sought staff with overall good business skills and a penchant for innovation and learning. Because of these criteria and since the working hours were 4 p.m. to 9 p.m. (our highest response times), most of the telemarketers were students and foreigners. It was the League of Nations. We had callers from Iran, Gambia, India, Pakistan, Jamaica, and France, plus a few Brits. Why was their performance so good?

Besides the hiring criteria, the training was great. We brought in telemarketing experts as guests. Citibank's incredible training department was thrilled to be teaching a new skill (and learning one themselves) and training such enthusiastic, eager new employees about the company's products. Ambitious folks from other departments joined our group. Other entrepreneurial types (Citibank had a lot of us then) saw our success and asked us to do tests and surveys on their products or services. We welcomed their invitations to better the company, and our telemarketers were thrilled to learn more about the banking business—training they would benefit from for the rest of their lives.

Fun was at the top of the job-requirements list. Since we spend most of our waking lives working, our day needs to be full of surprises and delights, or it's time to find a profession that makes us smile and laugh.

We introduced Games Nights. The only issue we initially had faced was the high absenteeism rate. Students felt pressured to miss work when faced with heavy homework assignments or upcoming tests. Games Nights happened on ad hoc, unannounced dates. When you missed one, the call center buzzed about the fun the others had. The phone stations were set in a semicircle with the center ring for activities or up-to-the-minute news. There were simple games like putting your name in the raffle drum each time you got a sale, with prizes being given out at the end of the night (more sales, more chances to win).

The games got bigger and better. Get a sale, run to the line in the activity circle, and throw a dart at the balloon board. Break a balloon, and get the prize written on the paper inside the balloon. Piñata night was crazy, with one blindfolded caller knocking out part of the ceiling instead of hitting the telephone-shaped piñata (yes, we found one!).

We had theme nights, with games around Bart Simpson and soccer teams. We cleaned up after ourselves too.

Customers often bought our products when telemarketers described what was going on in the activity circle, because we made them smile, and they knew the employees loved their jobs. Consumers assume that companies who treat their employees well will treat their customers 10 times better. Maintenance didn't get pissed off at us for knocking out the ceiling either. In fact, now visitors were coming from other floors to see what all the fun was. The whole company knew about Games Night.

We distributed yo-yos with trick instructions to every employee (and to our customers) to educate them about our insurance product, "For the ups and downs in life." Work was supposed to be a blast. When you woke up each morning, you couldn't wait to get to work.

None of this ever would have come to fruition without great business managers like Jeff and the *lack* of process managers. This would have been project mismanaged, specialized, or Six Sigma-ed to death. Within a year, personal loan sales had doubled and profitability quadrupled. Best of all, we had fun doing it.

Our division was successful because we ran it like a small company. We specialized in running a business, rather than being niche specialists. We owned the decisions to change, create, or discontinue products, and how to price and market those products. We manipulated our environment. Each of us felt as if he ruled the world. There was no reason to leave to create another one.

Silly Process Role #6
Customer Relationship Manager (CRM)

This title should be "manager relationship manager." The title ought to have a subtitle: "Warning: cross-functionalist in silo organization."

The company harboring this position has lords and ladies who insist on running their fiefdoms their own ways. Since there's clearly no intention to dissolve the feudal fiefdoms in favor of one big, happy, modern kingdom (and revenue is funneling down the keep as a result), a customer relationship serf and posse are brought in.

Having several fiefdoms is often an effective way to ward off tyrants from other lands (also called "competition"). As in small, independent corporate divisions, autonomy builds pride and covers more territory. Leveraging resources of other fiefdoms could deflect attacks from a wider area.

When a king and queen hire a serf, the messenger heralds to all lords and ladies that none of them will lose their fiefdoms due to their failure to collaborate or attain their share of the kingdom goals. If the royal couple doesn't take away their power for mismanaging their fiefdoms, what chance does a mere serf have to make a difference?

The serf will never become a lord or lady, who never leaves the castle walls, terrified of the outside world. Eventually, the serf who has traveled between the castles, and has seen the outside world and the inner sanctums, will create a serfdom. One by one, the fiefdoms will crumble as other adventurous serfs leave and join the new serfdom. And they live happily ever after.

It's a tragedy when a corporation admits to the world by creating a customer relationship management (CRM) department that its top leaders can't agree or don't know how to market to their customers. Even if they could, it wouldn't solve their problems. Why? The strategy is flawed. **Customers don't want "relationships" with companies.**

I like Starbucks coffee. I do not want a relationship with Starbucks. I don't love *you*, Starbucks; I just like your coffee. Uh, oh. The advertising groupies are chasing me while screaming, "You'll love our *brand*!" I like the coffee and even oat scones. The staff are cool, the lounges are tastefully designed, and Starbucks is great place to hang out. Ok, I like the brand. But I still don't want a "relationship" with Starbucks.

Starbucks may be in love with getting my business and want a serious relationship with me. So what? It takes two parties to have a relationship. Consumers want things or services from companies, not relationships. Even if your product makes me feel good (and caffeine definitely does that), you're not my soul mate (another ridiculous concept) and never will be.

A customer relationship manager position or CRM department would never exist if a company understood people as much as their own products. When asked to describe what CRM does, the most frequent answer is "build loyalty."

You'll read more on innovation and customer loyalty in later chapters, but for now, rest assured that customers are not loyal. Loyalty programs don't make them any more or any less so. I am not loyal to my grocery store because I have its frequent shopper discount card. I have its competitors' discount card too. In fact, 76 percent of us have at least one of these supermarket "loyalty" cards according to EMA Marketing Research for Standard Register. Where I'm driving when I need food determines my choice of store, not the loyalty card. I'm in eight frequent flier programs, too. I loathe some airlines, but I'm loyal to none.

Since every supermarket offers exactly the same program, it's not going to make me loyal to one (duh). I'm actually pretty pissed off that every supermarket makes me carry around its me-too program card, when usually the cashier will swipe a generic one anyway if I forget mine.

I know they're actually collecting or trading data about what I'm buying for giving me a discount. I've not seen an original or motivating use of that data yet, just a lot more discounts on stuff that I can get cheaper somewhere else. Wouldn't you be more likely to visit a supermarket if it gave you discounts *without* having to use a card or coupons? There's a novel idea! (That's how Costco ate their lunch.)

I don't want a relationship with either supermarket and I'm not loyal. I really want to break up.

You don't see Whole Foods or Trader Joe's cutting their margins and battling on price with parity products. Chock-a-block with well-traveled, well-heeled, and eclectic hunters searching for treats. Paying top dollar for them. They achieved success without a discount card.

I hope Whole Foods won't mess it up by launching a "loyalty program." It'll be the first sign that the place has nothing unique or special to offer anymore. When your business becomes a me-too operation because everyone who wasn't a me-too employee has left, you'll create me-too points programs, me-too discounts, a me-too membership card, and a me-too club. Then, after treating me too as if I'm nothing special, you'll want a relationship.

Department stores are also discovering how their best customers are not loyal. After analyzing the spend patterns of their best customers, retailers discovered that their highest spenders were their competitors' best customers too. Each erroneously assumed that if you were one of its best customers, it must be your favorite store. For years, each store believed its biggest spenders were exclusively loyal. It's tough finding out your best girl's been cheating on you with the whole village. Big spenders are everybody's big spenders. They're not loyal, and guess what they think about having seven more "loyalty" cards in their wallets? Some stores want you to have separate "memberships" in each of their departments!

Consumers are not loyal. They are simply creatures of habit. We do what we're comfortable with, over and over again. We know where they put the peanut butter, they have Hanes in my size and style, or there's a wide variety of merchandise to browse through for me to be entertained. Sometimes, slowly or painfully, our habits change. We quit smoking or lose weight, and it could be because of a relationship. But not one with Starbucks. We may change buying habits for many reasons: enjoyment, convenience, offers, price, moving home, being pissed off, etc. Having a relationship is not among those reasons. Target marketing is about making the right offer to the right customer at the right time. Forcing a customer to provide you with data to do that or carry another plastic card does not mean that you have a relationship. If marketing staff can't come up with a cohesive strategy for target marketing, ditch them. Don't take away this key element of marketing strategy from your competent staff by hiring a customer relationship manager.

Let your marketers market, let your salespeople sell, manage your managers' relationships, and stop trying to manage customers' relationships. If your leaders can't manage to make and market products or services that consumers or other businesses want to buy because they're *better*, it's time to manage those people out of your company and hand over the reins to people who can.

Silly Process Role #7
Integration Manager

If you can't beat 'em, buy 'em. When corporations have successfully squelched all new ideas and the people who generate them, they usually go on a buying spree—looking to acquire great little businesses that haven't squelched originality and advancement. Ironic, isn't it? Spot a big business on an acquisition binge and you've usually found an innovation-anorexic company that purges organic great ideas.

Many large corporations have earned accolades as "best in market" by buying the ideas *and* the companies that created them. In many cases, they eventually killed the golden goose after allowing the same incompetent managers who necessitated the acquisition to oversee egg production. Butterfingers. If you want the acquired company to keep rolling out winning products, keep the P&L executives with the history of new product success in the driving seats. Leave them alone. They were successful for a reason—you didn't manage them.

Leave them to grow as separate companies. Don't make them use your processes, or your people, or your vendors, or sell to your customers.

If corporations fostered dynamic growth organically, those little businesses that habitually generate patentable products and services would be cropping up from within. With their massive financial and human resources for cross-fertilization, ingenious offshoots should bear fruit everywhere. They don't because big companies don't believe that a meal should consist of a number of individual dishes, each a gastronomical delight in itself. They throw everything into a stew, serving up an overcooked, tasteless concoction.

In much of Asia, the main meal is a bevy of dishes, each stimulating a carousel of taste buds and senses. Sweet and sour, hot and cold, salt and spice, bitter and buttery. An Arabic mezza, Spanish tapas, or Chinese dim sum rouses the palate throughout the meal. In 2002, the most expensive meal I had in Vietnam was in one of Hanoi's top restaurants: 10 courses (served simultaneously, of course) with wine. Total: $3. The distinct flavors were mint, coriander, lemon grass, shrimp, peanut sauce, fish sauces, ginger, black pepper, garlic, basil, sugar, lime, chili, and green onions. Fabulous, fresh little morsels rolled in rice paper or lettuce wraps, or flash fried crisp. There's little resemblance to Americanized versions of Vietnamese, Chinese, and Indian food that are bastardized to suit bland, familiar U.S. tastes. I often hear people who have never been to Asia professing, "I love Thai food!" How would they know? I suppose it doesn't roll off the tongue to say, "I love Americanized Thai-style food served in U.S. restaurants." I doubt many who claim to love Chinese food have tried dog, horse, and duck intestines or webfeet, knowingly. While curling their noses at this, they readily scoff sausages, made from unmentionable animal parts all cased beautifully in a strip of intestines or beef bung caps (guess where that comes from).

The other difference between stew and these Asian meals is that while both meals are shared in different ways, the Asian meal allows for individual tastes. You can take more of one dish and ignore the other. If you don't like stew or one of its ingredients, tough luck. You starve.

It's the same in American companies. They stop organically producing a number of delicious side businesses or divisions to dress the dinner table and satisfy many customers. They destroy the very flavors and notes of acquired businesses that made each one special and desirable. They insist that everything must have the same potatoes and be cooked at the same temperature, and that everyone approve. Introduce a new side dish? Why, never! One person may not like it. Instead of embracing the philosophy that diversity in product offerings is good, they stick to the bland monotony to avoid new complaints, from within the company from the anti-change brigade. The menu always stays the same. Worst, all who walk through the kitchen (and have no culinary training or acclaim) criticize anything new based upon their dulled taste buds. Haven't they heard that "too many cooks spoil the broth"? Which is exactly what they end up with—broth. It's the only thing they can agree on.

Finally, when regular diners are so sick of the same stew that they leave to go to the competitor's restaurant to sample variety and no new diners appear because they don't want to be in a restaurant that only serves one type of broth, the company realizes it has a problem. The top chefs, without challenge and flooded with criticism for trying new dishes, quit. They go to work in a kitchen where not everyone has his finger in the pot; a place where the service quality manager isn't yelling for them to reduce the number of blueberries and serve before the meal is fully cooked. A place where dozens of project managers don't need to be employed to police the cooks to wash their hands after going to the restroom. A place where rhubarb pie is offered to see if customers like it even if Sammy the busboy doesn't like rhubarb. Away from where Janey the buyer criticizes the chef because she doesn't want to have the challenge of finding wholesalers of rhubarb, and where Suzy is jealous because the recommendation came from Joe, who is not a pastry chef. You can bet that Janey and Suzy will never leave, but the talented people concerned about brain atrophy will. As the talent pool and customer base drain and fill the pockets of the competitors, management never consider getting rid of Janey or Suzy. They buy another restaurant overflowing with the talent and customers they once had, and "integrate" it, sending Janey and Suzy in to spread their malignant culture.

Companies acquire what they lack. The excuse that they only buy to get to market faster is flawed because the big company has always had greater resources to produce faster and better. The large company with its greater access to talent, legal advice, market data, suppliers, and cash should have started building those products and services long before the little business ever obtained the financial resources to fuel the idea. While big brother claims to have bought the bright underling because it fills a "product or service gap," it's really buying businesses because of different gaps it needs to fill: nimbleness, ingenuity, marketing savvy, double-digit growth, extraordinary people. The logical conclusion would be that, after acquisition, the large company would abandon its stagnant culture (read "people") to absorb the one that has the traits (read "people") to build and market innovative products and services. Quite the opposite happens. Along comes the giant saying, "This little business will be so much more successful with our bushel of bureaucracy and a larger portion of politics."

In comes the "integration manager," appearing shortly after acquisition or a so-called merger. The title announces that, yet again, here's a big company with people who are unable to work together or communicate, so they need a "special" person to "integrate" them. I'm not sure what skill set or expertise it takes to be an "integration manager" and how exactly this person's performance can be measured. However, the jobs are rarely posted externally, so you may safely assume they are given to someone who's in with the in crowd and isn't currently doing anything that will be missed should he or she suddenly stop doing it to "integrate" people. You can also assume that the company doesn't have managers who know how to manage people and business, since the company doesn't expect its own leaders to be able to integrate successfully without a, tee hee, specialist in integration.

The Random House Webster dictionary lists a number of definitions for "integrate." While the acquirer may describe "integration" as "to incorporate into a unified, harmonious, or interrelated whole or system," the acquired is more likely to see it as "to become part of the dominant culture."

Since the dominant culture is one that discouraged innovation or growth, the first step of an integration team is to get rid of the new troublemakers who try to innovate or grow, starting at the top. The very reason the small business was successful was its people, and the bigger the acquirer, the faster the successful people leave. I've witnessed the aftermath of an acquisition where the big boys were so arrogant and incompetent that the "integrated" employees sadly hoped for their own business creations to crash and burn, to get even. They didn't have to hope for long. When the business was acquired, it was in its heyday. After replacing all the senior and mid-level leaders, submitting every aspect of the business to process roles, instating "quality" rigor, and integrating the innovators right out of the company, sales plummeted. Pink slip recipients were disproportionately from the bought company. Four years later, the integrated still refer to their side of the imaginary battleship by the old company name. The big boys, who bought a profitable company, and have posted a loss on the division ever since, blame everyone but themselves for the mess.

"The market changed. The biggest client went away." Put away the violins. The innovators and growth cultivators would have kept up with the market and introduced a stream of exciting, profitable products that would have attracted bigger clients. Stop whining. When acquiring great companies, you must acquire the philosophy that made them great.

Acquisitions work best when neither party is treated like the poor, sick sister. Each business is superior in a different way, and its employees should have the intelligence to take the best from its peer and ignore the rest. Truly complementary companies with exceptional staff can not only lead to better products and profits, but provide motivation and opportunities for ambitious, brilliant people to learn horizontally and vertically about their industry.

With mediocre talent, neither acquisition nor organic growth is likely to be successful. Look at the world of advertising. In the 1980s, geniuses like Lester Wunderman and David Ogilvy preached the benefits of direct marketing, a type of advertising where the results were measurable because you elicit a response from your audience. Not only could you know how many people saw your ad, but also you could determine your return on investment for your marketing expenditure, something nonresponse TV and radio spots and magazine and newspaper print ads couldn't tell you.

My focus in graduate school was international business, focusing on marketing and advertising. After moving to London shortly after graduating (I stink at learning languages), I temped while searching for a "real" advertising job. I went to a firm that specialized in advertising temps and landed a position at Wunderman, as a copytypist. My joy wasn't due to my position or because I was working for the largest direct marketing agency. It was because since 1973, Wunderman was linked with Young & Rubicam, then the largest advertising agency in the world, sharing the same building. At least I would be physically close to my goal.

As the largest direct marketing agency in Europe, we had 27 employees, and my job was one that has thankfully disappeared due to technology. It's easy to forget that photocopiers (or "Xeroxes" as they were called) were uncommon before 1980. Most direct marketing was direct mail then. Without PCs, the agency's recommended words for future letters and brochures, or "copy" as it is called in the ad industry, had to be typed. Just like today, everyone takes a stab at making copy changes. The copywriter's work looks like a dog's dinner by the time everyone is through. Agency colleagues (account staff, proofreaders, managers, art directors, etc.) will make amendments, and then the client will usually make several rounds of changes. Every time someone added a sentence or even a word that couldn't fit at the end of a line (anything that Wite-Out couldn't cure), the lowly copytypist would have to retype the entire letter or brochure double-spaced, to produce a clean version for another round of edits. If you left out a few words while retyping and didn't spot it until the end, you'd have to start all over again. It may not sound like a big deal, but in the early days of direct mail, longer letters got higher response levels. Therefore, most letters were a minimum of four pages. From the conception of the mail package to the start of print production, I averaged retyping the same material about 30 times and often had the copy memorized. Fortunately, Wunderman's biggest client at the time was Rank Xerox, which had just introduced a revolutionary electronic typewriter, and I was among the first to get one. Its memory chip could hold a whopping five lines of copy at a time.

What started as a stepping-stone became a passion, because of the brilliance of the Wunderman crowd. The little division was growing fast, and the only place big enough to sit was in a small "media department" inhabited by Neil the media director, Paul the media manager, and now, me. Staff scrambled to tidy offices and prepare for Lester Wunderman's big visit from the U.S. They felt on the verge of something big—the infancy of direct marketing—and a visit from the man who had coined the phrase "direct marketing" was a cause for celebration.

In this welcoming environment, even I, a temp copytypist, was invited to hear and talk with the agency namesake, Lester Wunderman, who truly is a wonderman. Personable, astute, charismatic, and intelligent, he is an inspiring leader who fostered the spirit of innovation and attracted people as hardworking and confident as himself. I was awestruck by his simple logic applied toward giving each customer what he really wanted and revolutionizing the way we delivered it. Wunderman is the consummate teacher. I learned so much from my colleagues, who generously shared their expertise and enthusiasm. They challenged me to think creatively and broader in looking for business solutions. Lester Wunderman didn't change what I wanted to do—he added to it! He preached how advertising and direct marketing were all media, and knowing how, how much, and when to do each, or both, was invaluable.

I let my coworkers know I was also interested in becoming a permanent member of their account team, the sales and management group that liaises between the clients and the agency teams. One of the staff in charge of hiring was someone we'll call "Endora." She told me there were no openings, which I found surprising because of the company's recent account wins and rapid growth.

Undeterred in my quest for my ideal job and eager to use my newly acquired master's degree, I wrote to the top guy upstairs at Young & Rubicam, in my fifth month at Wunderman. I enclosed my résumé while telling him that I was temping downstairs for Wunderman where I'd been told there were no openings, so I wanted an account position with Young & Rubicam. Although I had a little typewriter at home, I stayed late at work to type the letter on the electronic typewriter so it would be perfect, Wite-Out-less. I used my own expensive cream bond paper and envelopes. The top guy routed my letter to Endora with some written scribbles. Endora obviously did have open positions (that's called a lie) and had neglected to tell him about our sole, snapshot conversation.

In five months, Endora had rarely come out of her office to speak to anyone. Now, she was *inviting* me into her office. Her face got bright red as she snapped the door shut.

"You, you, you," she puffed. "Just who do *you* think *you* are writing to somebody like the CEO of Y&R? Do *you* know who he is? *You* are a nobody. A nothing. A temp. Using *my* typewriter! *You* are never to write or speak to anybody again. Now get out. GET OUT!"

The next day, I, the desk, chair, and *her* electronic typewriter were moved into a storage area so tiny that I could touch all the walls while sitting in my chair. Apparently, it wasn't my typing, writing, or speaking Endora didn't like—it was my laughing, and everyone else's. Endora appeared alone and lonely.

My office mates felt bad but couldn't defend me lest an evil spell be cast upon them. (See Chapter Seven on bullying.) They explained that she hated all of our laughing and joking (although we were twice as productive because of all the positive energy), my American-ness, my master's degree in international business, my guts (in writing directly to her boss's boss's boss), my delirious happiness as a newlywed (okay, it was a bit annoying), my lack of cynicism (so I've changed a wee bit), my ability to make friends and integrate, and countless other aptitudes she appeared to lack. Imagine how many others left Wunderman because Endora was envious of their green eyes, magic recipes, or fancier broomsticks. One poison apple...

Endora did me a big favor. In an effort to avoid her evil eye, I job hunted. I got a "real" job a month later at Kawasaki Motors UK Ltd. where, after one year, I was promoted to head the marketing department. I used what I'd learned at Wunderman (thanks to all the other super-smart people there who taught me well) to build the first commercial, computerized marketing database of motorcyclists in the country and used my direct marketing know-how to increase Kawasaki's share of the 500cc-plus U.K. motorcycle market to 65 percent. We clobbered our competition in the most profitable sector of the market. Big bikes equaled big bucks for manufacturers. Plus, I had a company motorcycle, a fresh-off-the-new-production-line Ninja 600—something I would never have had at Wunderman or Young & Rubicam. I experienced testing crotch-rockets around Grand Prix circuits across Europe, more exhilarating than the fastest electronic typewriter. Moreover, I combined two loves, motorcycles and direct marketing. As the client from Kawasaki, I got to work once again with Wunderman friends who had gone to other agencies (wonder why?).

Later, with the support of two great advertising men, Waring and LaRosa, I went on to create, lead, and build a direct marketing agency in Manhattan, which was eventually bought by, you guessed it, Young & Rubicam. Although Y&R had some super people, I didn't wish to be "integrated" into Wunderman, although they had many terrific direct marketers. And yes, they did appoint an integration manager for the, ahem, merger.

By 1980, Young & Rubicam had made impressive acquisitions toward offering a full-service communications agency with Wunderman, Burson-Marsteller public relations, Cato Johnson promotions, and Sudler & Hennessey health care advertising. In Britain, any of these marketing disciplines was coined "below-the-line" while advertising alone was "above-the-line." I still don't know what "the line" is, nor does anyone else I've asked. However, if you worked at a below-the-line agency, the above-the-line crowd at most agencies would react as if Pepe Le Pew had just entered the room. The agencies weren't integrated since most of the ad folks were afraid the smell might rub off on them, which suited the below-the-liners just fine.

Peee-yeu. In 2006, one of the oldest above-the-line ad agencies, Foote Cone & Belding, decided to, ahem, merge with another of my former employers, direct marketing agency Draft. Howard Draft got to put his name first on letterhead of Draft FCB. Way to go, Howie. Deal. The *Chicago Sun-Times* lamented, "We hope your black armbands are securely attached…. Without question June 1, 2006 will go down as one of the darkest moments in the history of an increasingly troubled ad industry, which, with each passing day, shows new and disturbing signs it has lost its way."[3] You know the old saying, "Don't kick 'em on the way up, because you might see 'em on the way down.

What advertising's top brass didn't want to admit is that *clients* were integrated, and are becoming more so. To stay ahead of the curve, clients have to use a combination of research, PR, direct marketing, promotion, advertising, event marketing, in alternative media, toward new or narrower targets to be more cost-effective, and their marketing departments' evolving structures reflect this. Because of economic recession in the early '80s, businesses scrutinized marketing budgets and demanded accountability. When your mom checked if you ate enough dinner, you didn't leave the uneaten hash in one big heap. You spread the food across your plate to make it harder to measure. When your company president asked if you had too much marketing budget, you didn't leave it in one big advertising heap. You spread it around among the marketing disciplines and in different agencies, so there weren't any big easy portions of budget to slice off. Marketing budgets, instead of growing, were divided, and the biggest chunk went toward advertising, and the advertising agencies. The biggest hurdle for the ad agencies was that the profit-and-loss statements (P&Ls) worked very differently for above- and below-the-line.

For decades, advertising agencies made most of their profit by charging clients the standard 17.65 percent net markup on the advertising media cost (that's 15 percent gross), plus billing production costs. The average 30-second Super Bowl TV spot costs $2.4 million.[4] If the commission structure was still the same today, CBS would bill $2.4 million but would collect $2.04 million while $360,000 would go to the advertising agency as commission. Three hundred sixty thousand bucks commission for one TV spot. It was in the interest of the advertising agencies to keep labor costs to a minimum by recommending one medium (e.g., just magazines): Produce one spot or print ad, and run the same ad as many times as possible. The major car manufacturers have spent more than $100 million on media advertising alone to launch one key model. When the old commission structure was in place, advertising was a lucrative business.

The shift toward integrated marketing changed this. How could you charge 17.65 percent for a sales promotion when it was on the back of your own cereal box? How did you pay when the direct mail piece went to your own customer list? How did you pay the PR agency when the media space might be free, based upon the interest level of the story for the newspaper's readers? Furthermore, direct mail was labor-intensive, scientific, and highly technical. You could measure response and/or sales. You might need IT staff for database modeling, analytics, and management and production specialists to ensure your pieces could be mechanically produced to a high standard and met post office requirements. One small mistake could mean millions in losses.

Technical expertise is paramount for direct mail execution. One time-sensitive, large newspaper insertion of a direct mail piece I created was botched by a minor mistake by the printer. It was a teaser envelope with a special offer inside for motorcyclists, with an expiration date. We planned to insert the envelopes mechanically into the leading U.K. publication for motorcyclists, a weekly newspaper. I received my samples; they looked terrific; I signed off. The print quality was beautiful, colors in register, crisp, contents in the correct insertion order. The newspaper invited me to the printing plant to watch the insertion. Opening the boxes to place the envelopes on the inserter revealed that most of the envelopes were stuck together and would feed on the inserter. The reason: During the application of adhesive during the envelope production, the position of the glue strips that seal the envelopes had shifted half a centimeter, so that the glue bled past the flap and stuck to the next envelope placed on top. My samples came from the beginning of the run, before the applicator had started slipping on the web press. Even if the printer ate the cost, I'd missed the window for insertion, which had to be booked in advance since only so many insertions were possible per issue. In short, if you're in charge of marketing, you're responsible whether or not you put the glue on yourself because vehicle sales dip that month, and in a seasonal business, it's often not recoverable.

You get the sticking point. Direct mail is labor-intensive and requires a high level of technical expertise and experience—which 99.9 percent of those in the advertising industry did not have. As many large companies, particularly those in financial services, shifted their advertising budgets to direct marketing (DM) agencies in the 1980s and 1990s, advertising agencies bought the DM agencies. The same happened with online or interactive agencies later on. Because the agency owners wanted to sell what they understood and were comfortable selling, rather than what the client wanted, they used their proprietorship control to attempt to steer clients away from direct and toward more advertising. Or worse, they imagined they were capable of doing direct themselves with no technical knowledge. There was no integration of agency services. As a result, the majority of large clients still use different agencies for different marketing disciplines.

The agencies would have been successful if they had integrated *employees* to handle integrated clients' businesses. With rare exceptions, the agency chiefs did not hire account staff, creatives, and production people who had expertise across the marketing mix. And in the few cases where they did, it was largely unsuccessful in the clients' eyes, because the integrated businesspeople were not empowered—they were still being directed by people who understood one discipline, usually advertising. Meeting after meeting I attended as a consultant to the agency world had the advertising big boys developing the so-called umbrella strategy for the client and then serving it to the poor sisters, the below-the-line crew. The advertising elders believed themselves to be superior beings, the only ones who could understand business strategy, although they'd only worked in one slice of the marketing mix for most of their lives. This always came across to the client, who often had 90 percent of his budget allocated toward the "poor" sister.

With that attitude, it is not surprising that more than a decade later, there are still few integrated *people* in most advertising agencies, and the online, direct marketing, PR, sales promotion, and ethnic divisions are still separate poor sisters, only allowed to eat dinner at the main table when invited by the big brother. Perhaps they would all live in a better house if they all shared the same knowledge, but the big brother is too afraid of losing the biggest room to risk getting a much bigger room in a much bigger house.

The same reason for not hiring integrated people to manage agencies is the reason why most process roles have been created. HR managers claim that people who are strategic and tactical, or people who have multiple skills (such as being able to program software *and* communicate with other departments), don't exist. They do exist and are tired of being asked if they are strategic *or* tactical by someone who is not both. They are easy to find—managing small businesses.

I've been told that I am not analytical because I am creative. The departmental manager who said this rationalized his statement this way: "You can't be both, because I'm analytical and I'm not creative." (Well, he was certainly right about not being creative.) When I explained that my business ideas were generated by data, and gave a few examples, he asked me to give him my "formula" for using the data to be creative so he could be creative. too. (He just lost the analytical vote, too.)

Your bank does the same thing. It wants you to be an integrated customer—owning several of its products. But you have to talk to a different customer service rep for each product. Listen up banks: If you want to cross-sell your customers, you've got to cross-train your staff. If your own employees don't understand several of your products, why should I?

The lesson is that if you want to have staff who are multitalented, ensure the people who manage and hire are multitalented. Today, most agency heads have expertise in only one area, despite the fact that their primary clients need many. Integrated people will keep integrated clients happy.

Unsuccessful at getting their clients' total marketing budget, the agencies were about to get another blow, and deal with it in an even more humorous way. McKinsey and The Big Eight, seven, six, five, four accounting firms started business consulting in earnest in the '90s. The ad agencies missed the boat again. Because they hired people with communications expertise and not marketing or business people, agencies had focused on how to communicate what businesses already had, rather than make what the business offered better.

Strategic and multitalented people in corporations, fed up with inept leadership, blocking of new ideas, and can't-do attitudes, started leaving to start their own companies, leaving a gap that McKinsey, accounting firms, and the former deserters as consultants quickly filled. Corporations took more money from their advertising budgets to pay for business consulting in lieu of marketing communications. It was sensible. Better to have a best-in-market product with high word-of-mouth advertising than a me-too weakening product with lots of expensive advertising. The clients complained that agencies were more concerned with winning awards for producing exciting ads than driving profits. They muttered that agencies weren't proactive and were focused on a marketing discipline rather than business strategy. They were direct in telling agencies that they didn't have personnel who had broad business experience, were proactive, and had a track record of generating business solutions. They didn't even have people who understood more than one marketing discipline, let alone competitive business strategy, operations, and basic profitability models in other industries.

As a result, most major ad agencies created consulting divisions to compete with McKinsey, Anderson Consulting (now Accenture), KPMG, Ernst & Young, and the youngbloods who formerly worked for big companies, to prevent losing another chunk of their clients' budgets. Some feared the big consultancies would create advertising agencies, or even scarier, buy ad agencies. Most were angry that consulting seemed like easy money, not labor-intensive like their last growth strategy. Not having learned any lessons by the way they failed to integrate below-the-line acquisitions, they formed these consultancies in the most laughable way you can imagine. They staffed the consultancies with their favorite good ol' boys from their ad agencies—the same staff who had driven their clients to McKinsey, etc., through their lack of business strategy skills and client-side experience. Imagine their surprise when clients didn't line up to pay their new divisions easy money to do what they should have been doing in the first place, and would have been able to do had they hired businesspeople with advertising experience rather than advertising people.

Just last week I viewed the Web site of one of these major "integrated" agencies that positions itself (like most of its competitors) as delivering innovative "business" solutions that will revolutionize clients' industries to supercede competition. Yet the examples in all of its case studies were me-too advertising and promotional ideas: clubs, discounts, print ads, Web cast. Chortle, chortle. Not one changed clients' products or services.

Acquisitions succeed when the players are in love with the skill of the acquired company and want to become like *them*. It's about delight in learning new things, not about control. Acquisitions fail when the buyer wants the assumed business to change. Companies shouldn't need integration managers; they need to hire and lead with integrated businesspeople.

The fact that a company needs to hire an integration manager makes it pretty clear that it expects anything but a "unified and harmonious whole." Expectations are built upon historical behavior. Companies create integration managers only after major problems repeatedly arise post-acquisition. It's an easy fix: Remove the source of the integration problem, which is the people who squelched innovation and success at the acquirer—now on a rampage to squelch it within the new division. Since big companies are creatures of habit, they'll do what comes naturally—avoid their people who are the problem (encouraging them to continue on the rampage) and create another scapegoat process role. Unless they get a flash of insight.

Think of your company as a major league baseball team. The players are judged by quantifiable measures: errors, RBIs, home runs. Outfielders have to field well, throw accurately, and be good batters, or they don't stay on the team. They have to communicate clearly with teammates. When a ball pops out between right and center field, the outfielders aren't fighting to both catch the ball—one calls it while the other backs him up. It's clear who's accountable. Major league teams don't keep lousy outfielders who drop the ball just because they can bat, nor do they hire support players to stand in the field behind them telling them how fast to run to catch the ball or traffic managers to make sure they caught the ball when they should have. If the team stays near the bottom of the league, the manager is fired rather than allowed to hire dozens of process managers.

Coaches don't play the field or go up to bat. They don't do part of the outfielders' or pitchers' jobs to cover up for incompetence. They impart expertise they gained through experience as leading outfielders or pitchers. Adding more players to the outfield does not make a team better. They don't keep players who prevent their teammates from hitting home runs or catching fly balls. When a good pitcher gets tired, you replace him. When the team keeps losing, you fire the manager or replace players with better ones rather than hire more and keep them on the bench while the losers continue to play.

Is your company hitting home runs, or does it keep hiring more players who will never get up to bat? Does it have coaches who impart knowledge borne from experience to help others improve and progress, or hire news commentators to collect statistics? Are your players and managers competent and cooperative? Do they understand the game and how to win? Or do they need additional strategy managers, quality gurus, coaches to coach the coaches, and process directors to help them decide whether they should steal second, catch the ball, or bunt, and to inform them if they are called out or lost the game? Do they need human relations managers and project managers to encourage them to compete against the other teams and not their fellow teammates? The world's greatest players got into baseball because they love the game. All they want to do is play ball.

Process roles are prolific in today's corporations. It's why the top players don't want to play in the corporate sandbox anymore. There are now 10 hands on the bat, no home runs, and, funny enough, everyone's blaming the guy who was belting them out of the park before the rest put their two hands in. It's only a matter of time before he changes teams or, better yet, becomes a big leaguer for another team. Undoubtedly, you can name countless process roles in companies created to compensate for employees who don't or can't make good business decisions. This brings us to the process role most likely to fail.

Keep the Change

April 9, 1992. London. Election Day. A man with a clipboard approached me. "I'm conducting an exit poll. Would you mind telling me whom you just voted for?"

It should have been obvious. I was wearing a button that read: "I earned it, and I'm going to spend it. Vote Conservative." (The in-your-face ad constituted a form of British wit.)

The incumbent Conservative (Tory) Party promised the same-old same-old. Labour's manifesto was "it's time to get Britain working again." Labour promised change. In TV interviews, citizens railed about the Tory blunders and talked about how they wanted change. In almost every poll, the Labour Party was garnering a significant lead. The BBC's reports of exit polls throughout Election Day confirmed it.

Final tally: Conservatives 41.93 percent, Labour 34.39 percent.

This was no statistical margin of error. It wasn't a polling error either. People simply lied about whom they'd voted for three minutes before. People said they wanted change. More important, people wanted other people to think they wanted change. They didn't.

Fast forward to the 2008 New Hampshire Democratic Party primary. Barack Obama, whose platform was "change we can believe in" had a 9 percent lead in the polls. According to most analysts, citizens were saying they were voting for Obama because they wanted change. They didn't. Hillary Rodham Clinton won by a 9 percent margin.

Change. People don't. New is naught. That's why banks use credit (FICO) scores to decide whether to lend people money and approve credit cards. Late payers will pay late again. People in debt will stay in debt, even after winning the lottery. Because people don't change.

Fast Company magazine says the odds are nine to one that you won't change, even if your choice is "change or die." Dr. Edward Miller at Johns Hopkins University reported: "If you look at people after coronary-artery bypass grafting two years later, 90 percent of them have not changed their lifestyle. And that's been studied over and over and over again...they know they should change, for whatever reason, they can't."[1]

I did product launch consulting work for Eli Lilly, which commands 80 percent of the U.S. insulin market. About 7 percent of the U.S. population has diabetes, and most people with Type II diabetes are overweight (yes, there is a correlation). People with diabetes know the related risks of amputation, blindness, coma, and death. Most people progress from oral prescriptions to injections. You would think that before the disease gets so severe that someone has to inject several times a day, he would lose weight and exercise more. He says he wants to change. He doesn't. Often, starting daily injections leads to an increase in weight as patients justify how they can overeat even more because the insulin will "take care of it."

So if we're not willing to change even if it will kill us, what do you think the chance is that people in big companies, who are being rewarded (read paid and promoted) for doing the same thing every day, would want to do something new. Here it is at the top of the pile...

Silly Process Role #8
New Product Development (NPD) Director

In his best-selling business bible, *Innovation and Entrepreneurship,* Peter Drucker outlined how to structure companies for innovation:

> For the existing business to be capable of innovation, it has to create a structure that allows people to be entrepreneurial....

And innovative efforts...should never report to line managers charged with responsibility for ongoing operations.... The best, and perhaps the only, way to avoid killing off the new by sheer neglect is to set up the innovative project from the start as a separate business.[2]

Notice Drucker didn't say separate *department*; he said separate business. When the book was written, Drucker praised 3M and Johnson & Johnson for their promises that the person who "develops a new product, new market, or a new service and then builds a business on it will become the head of that business...." The venture didn't need to be a full-time job either.

This, Drucker preached, will retain the best and brightest in corporations; let them use their entrepreneurial skills and "reward them accordingly." Those whose driving force is constant creation will naturally keep moving ahead, to the benefit of the company and its employees. Everybody wins when owners of ideas become owners of businesses with the same passion witnessed today among the self-employed.

In most companies, employees differ on the description of what exactly the new product development role is supposed to achieve, ensuring that it will achieve nothing. Is the person supposed to develop unique or patentable products, products that are new to the company but copied from competitors, or enhancements to existing products? Ask the division managers, line managers, or account managers what new products their new product department should develop. If your division makes shaving products, the new products they want should be centered on giving the end user a better hair-removal result, remembering that better can mean faster, smoother, more comfortable, longer lasting, razorless, fun (yes, fun), etc., or never having to shave again. Profit is a by-product of producing a product desirable to consumers that cannot be obtained elsewhere and making it known and available to the right target market. If focusing on the end user is the top priority of the entire corporation's new product wish list, there's a good chance there's companywide support for innovation.

However, if the key executives of the corporation spew a shopping list of me-too products or that the lowest market price is the primary objective (an unsustainable value proposition for any company), it's time to bolt for the door. Wholesalers will buy what end users demand. If the objective is a better shave, the first assignment for NPD should not be making a three-blade razor that's better than the competition's (we really need a six-blade razor). There are countless ways to produce a smoother shave than by using three blades. By the time you get a slightly better three-blade razor to market, it will be practically obsolete. The competitor with the great three-blade razor is already launching a newer product that will make your copycat look ridiculous.

When NPD exists to support other departments' needs, rather than to change what other departments sell either by making those items obsolete or fulfilling another unmet consumer need, it will fail. As covered under Silly Process Role #4 (Any Title Containing "Support" or "Services"), marketing departments labeled "sales support" will attract mediocre talent who will produce mediocre results, because the sales support title shouts that marketing (and those who work there) is not important. Furthermore, sales is a marketing function—a way of getting to the market. It would make more sense to call the sales department "marketing support" if you believe in "support" titles. Do you know any great salespeople who would take a job with the title "marketing support?" Why would a top marketer take the title "sales support"?

To close the door on salespeople, potential clients often say, "If you had the same product as your competitor for less, we'd give you the business." We know this is bull. The competitor could simply lower its price again once you provided the price benchmark. For example, Home Depot would often seesaw between two bidders offering the same requested product, when it was clear who the winner would be from the start. After three rounds in one particular bidding battle, the winner became the loser—promising to develop Home Depot's bespoke wish list for a miniscule margin, while agreeing not to enjoy economies of scale by offering the same product to its other customers. Home Depot used each company to cut the other's throat. The winner, of course, was Home Depot. Both bidders were losers.

Had either vendor created a *better, patented* product that would have exceeded Home Depot's requirements and made all competitors' products obsolete, the bidding war would never have happened. The vendor could have offered Home Depot its product at a premium since the vendor was the owner of the invention, the patented product. If Home Depot was desperate to stop the vendor from selling the invention to its competitors, the vendor could have charged a premium again. The inventors of patented products, of ingenuity, are the winners in today's business world. The me-too companies with me-too products are the losers.

The counterbidding strategy proved so rewarding for Home Depot, and HD received so much positive reinforcement for pitting the two vendors against each other, that it simply used one vendor until it was all used up, then showed it the door for good. After losing the Home Depot account, the vendor's head salesperson was promoted, to show the company's employees what's important. The head of NPD, whose never-presented products lay in a heap on the floor, left and started his own business. And lived happily ever after. Just to show the others what's important.

When you hire new product developers to follow directions rather than steer one of your ships or with the intention of keeping all their ships in the harbor, you'll find they abandon the ship quickly.

Annette, who never said "no," was chosen to head product development in her health care services company, reporting to the marketing director. Annette was supposed to produce anything that the client account staff asked for. She'd never developed a single new product before or during her two-year tenure, but she got things done. (Translation: She did what she was told and often suggested that the membership ID could be printed in six colors, earning the label "creative.") With the prestigious title emblazoned on her résumé (and no hope of ever launching a brand new product, which is precisely why she was chosen), she easily moved from her NPD role to the next hot job of the late 1990s, Six Sigma black belt, another process role. Success.

Her abandoned NPD role was filled by popular Dave, who transferred from a field office to lead new product development but quietly disappeared after six months to another division. Since no one had been successful in developing new products, the company decided it was because the former NPD leaders weren't assertive enough. Extrovert Colin, the next unsuccessful new product kingpin, lasted four months before being told to find another job because he was too aggressive. When hired, neither Colin nor Dave had a history of new product development success.

After 15 interviews over six months, Bryan was hired from outside the company because of his impressive track record of inventing new health care products and successfully launching them. Unable to accomplish anything in this process role in this company, Bryan resigned after 18 months. (What Bryan should have realized is that the length and difficulty of decision making during the interview process was an omen of things to come.) Neal, a dot.commer who was also an outsider, replaced Bryan as vice president. Brought in for his out-of-the-box thinking, he found that all his ideas (adaptations of successful ones he'd created at other companies) were abandoned as "not practical" although they scored high in consumer research. After six months, the marketing director who'd actively blocked every new idea proposed because he couldn't understand them and was afraid of change, abolished the title. A year later, he continually whined to his line managers: "There's just no one here who's creative anymore."

The factor that is consistent for all those unsuccessful product development employees, regardless of whether they had a history of new product success elsewhere, is this: They all had the same manager—the marketing director. You would never guess that every division this boss had been a senior level manager for has either gone out of business, had a massive decline in revenue, or suffered a debilitating law suit. But he kept getting promoted. Imagine how everyone who has worked with him feels knowing that his appointment spells disaster for them and further rewards for him. Will anyone dare to propose an idea that would improve earnings?

It is clear that the decision makers in this company don't want new products. Why?

If the president wanted new products, by now he would have fired the Bozo marketing director. The organizational structure wouldn't have the new product position under Bozo. In fact, if the environment was conducive to developing new products, there wouldn't be a new product process role. The marketing director would have a history of new product success, as would the other senior leaders and the vast majority of marketing staff. It would be a natural function for people in the company to develop new products, particularly the people who make the hiring decisions.

Most corporations use new product titles as awards for popular or hardworking staff who have no expertise in development or market launches of new products. Even more surprising (except to people who work in large companies) is that the leaders of most product development divisions have never created and marketed a new-to-market product. Try to find an NPD director in a large company who has even one patent in the company's field. Give up? Then try finding one who even has a patent. Good luck. It's the blind leading the blind. Often, the same companies describe a copycat of a competitor's product as a "new" product. The people who have the ability to create and market new, exciting, profitable products, and see the new product kahuna title go to someone who hasn't, are probably designing their exit strategies or have long since left.

Try to find a small-business owner who has created a new or significantly better product. No problem. Find an entrepreneur who has a patent. Easy. Having the ability to create and deliver that new idea was the reason they bolted from the big brother. Lack of a support network is more attractive than a retort network.

The same companies who put people with no record of new product creation and market success in the top new product position (or promote finance managers to virgin marketing directors) are the same who would never dream of putting someone with no IT experience in the top IT role, or someone with no finance department experience in the chief financial officer role. The NPD leader and marketing director will have at least as much impact on the company's future financials as the CFO, yet the position is usually trusted to an amateur. The key characteristics for becoming CFO and NPD director are vastly different but should be similar. CFOs are selected for having shown their ability to affect the bottom line in ways their colleagues have not. Internally promoted NPD directors are typically chosen for their popularity. Their creative contributions have been limited to improvements that haven't threatened the jobs or egos of their colleagues, including senior managers. Change agents are rarely selected for this top position and leave the company to start their own businesses as a result. Change accomplished.

How many times have you heard that someone who's never even driven a different road to the office has been given the NPD role because "he's more likely to get a new product delivered because people like him"? This excuse not only indicates an absence of right-brain thinking, but indicates that the left brain is missing as well. Ingrained in that statement are two revelations. First is that the company does not believe it is possible to find a person who will be liked who also has a history of product development. Second, therefore, is the admission that people in the company will hate those who propose truly new products.

Hiring marketing heads or NPD heads without product development expertise is an admission that your company's heads don't want innovation or change. The best ideas should be adopted, regardless of their source. They know very well Mr. Nice Guy will never come up with a great idea, but they all sleep well at night saying they've done something about it—filling a job title. Brain-dead.

Here's the fundamental reason that a new product department or person should never exist. **If the new product group is successful, while ousting competitors, they will also create products that are better than existing products. Their breakthroughs, their successes, will put their colleagues out of jobs by replacing their products and know-how with new and better things. Established employees, as a matter of survival, do everything possible to ensure the destruction or failure of the new product director or department.**

When the idea (and the data supporting it) is so good they can't attack it, they personally attack the person who presented it.

The existence of NPD process roles creates nothing but new politics. Forcing new product departments to get approvals and build test products through an existing corporate infrastructure whose very existence depends on maintaining the status quo drives capable innovators to run for cover. The most dysfunctional organizations "hand off" the new products to be managed by or voted on by the same individuals who spent a great deal of their time criticizing rather than contributing to the new product and its inventor. After the handover, the people who are unable to develop new products because they lack expertise in new trends will often whittle down the differentiators that made the new product a breakthrough and use the same stale marketing techniques as for their old products until they feel comfortable with the new product. Making the new product like the old product reinforces their position as company experts, ensuring their survival. How many times have you seen products that performed brilliantly in research fail in the market for this reason? It's common in companies where there's a separate NPD department that doesn't continue to own the P&L for new products.

You know what happens when the NPD director has to get buy-in and support from other departments. The finance guy prepares a profitability model for the new product, putting in the standard 27 percent for corporate tax (although the company has never paid more than 10), adds a healthy portion of the overstuffed company's existing fixed costs (which should not be included in new product P&Ls—and if you don't know why, you shouldn't work in finance or NPD), uses financial assumptions from irrelevant loser products, and includes write off percentages that haven't been realized since the Great Depression. The IT guy estimates 3 million man-hours to build the product without researching or considering off-the-shelf software.

You can go Drucker's route and banish inventors to run new divisions. It might work. But you're still going to have a battle with the deadheads for overall resources. Drucker touched upon another alternative. He stated, **"Innovation must be part and parcel of the ordinary, the norm, if not routine."**[3] The same goes for quality, service, compliance, and every other characteristic that all competent businesspeople should possess. When you need to create separate roles or positions to get those qualities because your core leaders and staff don't have them, the good people will bail.

So while I agree that Drucker's theory of structuring NPD as a separate business (not department) can work, in most companies it is actually better to have new product development experts in all the key company roles—"part and parcel of the norm." This way, it is natural for all staff to drive for better and replacement products and services. Product development will be intrinsic, rather than threatening, since those who have responsibility for the existing products will be rewarded, not eliminated, with destruction of an existing product.

I hear shrieks of horror as business executives imagine their past and present new product developers in all their company's leadership roles. If you are shrieking, it is simply because you haven't had the right people doing NPD (and that's probably because it was a process role in your company). The new product developers you need in the company's key roles are businesspeople who also have a history of success in a wide host of functional roles such as finance, marketing, and IT, with management strengths. In other words, they have shown they know how to run a business *and* build/grow a business.

"But, but, but," says human resources. "It's impossible to find people who have not only created and marketed successful new products, but have great people skills, understand finance, marketing, IT, client relationships, etc."

Wrong. It's simple to find multitalented businesspeople. They are running small businesses. They left big businesses because they weren't allowed to do more than one thing or anything. Forced to "dumb down" and do a single process role in big business, they decided instead to make business decisions that utilized the broad skill set they had. Allow them to be business leaders again in an environment that is free of deadheads, and they will come back. If they lack a single skill, train.

If you want to work for a company that believes in change, look for one that epitomizes change and has mostly employees with a history of significant change. Because people don't change.

So those are the top eight silly process roles. Small companies don't have them.

If an existing employee lacks the training or experience to do the job right, fix that. If the employee can't integrate new skills, remove him or her. The solution is to increase the breadth of knowledge, experience, and expertise of existing, capable employees, not to hire a labyrinth organization of form fillers and checklist checkers. Creating process departments, like quality, is a sure sign that companies expect staff to deliver inferior products and service. As long as people can keep blaming the quality department for poor performance, no one will blame them. Convenient.

When you create a process department like quality, new product development, e-marketing, or project management rather than make those roles part and parcel of everyone's jobs, you don't really want any of them to prevail. You're just looking for scapegoats. List the process departments of any large company, and you can easily discover what senior management is keen to avoid (while paying lip service), and will never succeed at.

Structuring a company like an Internet of small businesses creates opportunities for employees to stay on a steep learning curve and provides avenues for individuals to impact the bottom line of the company, to make a difference. Remember the *Harvard Business Review* study? The top two reasons people quit were job content and level of responsibility. Customer service, IT, operations...you name it, it's been outsourced. Funny enough, departments like quality and project management that shouldn't exist usually aren't outsourced. Processes should be outsourced.

It's no surprise that one of the fastest-growing trends for product development is to outsource it to small businesses that specialize in invention. The problem is that big companies believe that innovation is a process rather than a job skill— which is precisely why the people who had that job skill left. Smart people read and listen. After watching their brethren beaten up for being creative, innovators avoid those companies like the plague. Without the ability to keep or attract new product developers, companies resort to outsourcing.

Small businesses (usually staffed by people who came from large businesses) are becoming the R&D departments and new product development departments for big companies that haven't managed them well in the past. What makes anyone think they're going to manage the small-business output any better?

A.G. Lafley, Procter & Gamble's CEO, told employees that their goal is to source at least 50 percent of innovations from outside the company. P&G gave around 50 employees the "position" of finding ideas from external creators.[4]

Call me stupid, but wouldn't it be a lot better to hire 50 serial innovators here instead of 50 project managers? Can you imagine a small-business owner hiring an employee whose only job is to find compatible great ideas?

It's not a coincidence that this drive toward an "open model of innovation" has happened right after P&G's migration from a brand management structure (P&L based and product based) to a process management structure. Open model equals closed process. Every college grad's dream job used to be to "own" a brand (be a *business manager*) at P&G. Now there are no businesses to manage, so the university students are loading up on courses on entrepreneurship instead, hoping they'll get hired by one of the invention firms that P&G outsources its product development to.

Nancy Rodriguez runs a $5 million product development company, Food Marketing Support Services. Like most product developers who are successful business owners, she worked in the food industry for a large company. How did her business grow? She hired top talent, who wanted to create and innovate. Guess where they came from?

American Pop Corn, which makes Jolly Time Pop Corn, allocated all of its new product development budget to Nancy's company, which created "Blast O Butter" for them. It became American Pop Corn's best seller, boosting revenues about 28 percent the first year.

> "Before we introduced Blast O Butter, our sales had plateaued and our market share was 3.5 percent," says Tom Elsen, vice-president of marketing at the 160-person company. "Now our market share for microwave popcorn is 10 percent and growing. Based on that success we're believers. We really rely on Nancy and her team. They are our R&D arm."
>
> ...A range of small companies—from invention labs and industrial-design firms to all kinds of entrepreneurs, from independent record labels to consumer-goods manufacturers— are behind corporate America's newest products.... Large companies don't have the time, talent, and patience to nurture seed-stage inventions.[5]

Large companies don't have time, talent, and patience to nurture invention because the talent most managers in large companies have is how to stop progress and change, and that includes any change required to *implement* ideas, whether from inside or outside sources. If product development was normal, and the people who worked for the company were normally developers, blockers would be exited quickly, saving time.

It's terrific that companies outsourcing product development finally realize that inventors are most likely to produce new inventions (because people don't change), and that a history of successful new product creation and implementation is the best indicator of future success. But it's an admission that it's not a core competency of the people they employ, or that if you're an inventor who is employed by the company, you're unlikely to have any success getting your ideas approved.

The way for large companies to attract the best and brightest and retain profitability and growth in the long term cannot be accomplished through obtaining product superiority through acquisitions, outsourcing invention, NPD departments, or hiring stacks of engineers. It can only be achieved by ensuring that the decision makers, the line managers, the leaders, the board, the president, in other words, the people with the power, have a track record of successful new product creation, development, and implementation. Where innovation is the norm, the best and brightest will flock to and nest.

Cheese. My first job was at a mall working for the cheese store, Hickory Farms of Ohio. It was summer and I was 16 years old. I hated cheese, probably the result of too much TV. Remember Chubby on *Little Rascals* and Limburger cheese? It was like a Pavlov's dog experiment. When I saw cheese, I saw goo and smelled gunk.

Hickory Farms had a rule: Every time you cut cheese for a customer off a block or wheel, you had to take a sliver for yourself. That way, you could forever associate the taste, texture, and smell of the cheese with its name. Customers would come in and say, "I'm looking for a cheese I had at a party last weekend, and I can't remember its name." Hickory Farms believed you had to know the product to serve the customer well. By the end of the summer, when I was 20 pounds heavier and looking more like Chubby, I'd become a cheese lover, craving the bluest blues, peanut-buttery Gjetost, and Wisconsin white cheddar, extra sharp enough to cut your tongue.

If a customer asked for a half pound of Jarlesberg cheese, it was easy to put the wheel on the cutting board, pull the wire through it at the right point, wrap it up, and exchange currency for cheese. Because I chatted with the customer while doing this, and shared a taste, I could also recommend and offer samples of other things the customer might like, and increase sales. I loved that job. Once the managers saw customers liked me (and I liked cheese), I got to make cheese logs (before they were mass produced) in the back kitchen, close out the registers, and balance the ledgers each night. All this without supervision. At 16 years old, I was even trusted to carry the cash to the bank and make the night deposit. Imagine how much I learned about running a business from doing *all* those things. Just think how loyal I felt toward my manager, and the company—and still do. I could see the direct impact between my salesmanship and the takings at the end of the day. I knew how the product was produced and the importance of sterility in food handling (after all, I was eating it too!), and could relay this care and pride to customers.

Although it was only a summer job, I remember the congeniality among all the employees. Competition was friendly and for the benefit of the company. Because we handled the customers start to finish, a lost sale was a learning experience to improve upon, rather than an exercise to assert blame. It was more like a game of golf: You compete against yourself to improve your own handicap and that's how you win the game. You don't see golfers slugging it out on the links.

What if that Hickory Farms store had had process roles? Would I, or my colleagues, have lasted the summer? Would their sales have increased? Would I enjoy only making cheese logs all day? Would I care as much about food hygiene? Would I still be an advocate? If I worked the cash register only, would I be able to increase sales by recommending another cheese or beef stick, or would it be too late? If all I could do was cut cheese and not converse with customers, would I care if they bought that high-margin box of crackers? What if a Six Sigma manager was standing over my shoulder as I sliced the cheese off the block or wheel, making sure that I was within five hectograms of a half pound under 3.4 times per million cuts? Instead of training and supervision from managers, what if headquarters had sent project managers to monitor whether I cut the cheese within 10 seconds of the customer's order? Did we need to hire someone to log in each customer's piece of cheese before handing it to an expert cashier? What if I had to use a script and couldn't try different sales approaches?

The key elements of job satisfaction at Hickory Farms were **the breadth of tasks tied to the ability to make a difference, the perpetual training from managers and peers, the uniformly high competency level among colleagues, autonomy, and respect. And,**

of course, the absence of process roles. It sounds simple because it is simple.

Today, these key elements are most often found as a small-business owner or as an employee of a small business. That's why there's a corporate brain drain.

Getting America's wizards back in big companies is just as simple:

1. **Eliminate at least 80 percent of your process departments within 180 days.**

   Put people back in P&L roles. If, for example, a quality black belt does not have the job skills to migrate to a multitalented functional role, say "good-bye" to that employee, regardless of how well liked he or she is. Use the 180 days to refresh staff to handle "business" roles and make quality (and other process functions) the responsibility of P&L owners.

2. **Eliminate employees who are unwilling or unable to collaborate or communicate** on corporatewide issues such branding, privacy policies, advertising agency choices or rate cards, product pricing guidelines, etc.

   Do not hire separate employees to police inter-departmental agreements. You will reduce your overall employee base, saving costs. Instead, fire employees who are unwilling or unable to implement agreed-upon policies or group business decisions that they participated in developing. By removing process police officers and other scapegoats, you will quickly see who the problem employees are. Do not make special sanctions for the anti-collaborators. This does not necessarily mean eliminating employees who are not liked, because in most large organizations, change agents are seen as threatening and are not liked. It means that you eliminate those who don't collaborate and communicate. Change agents like change and are usually more flexible.

3. **Outsource remaining process departments.**

   If it's really a process, you'll cut costs and eliminate politics by outsourcing it. If it can't be outsourced, you probably didn't need the process department anyway; it was just a cover for other people who weren't doing their jobs.

4. **Divide your company into smaller business units, and those into smaller business units**.

Make each business unit have total P&L accountability and responsibility. In a packaged food, that means that at some level, a person is responsible for one product. If you produce soup, at a higher level the business division might be between canned and dry. But somewhere in that organization, one person has responsibility for the profitability of minestrone. Make each business leader responsible for improving his or her product. Hire people who have the brains to investigate and introduce what works for the competition and for internal competitors, as well as what the market needs and wants *that no one else offers.*

5. **Put people who have demonstrated the ability to run businesses, not process departments, in the top jobs.**

Let them choose accountants, systems personnel, HR, etc., from the pool. To eliminate process departments (e.g., finance), transfer the best employees to the business units. You will quickly see which financiers none of the business leaders chooses for his or her business unit. Don't assume that the lowest paid and least competent will be the only ones not selected. Those who do not offer more profitability potential than their salaries and related costs can also be left behind when the company becomes a conglomerate of communicating small businesses.

Anyone crying that functional "best practices" will disappear when process departments disappear is missing the point. If a financier from one business unit doesn't proactively keep up with best practices in his or her own area of specialization and doesn't seek out information from colleagues, you've got the weakest link. Best employees want training in the newest methods in their function. Pay for training. Let the best employees decide which methods to apply. You'll have the funds because all the process managers who stopped progress will be gone. If you need to hire a finance director or seat someone next to other finance managers for them to be competent and use best practices, you can guarantee that the department isn't packed with geniuses. Following "best practices" does not mean treating every situation the same, no more than having "best service" means treating all customers the same. "Best service" is treating each customer the way he or she would like to be treated, as "best practices" means applying the most effective technique according to each situation, not the same old technique. Since business is not stagnant, neither should best practices be. "Have It Your Way," was a hugely successful Burger King slogan. The company didn't say, "Have It the Way We Determined Most People Want It."

Hire the best, and they'll use all the tools available to them to implement the most lucrative solution whatever the circumstance.

6. **For niche talents, provide training by current business experts, not a process department, to develop your existing business unit team, or outsource to fill gaps.**
   You get better results training existing employees how to run every facet of the burger business than making them flip burgers for eight hours a day. How long can an employee stay in the burger-flipping department? About as long as he or she can stay satisfied in any other process role.

   Everybody flips some burgers when he starts a business. No one minds rolling up his sleeves and doing the dirty work, when it's only a small part of running the big burger business. "Burger flipping" got a bad rap when it became a process role, with quality people screaming how to do it, and cashiers screaming orders. Run your own business, and making that burger best becomes a lifelong quest. Let employees own the business in a big company, and watch those burgers plump and sizzle right before your eyes.

7. **Employee gaps? Fill them with small-business owners.**
   The next 10 times you hear people say they're unhappy in their careers, they don't know what they want to do, or they don't feel fulfilled with their lives, scribble down whether they currently work for large or small companies. Then note whether each is a small-business owner or in a large-company process role. Guess what? Small-business owners are least likely to claim they're unhappy in their careers, don't know what they want to do, or are unfulfilled in their lives. Process role employees are most likely to be unhappy in their jobs, stressed, and confused about their future.

   Whom would you rather hire to run your company or any of your divisions? Whom would you rather hire to do any job that can't be done by a monkey? To fill employee gaps for people with proven ability to run businesses, look for small-business owners and employees in small businesses.

That's all there is to it. Even the gurus of quality and process management are changing their views:

> Michael Hammer, who is largely responsible for the spread of the reengineering movement throughout the world, has acknowledged that 70 percent of the efforts to replace corporate hierarchies with "process teams" have been unsuccessful. The main reason, he claimed, is that he and others who promoted this management craze had failed to address the human side of the process."
>
> Daryl Conner, *Leading at the Edge of Chaos*[6]

In a Reveries.com survey (almost half of respondents had 15+ years of business experience), the "need to break down organizational silos was by far the most frequently—and vehemently—mentioned challenge." Other top-listed barriers were management and having cross-trained staff. The respondents' recommendation: Replace "pyramids" with "pods." What business execs wanted was for each pod to become its own company. They wanted each pod staffed with people, diverse in backgrounds, skills, capabilities, and seniority, who were empowered to make their own decisions.[7]

In *The Conference Board* report by human resources managers called "Sustaining The Talent Quest: Getting and Keeping the Best People in Volatile Times," HR executives listed in their top five objectives multilevel involvement and accountability for talent, integrated talent strategies, and opportunities for career and personal development.[8] Yet companies do exactly the opposite, creating more and more matrix and process positions.

Given the responsibility *and* authority to run a type of small business with big-company resources, the best and brightest people will come back to big corporations. With a business full of small-business owners, the focus shifts toward products competing with each other, both within the company and with competitors, and away from departments competing with each other.

Big business can once again flourish. Say "cheese."

CHAPTER

6

Fast Track to the Sole Train

May 14, 2002, 7:01 p.m. "Here are your tickets. Someone will be waiting to meet you in Kyoto," said the perfectly pleasant courier in impeccable English.

"Tickets? There are two?"

"Yes. You'll need to change trains in Nagoya," she replied slowly, cautiously avoiding any grammatical errors.

I flipped through the tickets. They had assigned seats, and there was less than five minutes to change trains to make my connection. "I think there's a mistake. There's not enough time to make the connection." She gestured to see the tickets. I handed them to her, shuffling my bags, careful to remember that I must always use my right hand to pass or receive things in Japan.

"Aaawwww," she intoned, in a way that was typically Japanese, checking the times. "I think maybe there's almost five minutes to change trains. That's OK?"

"Umm," I would try to be equally indirect and, therefore, polite. "What if the train is late?" Buzzer. Failed.

She looked puzzled. Thoughtfully, she strained to use her tourist training: No question is a stupid question. It was obviously a stupid question. "Why would the train be late?"

To the courier, it was illogical to make allowances for trains to be late. In her experience, the train had never been late. My experience was 11 years of British Rail (BR), whose ambiguous, self-effacing slogan was "We're Getting There"... acknowledging their on-time record was appalling without making a quantifiable commitment to change. Until it did markedly improve, BR set itself up for years of lampooning by British comedians. Never have a tag line that lends itself to tagging adverbs on the end. It's like naming your newborn something that rhymes with a derogatory term. Perhaps its advertising agency convinced BR that any publicity was better than no publicity.

Growing up in a small city the United States, I'd never been on a commuter train. Trains in the U.S. didn't have the reputation for running like Swiss watches (or Swiss trains). Cars were considered more convenient and reliable. Or perhaps having one's own personal space to sing out loud or pick one's nose was more essential to the travel experience than in other countries.

Why did Japanese workers focus on ensuring trains ran on time while British Rail initially appeared to focus on developing a good advertising excuse for why they didn't? Have you worked in places where covering your butt takes priority over changing the status quo to solve problems? Who scores the points: the person who helps dwellers out of a burning building, or the one who proves he didn't cause the fire? Isn't the ideal to prevent the fire, rather than reactive firefighting? Let's extinguish the infighting and post-mortems. The death of a project is going to be attributed to the firefighter who didn't put out the fire fast enough rather than the pyromaniac anyway.

I did a Six Sigma project to reveal the leading cause of new product failure. The findings? Before the Six Sigma process began on designing a new product and before any research had been undertaken, the company decision maker who had no history of innovation or new product success had already decided which new product would be created. Therefore, the Six Sigma process that was supposed to be a method to determine the best offering was moot—a tremendous waste of time and effort, and therefore, money. When the products inevitably failed because their creation was predetermined rather than based on data on unmet consumer needs, members of the group who did all the work (including the useless Six Sigma fiasco) to build the mandated product were hanged. Everything was picked apart from the colors on the brochure to the business attire of the workers. The real problem was there was no market for the product offering. Most of the offerings were copycats of competitors, launched long after the market was saturated. For example, a business leader's instructions might be "Find the best sweepstakes prize to get magazine readers to renew their subscriptions" rather than "Find the best way to encourage subscription renewal" or even "Find the best way to increase the profitability of our publications among current and/or potential readers." In several cases, even the managers who ordered a Six Sigma project to "Find the best way to encourage subscription renewal" had already determined that the outcome was going to be a sweepstakes, regardless of the number of Six Sigma charts and meetings completed. A simple check of consumer behavior would have revealed that around half of consumers are not "players" or "gamers." They don't like sweepstakes, points collecting, or competitions and react negatively toward products that use these promotional tactics, believing they increase the cost of the goods. Even if the Six Sigma outcome was cost-efficiencies through better targeting (e.g., only advertising to players), the project still would have failed, since the listed objective (by the same person who wanted a sweepstakes) was increasing overall subscription renewals. Half the market will not respond to the sweepstakes, no matter what the prize is. Go on, laugh, but aren't the people who usually recommend sweepstakes the ones who claim they wouldn't dream of entering sweepstakes or buying a lottery ticket, believing their customers are not as bright?

According to a Gallup poll, 57 percent of Americans bought a lottery ticket in the past 12 months. You wouldn't think it's that many since the losers (most ticket buyers) don't go around bragging that they bought dud lottery tickets. Contrary to popular belief, the folks making the managerial salaries are doing most of the gambling. The Public Gaming Research Institute found that those with $45,000 to $75,000 incomes were most likely to play, with those earning more than $75,000 spending three times as much as the below-$25,000 income group. Funny, some people won't buy a lottery ticket, but gamble by working for companies that provide poor service and weak products.

More surprising than companies that can't add new products or services are companies that won't remove ones that customers loathe. Often, large companies keep using technology that doesn't work (developed by process management), increasing their (and their customers') costs, requiring them to pad their pockets with fees to make up lost profits of a dwindling customer pool. How many times do you phone customer service and the Interactive Voice Response system (IVR) aka phone menu asks you to punch in your account number on the key pad? And how many times is the first question the live service rep asks, "Can I have your account number please?" right after you've finished punching it in? Is this brain surgery? Either don't ask me to punch it in or don't ask me to repeat it.

IVR systems are a great example of something that took vendors years to sell into big companies, and now that they're ineffective and obnoxious, it'll take twice as many years to get them out. It's the anti-change brigade at work (or lack thereof). Don't you feel like The Scream when you get the recording that says, "Press 'one' to buy our new me-too product; press 'two' to speak to billing; press 'three' if you know your party's extension; press 'four' if you want to be rerouted to 'two'; press 'six' if you want to go to another menu of 99 of our most frequently asked questions; press 'eight' if you want to hear these choices again; press 'nine' if you want to go back to the first menu..."

My buddy Donna, who is a retired cop, tells me how they used to joke on the 911 board that they were going to put in an answering machine:

> Hello, thank you for calling 911. Your call is being recorded for quality assurance. If you'd like to take a survey at the end of this call, press 1.
>
> If you've been raped, press 2.
>
> If you haven't been raped, press 3.
>
> If your car is missing, press 4, but only if you think it's been stolen.
>
> Press 5 if your car is missing and you think it's been towed.
>
> If you're calling to report a murder in progress, please hang up and dial 1-800-555-1212.
>
> If you're having a heart attack, please hold for the next available operator.
>
> *Para español, oprima el numero seis.*

With IVR, you usually go through an average of four menus, after which time, you are put on hold anyway. After someone eventually answers the phone (and you have to give your account number), you usually discover that the person you got can't answer your questions (which is why companies say they installed these systems—so that you're routed to the correct agent). Then he transfers you, and

1. You are "accidentally" disconnected.

2. You are put back in the menu system.

3. After another bout of menus, you get another person who "doesn't handle that in this department."

4. You get a rep who criticizes the colleague who erroneously transferred the call.

5. You hang up.

When you call a small company, how often does this happen?

We all know that calls are not "recorded for quality assurance." They are recorded so the big company can cover its big ass. Since thousands of people have complained about IVR systems, there's obviously no quality assurance and no one listens to them, unless they're being sued. I've watched companies spend hundreds of thousands of dollars on gathering and paying research focus groups when the top brass can patch into customer service calls, listening in as a third party, at any time, for free! When I was a senior executive in big companies, I regularly listened to customers' inbound calls. Ask some senior executives when the last time is that they've patched into a customer service line and they'll give you excuses of all the times they talk to customers who aren't in the process of complaining about their products or service.

IVR menus were not developed to help customers. They exist so product managers in big companies don't have to work with other product managers in the same company (unless, of course, they hire some process roles). That's why the only time you can talk to ONE person about DSL, long distance land lines, mobile, AND cable from the same company is when they're trying to sell you a two-year service contract package with a hefty termination policy, because they know you'll want to leave when things don't work and you can't get anyone to help you. It's remarkable that they can train someone to *sell* all products, but they're incapable of *training* anyone to *service* all products. Yet they want you to *have* all products.

IVRs exist so that customer service employees will only have to cut cheese *or* take orders—in other words, so they only have to deal with a single product or single division. This is not what customers want, so if there's anything about listening to customers or serving their needs in your company mission statement, please remove it if you have IVR.

The facts on how much people hate IVR are readily available. So why don't big companies change their insulting, Cro-Magnon IVR systems? Whoever sold these systems to big companies decades ago convinced them that they saved money by replacing operators. After a few big companies did it, the others got in line as if they were following the Pied Piper. Most IVR systems now generate a net loss by pissing off customers, but the big boys are blocking their ears to what their customers want to deal with—people, not machines.

When people complained in research that they wanted to speak to a person when they picked up the phone, instead of a machine and punching phone buttons, the phone companies, banks, cable companies, health companies, etc., came up with a brilliant solution. They'll make the machine sound more like a person. Can you hear me now?

That didn't appease the masses, so the next "innovation" was to add voice recognition, so callers could *say* their replies to the machine, rather than punch buttons. Can you hear me now?

Customers were still complaining about machines, so companies installed caller ID to identify callers automatically so customers only had to offer two pieces of information "for security purposes" instead of 10 to be transferred to the "correct" representative.

Well, that didn't work either since people still had to repeat the information (including their phone number that was ID'd) for someone who couldn't handle the issue, because the company couldn't be bothered to install warm transfer systems (which transfer the customer's data with the call). (This happened to me today with my health insurance company, which raises my stress level to the point where I'm sick.)

So guess what? The banks finally decided to go through another cycle of opening up overhead, I mean, branches, on every corner because research told them that customers wanted to talk to people. Rather than remove IVR and replace it with people who pick up the phone, they opened branches on every corner, with more people. For some reason, they could train the people in the branches to understand all the products, but not the people on the phone. In five years, all the banks will be closing those unprofitable branches, just as they did in the 1990s. The expense didn't give them a competitive edge, because they were copying their competitors who were also opening branches next door. So now we're expected to drive to a branch rather than use the phone or Internet, if we want to deal with a person. How incredibly forward thinking.

On average, 60 to 70 percent of women "zero out" of IVR (press "0") to reach a live operator, and they're still on hold for just as long as they were before IVR was installed. Twenty percent of callers who get IVR immediately hang up. Eighty percent of us prefer live agents to automated systems. In Britain, 52 percent of banking customers described automated answering machines as "infuriating."

Is it surprising that more people want to do business with *people* in small businesses? Is it surprising that intelligent people don't want to work for companies that treat their customers this way? Is it possible that most of the best and brightest have already left big companies, and that's why you still get a machine? Is the reason for the brain drain becoming clearer?

Any wonder that those with a brain have hopped on the fast track to sole proprietorship?

Where IVR doesn't work, which is now the majority of cases, why haven't corporations done something about it? Which numbers are they looking at: staff costs (which are increasing due to zeroing out), or total net profit (lost custom), or none? Can you expect corporations that can't make simple, obvious changes to offer best-in-class products or have best-in-class people?

In the 21st century, when

- caller ID technology can identify me and match me to my account details in nano-seconds,

- then automatically route my call to a customer rep in any location or with a relevant license (resolving state law compliance issues) who can answer all my questions,

- then incorporate consumer behavior modeling software that predicts the three most likely reasons I'm calling based upon billing cycle, correspondence, account activity, etc., and flash those instantly on the customer rep screen along with the answers in a few more nanoseconds,

is there any excuse for having IVR, or transferring customer calls?

Based upon a ton of research and customer complaints, Citibank created TV commercials showing the stupidity and annoyance of phone menus. They promised to "treat you right" by ensuring you "get through to a real person to help get your life back." Their solution: "Press '0' to speak to a live person—anytime." This solution was created by a bunch of zeroes.

Hello? Hello? Hello, is *anybody* listening? Customers don't want to press "0"—ever! **We don't want to speak to a machine AT ALL! We want a human being to answer the phone, AND THAT person to answer EVERY question we have about ALL the company's products.** We don't want to be transferred, put on hold, or press anything. Why can't companies LISTEN? Stop devising "solutions" based upon what you don't want to deal with (which is the people in the other departmental fiefdoms who won't work together).

And this is why America hates big companies. This is why Americans don't want to work there.

When I call the local dry cleaner, a human being answers the phone and answers all my questions. Big business, if you can't connect with that, good-bye.

Before I signed up on the National Do-Not-Call Registry, a telemarketer called me to sell long distance service. "It's only five cents a minute," the caller claimed proudly, reading the script.

"Why would I pay five cents per minute plus all your gargantuan extra monthly fees, when I can use a calling card for three and a half cents a minute and no fees, or my cell phone?"

"So you don't have to dial all those extra numbers. Convenience."

Who writes this stuff? People who never heard of speed dialing or voice recognition dialing?

They all sell the same thing, and they all sell it the same way. If one or two companies were telemarketing, no one would complain. Not only did they all do the same thing, they kept doing it until outraged consumers provoked legislation and the National Do-Not-Call Registry put them on hold.

So they bombarded them on the Internet instead. As mentioned before, the e-business departments, full of young Internet-savvy entrepreneurs (because big business boys were afraid to learn), were resented by the old school. When other departments refused to integrate e-business, customers started getting e-mails, direct mail, and telemarketing calls simultaneously from the same companies. In most large companies, there is no single up-to-date source to find when each customer will be receiving which promotions. The deluge of e-business departments cropping up created a flood of junk e-mails. The anti-spam, anti-pop-up, anti-e-mail backlash started long before the marketers of Viagra and penis enlargers started abusing the medium. And companies wonder why response rates are flaccid.

In 2007, *MSN Money* published the results of a reader study called "The Customer Service Hall of Shame." The top, um bottom, 10? Three banks, three cable companies, three telephone companies, and Wal-Mart.[1] Are the same incompetent people playing job musical chairs within their industries, or are these companies simply copying the same worst practices from their competitors?

I do know that banks have won most of the awards in my Hall of Shame. Let's start with my mortgage lender, Bank Rupt. That's not its real name, but it has more lawyers than I do, which matters when a big company is more concerned about its image than its service. Having worked in the mortgage division of a large bank, I was careful to specify that my mortgage with Bank Rupt had "no settlement fees" before signing on the many dotted lines. Imagine my surprise when the bank tried to charge $60, yes, $60, for an *e-mail* of my settlement statement (a letter with the calculated total amount to pay off your mortgage on a specific date) that is computer generated. When I responded to the bank saying that I refused to pay that fee because our agreement was "no settlement fees," the politician-type reply stated the $60 fee was "***required*** to pay the account in full, as is the payoff statement." So I wrote back to say that my understanding of calculation of APRs is that legally any mandatory fee must be included in the APR, which Bank Rupt did not do. Therefore, it must not be mandatory, so I wasn't going to pay it, as we previously agreed. Bank Rupt's reply was that it wouldn't charge me $60 for an e-mail but would charge me $10 instead to send the information to me via fax. Thanks, tons: a "savings" of $50 while still sending the same data over a telephone line, but pushing one different button at the other end. Lucky me! In the end, I got my payoff statement and did not pay anything for it. I'm sure I cost the bank more than $60 in staff costs handling my complaint. After I paid off the balance, it took four letters and six months to get my promissory note and deed of trust returned. Boy, they sure taught me a lesson. Guess what the chance is that I will do business with Bank Rupt again?

A dissatisfied customer tells an average of seven people about his negative experience, and I've just helped boost the average. Why was I so adamant? Because Bank Rupt decided to expand its bank branching network and put a bus shelter advertisement right outside my door criticizing other banks by telling me to "Reject Fake Free Checking." How about "Reject Fake Free Mortgage Settlements?" Odd that its "free" checking account didn't include checks unless you bought the "plus package option" for $4 per month.

So let me understand this. A free checking account that you have to pay for the checks unless you pay the $4 a month. (Perhaps the in-house lawyer approved this because it's the *account* that's free, not the *checks*. Of course. How could the average consumer be such a simpleton to misunderstand *that*?) They don't charge for the checks anymore, perhaps to copy competitors with "*Totally* Free Checking" offers. Then there's a mortgage with no settlement fees, unless you want to settle, in which case you must buy a mandatory $60 settlement letter (or a $10 settlement letter if you're in the minority of households that has a fax machine). So the mortgage has no fees, just the letters required to do business with the lender. Just like the catalog and Internet companies that charge you a shipping fee (that is more than the cost of shipping) plus a massive handling fee because they didn't have to put it on a truck and stack it on a shelf in a bricks-and-mortar outlet with high overheads, and make you go through their lengthy ordering process before telling you what the fees are. Just like companies that charge you a fee to pay or do business electronically, when it saves them money and time. Just like stores that nail you for buying, but not using, their gift cards while they benefit financially from the float (even though they don't recognize the sales revenue until merchandise or services are exchanged). Phew!

Stop! News flash! I just opened my mail and my credit card company just said, "Congratulations. Your excellent credit history has earned you an upgrade to the enhanced benefits" of the Platinum Card. Lucky me! The annual fee is only $30 more per year and for that, the cap on miles I can receive goes from 60,000 (which I've never come close to) to 100,000. Whoopdedoo! That's a great deal! And since only 70 percent of new card offers are platinum, I felt reaaaallllly special getting this offer. And I'd also get a free companion airline ticket. Of course, "certain restrictions apply" like limited seat availability, blackout dates, minimum price of the noncompanion ticket, taxes and fees additional, only on one airline, etc. Too bad; I just applied for a fee-free card that gives miles on several airlines and I'm about to cancel their old card.

Who is making these business decisions? Would you want to work with them?

After feeing us to death, now companies are all fighting for the last seat on the "no fee" bandwagon or stagecoach. Bank One, which couldn't figure out that charging its own customers $3 to use a teller would hurt business and get bad press, sent me a mailing in which the words "no...fee" or "free" appeared in bold type in the first two paragraphs eight times. Bye, bye. Because now it's Chase. Whether it's yes fees or no fees, it's still price focused rather than product focused and people focused. Easier to "improve" the price rather than improve the product, if that's your management's skill set.

You can live without a mortgage, but it's harder to live without a bank account although the Federal Reserve says 8.7 percent of households are still stuffing the cash under their mattresses. After my experiences, I'm considering calling 1-800-MATTRES, leaving off the last "s" for so-long-big-banks.

After the bank where I have my checking accounts made three strikes in a month, I decided it was out. Foolishly, and I do mean foolishly, I gave Bank Rupt another chance figuring, foolishly, since bank departments are so siloed, I'd be dealing with more competent people than the mortgage fools. Maybe, I foolishly thought, they have their act together now because they've been winning some of the J.D. Power satisfaction awards. One week after opening business and personal checking accounts, I hand delivered this letter to them:

15 January 2008

Dear Mr. [Big Bank Employee],

Here's why I'm canceling all my [Bank Rupt] accounts one week after opening them:

As I told you, I opened the accounts because my primary bank kept making mistakes.

Problem 1: When asked to sign the agreements for opening my accounts, I noticed my surname was misspelled. I asked it to be fixed (no big deal). I was promised it was.

Problem 2: A few days later, I got my ATM card and checks— name still misspelled (big deal).

Problem 3: I logged in online where my two [Bank Rupt] accounts were supposed to be linked (which we discussed AT LENGTH due to the problem with my former bank). They weren't and the customer (that's me) is unable to link them.

Problem 4: I went online to activate my ATM card (because the activation sticker says I could do it that way). The online activation system gave me an error message. It didn't work.

Problem 5: I called the customer service center about my misspelled name and problem activating. The "zero out" function was disabled, and I don't yet have a phone PIN required to bypass the menu and speak to a rep, so I spent 25 minutes trying to reach a human being.

Problem 6: I went to the branch and relayed the above, saying I called the CUSTOMER SERVICE CENTER, NOT the activation phone number, explaining I tried to activate ONLINE. You called the activation phone number and activated my ATM card AFTER I said twice, "DO NOT ACTIVATE my card—I want to close my account, then said, "See, it works." (This is the biggest deal of all because instructions I gave twice were ignored.)

Thank you for making an offer that every time [Bank Rupt] makes another mistake I can spend my time to come to the branch to sort it out, but I do not want to spend my life in the branch sorting out problems created by your bank. Oddly enough, I want a bank account that doesn't create problems in the first place and one that just works the way it promises to. Oh, yes. I also want people who answer the phone (not machines), and listen.

So please close my accounts immediately.

Babs Ryan
not
Babs Rayn

The saga continues.

There are bankers who get it. One of my former clients, John Harris, who was the head of marketing at a midsized bank, directed me to avoid putting small type and asterisks in his bank's marketing materials. He was a maverick and has since become a successful business owner. These are people you want to work with and for, and do business with.

The people and places you don't want to work with are the ones obsessing with price structure in lieu of innovation. And price is usually not the real driver of choice, even though people say it is. The proof? The majority of credit cardholders cannot accurately tell you what the current interest rate is on their primary credit cards, although in research, the majority tell you that's how they choose a credit card. In January 2008, the average APR was around 18 percent. Since there are tons of cheaper cards, why don't cardholders switch? Because they don't like change either, even though they say they do.

Think about the most of today's products laden with fees. They are commodity products whose core benefit (why you buy them) offers little differentiation. Like their competitors, they add copycat points and "programs," sales, cash back, and discounts, and when those don't work, they start to charge fees—lots of them.

When you see this cycle, the company has lost its best and brightest, and even its desire to seek out the best and brightest. It adds peripheral features to its products (usually mimicking competitors) instead of developing a superior core product, just as it creates more peripheral process roles instead of hiring and promoting superior core management. Can the last innovator out the door turn off the lights? Big companies think they are getting ahead of the game by hiring the competitors' leavers—the people uncomfortable with innovation who can only make their mark by going to a weaker competitor and helping them copy the industry leader, their ex-employer.

Charging semi-hidden fees is often legal, but it's not too clever. In 2008, major credit card companies will be sifting through millions of dollars in claims (including mine) to settle a class action suit alleging that they "conspired to set and conceal fees" on foreign transactions. Tisk, tisk.

Companies who charge masked fees to cut a profit on me-too products have something in common—everything. They have nothing that differentiates them. When you offer value that's over and above your competitors', you openly parade your fees, if you charge any. Country clubs whose draw is exclusive clientele openly advertise their fees. It's part of their cachet. If you want to be part of something special, you expect to pay through the nose. If you get extras such as VIP invitations, you feel you got an inside deal, rather than having won a battle with a bloodied nose. If you want to own something special, you may have to pay a premium. That's the basic principle of supply and demand. Look at what Starbucks charges for a cup of coffee, with no hidden fees. In the past week, 35 million customers walked in for a cup of joe or some other drink with a longer name; a typical customer makes 18 purchases each month, making Starbucks the U.S. leader in frequency of customer visits.[2] (And it is No. 16 in *Fortune* magazine 2007 Best Companies to Work For.)

In case you were wondering, only two of the top 10 Best Companies to Work For have more than 10,000 U.S. employees. Half have fewer than 5,000. Small is beautiful.

A segment on the *Today* show talked about the terrific new autos from Detroit being launched at the Detroit Auto Show. Matt Lauer and the editor of *Car and Driver* magazine talked about how Detroit had really changed with the products it was launching this year. Now, said Matt, Detroit is coming up with fantastic cars that consumers really want and, therefore, won't demand rebates. What a huge leap forward. Duh, duh, duh, Detroit.

Jeff Bell left Duhhhhtroit and got a much longer title: Corporate Vice President of Global Marketing, Interactive Entertainment Business at Microsoft. He is one of my big company heroes. I worked with Jeff at his direct marketing agency when he was a regional manager at Ford. (Toyota surpassed Ford and, in first quarter 2007,

GM to become the world's leading automaker.) Jeff made his dealer region tops with exciting joint promotions with movie rental and pizza companies. His promotions weren't based on price; they were based on family fun and entertainment. He surrounded himself with what he called "can do" people. He handpicked brilliant people, and, boy, he had fun. So did everyone else around him. Full of life and passion for his work, he brought sparkle by embracing innovation. He made me want to work with his company and make it great.

After one of our meetings, Jeff spotted a driver in Ford's new-model Mustang in the parking lot. "What a great-looking car!" he said to the driver, who was beaming with pride. He spent a few minutes chatting with the guy about his new motor and about his great choice, throwing in a few semi-technical details. The guy was partaking in Jeff's spontaneous research study too, offering tons of honest feedback on product hits and misses.

"What did he say when you told him you worked for Ford?" I asked.

"I didn't tell him, but he feels so good right now, he'll be buying Fords for the rest of his life." Jeff was going to understand the customer, even if he had to knock on every car window. His pioneering spirit, ebullience, and broad smile are infectious. He is responsible for good people staying in big companies, because he's the guy who'll knock on your window or door to hear your ideas whether you're getting your learner's permit in business or are an experienced driver.

One man can make a change, but Edmunds.com found that the average rebate for the big automakers is still $3,445 per vehicle compared to $931 for Japanese brands. When U.S. carmakers were insisting that American SUVs were just what consumers ordered, they were still offering big wheel rebates. Has discounting worked as a winning strategy?

Me-too products are usually laden with fees because the company offering them has built its "strategy" (actually, lack thereof) around price rather than innovation. Phone companies will fight on "cents per minute" while soaking customers with additional fees. A price-based strategy is *never* sustainable. It's what companies do when they have nothing unique or better to offer. It is inconceivable that your company will remain the lowest cost provider forever, unless it is the only provider (in which case, it is also the highest cost provider) or the product is defunct. You'd be amazed how many companies think adding or subtracting a fee is *product* development.

Rebates. Rebates. Rebates. Let's treat customers as if they're imbeciles. Surely, no one can figure out that if you're giving rebates, you were trying to overcharge them or making the profit somewhere else. Has anyone missed the fact that credit cards with points programs charge annual fees? Is the $200 airline ticket worth the $300 you paid in fees for four years? At least you got *something*—50 percent of points are never redeemed.[3] How about the credit cards charging higher interest rates and/or fees while telling you the card gives you "up to" 5 percent cash back. The "up to" cash back on those cards is typically scaled to annual spend with the real percentage between 0.25 percent and 1 percent for the vast majority of customers. (One of the best known advertising "up to 5 percent cash back" has a hurdle of $15,000 in annual spending before you get *any* cash back! Another advertising "up to 2 percent cash back" only gives 2 percent after you've spent $50,000!) The maximum cash back advertised is often restricted to using that credit card at a few specified retailers where you probably don't shop, you'll rack up limited charges (e.g., gas stations), or you have to sign up for some telephone service and pay the bills on your credit card. There's nothing special about these products that are price focused and actually create price-sensitive shoppers. The only thing that's "transparent" about some cards is their attempt to mislead customers because they don't have new ideas to satisfy real unmet desires of consumers. Consumers are up to here with cash back when the credit card companies keep the cash behind their backs. Consumers are up to there with rebates that make you mail in 10 pounds of box tops and forms to a P.O. box number so you can't get proof of delivery, which you'll need when they don't send you the rebate.

You may argue that Wal-Mart has been successful with a strategy based upon discounting. Securing a great deal from wholesalers and passing those savings on to consumers has worked for Wal-Mart. But its positioning is not "discounting" or "sales," although its tag line is "low prices, always." (Low is a relative word and therefore meaningless. "Low" compared to what? The most expensive place?) Sales, discounting, and rebating say to customers that your "normal" price is high and it takes a discount, sale, or rebate to get a deal. Retailers have trained consumers to be price sensitive and not to shop without a sale. In other words, their message is, "We normally overcharge, but today we won't on these items." Wal-Mart's message is that it never overcharges, on anything. It's customer-centric rather than retailer-centric. Wal-Mart is about "affordable abundance," meaning that a consumer sees the shelves stacked and feels, "I can afford *all* this."[4] Were it simply about price and money, customers would walk out with only what they walked in for. Research shows that I don't and you don't. In that checkout basket are often several items that we could have bought elsewhere for less. Somewhere in that basket, though, is the great deal that I tell the family and neighbors about, always.

Furthermore, Wal-Mart isn't focusing on cutting *its* margin (or adding fees) to charge consumers low prices, although that is often what consumers receive. Wal-Mart gets the savings *from the wholesaler*. (I've been in the sparse bartering rooms in Bentonville, Arkansas, that are often compared to interrogation cells.) The savings, when passed on to the consumer, are called "rollbacks." You won't hear Wal-Mart pushing "sales" or margin cutting. It doesn't cut its own throat. The difference may seem subtle but it's what's made Wal-Mart huge.

Americans hatred of big companies does cross the line. Since Wal-Mart offers the same products as many of its competitors, and its service is on par if not superior, my guess is that Wal-Mart got in the Hall of Shame top 10 not because of customers' experience shopping there, but because of bad press. And since the Hall of Shame was supposed to be about "customer service," that's not fair. Americans turn against anybody too successful. I've seen it in almost every group I belong to. It's called the Underdog Syndrome.

When Wal-Mart became the biggest, Wal-bashing became a popular sport (see Chapter Seven on bullying). People protested the opening of Wal-Mart stores supposedly because of big-box employee benefits and the effect on mom 'n' pop stores. But they didn't seem to have any problem with Target, Home Depot, etc., opening up in their neighborhood. Of course, the same self-righteous critics wouldn't pay higher product prices to compensate Wal-Mart if it paid for massive benefits for every part-time employee. Those horrible people at

Wal-Mart sell clothes made in China. Uh-huh. Probably because that's what horrible U.S. consumers buy—"96.4 percent of apparel sold in the United States is imported."[5] Before you squawk about toys being made in China and make generalizations about quality, ask how much more you'd be willing to pay for those foreign-made items if they were made in the U.S. Ask again if you want to close the borders to lower-paid immigrants. Hear again the unemployed's excuses about being too "special" to take entry-level jobs in manufacturing, retail sales, McDonalds, or Wal-Mart. They don't need *work* experience and they don't need track records of producing profits for companies to get high-paying jobs, because they took business courses in college on strategy. And that's what it takes to tell all the other experienced, revenue-producing employees what they should do every day.

Hey, Wal-Mart *is* different. Their employees are innovative. They hire people who *want* to work part time. They hire people who want to work. As my client, they were exceptionally open-minded, professional, and ethical, and had manners. Please open a store across the street from my home.

While it's true that you'll work with more riffraff in a big company (because they can't cut it in a small company and are incapable of managing their own), tarring all big businesses with the same brush isn't right. Another case of we-love-to-hate is McMurdering McDonald's. C'mon, America. We are not fat because of McDonald's. There are loads of middleweights and flyweights who eat at McDonald's. We are fat and in debt because we are gluttons. People in other nations who have McDonald's and credit cards are not obese with massive debt.

McDonald's doesn't make you eat 4,000 calories a day, and the credit card companies don't make you buy stuff that you know you can't afford to pay for or force you to lie on your mortgage application about your income so you can have a bigger house than your brother-in-law. Again, the people crabbing about McDonald's have nothing to say about Wendy's or Burger King, because McMurdering is about massacring the most successful, not the most incompetent. They provide phenomenal training that you benefit from for the rest of your life, they serve clean products quickly that represent excellent value for money, and they listen to their customers. What's sad is that a positive exception in big corporations has now become the place where most people say they would least want to work. How many times have you heard an unemployed, healthy person say, "*I'm* not going to flip burgers at McDonald's." Most people should be so lucky as to have a job at McDonald's. I've never heard anyone who worked for McDonald's complain about management mistreatment, lack of opportunity, or having to work with stupid people. I have never received anything but outstanding service from their employees, in many countries. They contribute to communities. Best of all, they have made millionaires out of entrepreneurs who invested in their franchises. All big businesses don't suck.

While it's hip to hate Wal-Mart and McDonalds, we all love Harley-Davidson, the lone survivor of America's motorcycle industry, because it almost went out of business. When Harley-Davidson motorcycles were in short supply, purchasers succumbed to yearlong waiting lists and paid more than the sticker prices to own them. Meanwhile, U.S. dealers selling the Japanese brands were discounting. Why? The difference between the four major Japanese motorcycle brands is minimal. A couple of horsepower, a few seconds on the 0-60, a tweak to the styling and graphics, and a few barely detectable improvements in weight, suspension, braking, engine configuration. But H-D motorcycles? You can't get anything like them anywhere else. Indian Motorcycle Company tried to rise from the ashes but failed to knock a dent in H-D and crashed after executives from the copycat car industry zoomed in (no surprise). So H-D still doesn't have real competition today. Therefore, it can charge a premium. It doesn't have to charge fees. The average cost of a Harley-Davidson motorcycle is $16,000. The typical new H-D bike owner adds more than $3,000 in aftermarket parts and extras in the first year. H-D can charge whatever it likes for apparel, parts, and, yes, fees (e.g., delivery), which it doesn't have to hide. (The fee thing was copied from the car industry.) H-D has no competition. Although recently, sales have been slipping, it shipped more than 300,000 motorbikes and sold 7 million pieces of clothing in one year plus closed profitable financing deals. If it eliminated those delivery fees and included the amount in the recommended retail price of the bike, H-D would not lose a single customer. Can you say the same about banks or the car industry (e.g., leasing agreements)? When charging separate fees is the only way you can make your product appear competitive and your primary selling point is price, your company is unlikely to be in hog heaven taking home the bacon. Your best and brightest staff have ridden into the sunset long ago.

In 1993, I applied for a marketing position at H-D. I'd been head of the marketing department at Kawasaki in the U.K., where I'd increased our big bike market share to 65 percent. My knowledge might have been heavyweight but the Japanese/American motorcycle rivalry (mostly just talk) had my mind revving. Would H-D even talk to a "crotch-rocket" enthusiast?

H-D's now-chairman, Jeff Bleustein, called me to Milwaukee for an interview. "Your experience and results are great," Bleustein said, "but you'd have to start in a junior position. There aren't any open positions at higher levels, and frankly, there may not be any openings for a while. Our employees tend to stay around a long, long time."

He was being entirely honest and fair. Harley-Davidson's employee turnover rate (4 percent in 2002) was way below the national average, which exceeded 38 percent (23 percent voluntary). About 50 percent of the employees own an H-D motorcycle: They are fans. There are no real competitors to switch to. Having unique products not only ensures that customers will pay a premium, but it ensures that you will attract and keep premium employees. When you get lazy and let the competitors catch up instead of continuing to change, your best employees will fade away.

Compare a job description for an HR position advertised at Harley-Davidson with the ones you perused for process jobs. The job summary starts out: "The major *responsibilities*..." There's a change! The employee is actually going to be responsible for something instead of just monitoring and coordinating. Here's more:

- Designs **and implements** internal promotional and external recruitment programs...
- Handles any on-site investigations the government may initiate...
- Evaluates the status of personnel programs, recommends, **and implements changes**...

This is one of the few job descriptions that actually contains the word "changes." It notably repeats the word "implement."

Once a brand criticized for hanging on to its 1950s technology, H-D has changed gears. Bleustein knew he didn't have exactly the job to utilize my experience when he met me at H-D on July 7, 1993 (and I knew it too). But he was open-minded enough to explore all possibilities with potential employees. I'm certain this is how he treats his existing employees' ideas—with an open mind. For that, despite still riding a Japanese sports motorcycle, I have always admired him.

Are We There Yet?

OK, let's get back on track. How do you drive innovation in big corporations so the best and brightest don't leave for sole proprietorship or, if they already have, go back?

I'd arrived at Odawara Station to meet the Japanese greeter 15 minutes early. I craved a final visit to the sushi bar in the station. The sushi train. The cost of living was higher in Japan. There seemed to be a lack of immigrant labor. Labor costs, and therefore goods and services, were relatively expensive. One thing was cheaper than in the U.S. Sushi.

It was served up as fast food at sushi train restaurants called *kaiten-zushi* (translated as "rotating or revolving sushi") in every nook and cranny in the country. You sat on bar stools at a counter in a circle, as a conveyor belt passed around the counter. In the center, the sushi chefs kept the conveyor belt well supplied with an assortment of sushi—a pair of nigiri sushi on each small plastic plate with a different color rim. Each plate's rim color indicated the price of the dish, with a color/price guide posted on the wall. As your favorite tidbit rolled by, you'd take it lest the person seated beside you grabbed it before it made another round. When you were full, the cashier would count your plates, multiplying them by the appropriate amounts, and give you the bill. If you didn't see your favorite morsels, you could ask the sushi chef to prepare a special order. No problem. No extra cost. You had pictures of the items on the menus or cards (an idea adopted by sushi restaurants in the U.S.) so you could point to what you wanted. The other great idea was that there was a hot water tap at each station with an ample supply of green tea bags, so you could serve yourself.

My frequent trips to sushi train bars left me not only satiated, but stuffed, for less than $10. Often, I would feel embarrassed by my huge stack of plates, typically 10. It's hard to break the habit of gluttony derived from the obscene portion sizes in America where less is not more, and big is better.

The sushi train was a brilliant idea, the brainchild of an inventor named Yoshiaki Shiraishi. Ironically, he'd previously invented a portable toilet (there's a lot of innovation surrounding toilets in Japan, no correlation). *Kaiten-zushi* is a $2.1 billion business in Japan. Shiraishi made the parallel after watching beer bottles on an assembly line at the Asahi Brewery. And what goes better with sushi than beer? He perfected the conveyor belt to run at eight centimeters per second in a clockwise direction, making it easier to remove the desired tidbits with the left hand without dropping the chopsticks that are always held in the right. At the exact speed of eight centimeters, the sushi stays fresh and on track, while the patrons stave off boredom. Yes, he even measured the boredom level at different conveyor speeds.[6]

Since Shiraishi's death, the sushi trains are following a new route. A game that looks like a screen saver with an animated aquarium lets you select your fish choice on a touch screen. Within seconds, your selection arrives via the conveyor belt. This has reduced waste from 8 percent to 2 percent. A train journey is only exciting if the view keeps changing. Great ideas only stay great if they evolve.

Doesn't it make you wonder why we need waiters to take orders? Aren't you tired of waiting for <u>wait</u>ers (aren't they supposed to do the waiting?) to come when you know what you want and are starved, or tired of shooing them away when you haven't looked at the menu yet and are engrossed in an important conversation? When are restaurants going to adopt innovations like Microsoft Surface, the flat touch screen menu integrated into your table, so you can choose what you want and your order can be wired directly to the kitchen? Surely, it would be simple enough when, for example, you order steak, the pull-down menu has a choice of how you want it cooked. Which potatoes would you like: Baked, fries, mashed, hash browns? Baked? Is that with sour cream, butter, both, none of the above? On the side? Special orders or instructions—type them in. If you want to talk to a "real" person to place your order or at any other time, press the little waiter icon on the screen. Even better, how about getting a confirmation that the kitchen has received your order and a countdown clock pops up showing when it will arrive at your table? Get a few appropriate options to go with that steak, the best wines, or a thirst-quenching cocktail.

In kids' restaurants, they could just push the pictures of what they want. What about a sleep button to push when you want the screen off for a while? Remember those mini juke boxes at each booth in the diners? Add other functions, like music. Why have to wave down the waiter to get the check? As you order, your bill is tallied on the screen. Dip your credit card in the slot, add a tip on the touch screen calculator (which can tell you exactly how much 15 percent would be, and pay instantly. Add a button to round it up to the nearest dollar. Of course, there is an electronic pressure signature pad like the ones at Target, so you can pay your bill and leave when you want to.

At this point, the entrepreneurial readers are wondering why restaurants have so many wait staff. They are not only thinking about which types of restaurants are most suited to touch screen menus for instant ordering, but they are thinking of 20 ways to make the above idea work better. The smartest and glass-is-half-full readers are already visualizing images of what the above could look like. Correlations of how to apply this idea to things other than food are swimming through their heads, as they recall what they read or what they saw customers doing in restaurants (data). They are considering the strategic and tactical considerations, including the financial opportunity. They are pondering which target market is most appropriate. Teens? Tweens? Generation Y? Boomers?

At this point, most of the *corporate* people who read the idea are initially thinking of 50 different problems with self-ordering. They are concentrating on why the above idea *won't* work, seeing each problem as a reason not to consider developing the idea at all. Instead of improving on the main concept, they are focusing on why the specific touch screen shown as an example is all wrong and making lists of every reason why that's dumb instead of considering other automated or different ordering systems. They've not thought of any alternatives to the way restaurants treat them now. They are criticizing every word of the existing proposal instead of imagining working with the proposer to understand the objective of the idea, the data that prompted it, and which aspects consumers would like. They've yet to make a correlation to anything not currently in a restaurant (like the iPhone). The corporate people are visualizing nothing and focusing on words such as "work," "cost," and "problem." Everything but "opportunity." They are not imagining people at tables in restaurants; they are thinking about people in *their* company, about meetings and the difficulty of getting the necessary decisions and changes made, the costs, how much time it would take to implement, and the three customer complaints they might get. The dread of a system meltdown or glitch, or a typo on the menu, immediately flooded their minds when hearing that there was technology involved. They are focusing on the long-term negative impact on wait staff employment levels while never considering the growth of employment of skilled workers to develop, program, install, and maintain the touch screens, electronics, wi-fi menus, or the construction and refitting of more restaurants for the chain. The cost of the system was entertained before the benefit of economies of scale from increasing customer traffic. Next, they'll begin to criticize the person who generated the idea for not having every detail set in stone and in writing before mentioning the idea (so there'd be more minutia to criticize). They believe the person who had the insight to think about making the world a better place to live doesn't understand the "process" to build the product, and they are thinking about processes, not consumers. They're troubled because the innovator showed a green menu screen instead of a blue one, so the screen idea should be killed.

Which were you? Where do you work? This latter is the status quo in most large companies and that is why positive, innovative, smart people leave.

All the processes in Six Sigma, all the training on earth, all the brainstorming sessions in the solar system, and all the job titles in the universe are not going to change whether someone is idea receptive or idea averse. It's hot wired.

Some men see things as they are and say 'Why?'
I dream of things that never were and say 'Why not?'

Robert F. Kennedy

The best and the brightest will continue to depart from places where they'll be stuck in the weeds. Companies only need people who have the ability to see both the weeds *and* the sky. Said one Home Depot manager: "People want 'elbow room'—a job that's pretty big, where they have responsibility for a number of functional levers.... They also want 'headroom'—a job where they can make decisions on their own, without having to go through a bureaucracy. The best companies are beginning to appreciate these aspirations."[7]

Corporations are uncomfortable with those who don't stay down in the weeds and want headroom. The taller entrepreneurs have their feet in the weeds and their heads breathing the fresh air. Having the ability to do both is why the ones who are breathing fresh air start businesses and are successful.

There are multitalented individuals still in corporations who have leadership and entrepreneurial qualities too. Unfortunately, you'll be hard-pressed to find many in decision-making roles. The last of the species are in process roles or working for managers who are single-minded. When corporations crowd their top tier with people who have their heads in the clouds, their feet in the weeds, and are hands-on, the rest of the do-it-all employees will come back. The moral of the story is that too much weed does not make you creative.

The big office reminds me of Bart Simpson with Homer in their car, heading for a mutually desirable destination. Without stopping for breath, Bart enthusiastically repeats, "Are we there yet are we there yet are we there yet are we there yet?" And Homer, without listening, keeps repeating, "No no no no no no..." As soon as he is able, Bart is going to get a driver's license and run away.

Entrepreneurs prove they are not only able to generate marketable ideas, but also to implement them by starting their own businesses. After two years, 76 percent of new small businesses are thriving,[8] about the same as the two-year retention rate in large companies.

Unfortunately, most big companies aren't comfortable hiring entrepreneurs who have proven idea innovation and introduction skills. Former Pepsico Chair/CEO Craig Weatherup said, "We want to avoid the tendency to promote the person working in the next office, the one that you're comfortable with, rather than the person in the next continent who's really best but who you don't know."[9] (In 2003, *Fortune* named PepsiCo the most innovative company across all industries. However, *Fortune* had also named Enron "America's Most Innovative Company" for six consecutive years, and some kinds of innovation are not necessarily a good thing.)

Innovative leaders comprise 2 to 4 percent of the population.[10] Most have already left to start their own companies. The majority of people in large corporations making the hiring decisions have invented nothing of substance. Look around. They are not among the 2 to 4 percent. They are not hiring original leaders. They are hiring people like themselves, while the small-business owners are doing the same. Hence, the exodus.

Things haven't changed much in a century. With all the psychobabble in the latter part of the 20th century, we've still made the people who like to solve problems **the** problem. Read this excerpt from *U.S. News and World Report's* American Ingenuity Special Issue:

> In 1958, British economist John Jewkes assembled a representative list of about 60 major inventions from the previous half century, ranging from acrylic fiber and the long-playing record to television and the zipper. More than half, he found, had come from individuals working on their own. One reason, he wrote, was that "men with great powers of originality are in many ways a race apart." They tend not to play well with others, wrote Jewkes, "because their great gifts arise from the habit of calling everything, even the simplest assumptions, into question."[11]

That is the prevailing view of creative people: They don't play well with others. The reason, as stated above, hasn't changed: because they ask questions. It seems that the folks who believe creative people generally don't work well with others have followed this deductive process:

1. Creative people ask a lot of questions.

2. If you ask questions, you are hard to get along with.

3. People who don't like being asked questions are easy to get along with.

4. Getting along with others is essential to being a good employee and manager.

5. Good managers don't ask questions.

6. Therefore, creative people are not good managers.

Why doesn't the current majority of "good" managers like being asked questions? Remember when Sherron Watkins asked questions at Enron? Were they answered?

Apparently, a lot of "good" managers get tired of dumbing down and not asking questions, to be perceived as not throwing sand in the sandbox. The Center for Women's Business Research in Washington, D.C., reports that women who started businesses within the past 10 years are much more likely to come from management positions than clerical posts prior to starting their businesses. They were good enough at managing to be promoted to management positions at their former companies but left because they weren't given the opportunity to manage *and* innovate. Starting a business gave them the opportunity to do both. Until large companies give their managers the chance to innovate, they will continue to go elsewhere to build sandcastles, without question.

Isn't it time we stopped pigeonholing the chronically inquisitive as devoid of all other jobs skills, and answer their questions? When are we going to stop accusing the what-if people of being incapable of having commercial common sense? How many Bill Gateses have to become billionaires before we believe that some of the 27 million small-business owners who asked about possibilities or the 2 to 4 percent who invent solutions might be good candidates to hold the leadership positions in our big businesses? **Is it possible that the innovators are playing well with others, and the people who don't like questions aren't?** Aren't they trying to provide better products for the customers? Perhaps people just don't want question askers on their teams. It takes two to get along. Who's really stomping on the chessboard? The person with the winning ideas or the one who thinks he's about to lose?

You know those motivational posters by Successories that have the soft-focus nature scenes with words like "Teamwork," "Success," and "Risk" with a meaningful quip below? I had to laugh at this innovation. A company named Despair, Inc., parodied those posters. Here are a few of their posters:

<u>Teamwork</u>:   A Few Harmless Flakes Working Together Can Unleash an Avalanche of Destruction.

<u>Discovery</u>:   A Company that Will Go to the Ends of the Earth for its People Will Find It Can Hire Them for about 10 percent of the Cost of Americans.

<u>Change</u>:   It's a Short Trip from Riding the Waves of Change to Being Torn Apart by the Jaws of Defeat.

<u>Cluelessness</u>:   There Are No Stupid Questions, But There Are a LOT of Inquisitive Idiots.

The last one says it all. It's the real deal. It's not the questions getting attention; it's the questioner. The attention is not always positive.

Entrepreneurs welcome the questions and interaction about *how* their and others' ideas might work in the marketplace. I've often told clients who are frustrated by endless internal queries that as long as questions are being asked about the product idea, there's a chance that the idea might see the light of day. However, what creators are tired of is questions or judgments about why it *won't* work. They're exhausted by negativity euphemized as due diligence (which eventually becomes bureaucracy). They answer all the questions and still get nowhere in a corporate environment. Because the real dangers are the people who ask no questions and go around slamming every idea behind everyone's back where they can't be explained or clarified. They misrepresent the ideas or take them out of context. They wouldn't know which questions to ask. Usually their criticism stems from their inability to develop or understand anything new or from being envious of anyone who's not afraid of change. If there's sand being thrown in the sandbox, they'll bury whoever is moving things around. They want the play area to remain the same, with the biggest pile at their corner. To block the shifting sands, they have their doors closed often and do the majority of talking in private one on ones, including with higher-ups. This way, they can deny saying everything. They're great at conversation, and not so great at generating ideas for future profitability. Afraid of new ideas, they'll slip in disparaging remarks about the creative person and his alleged intentions rather than the proposal. They lie. They misquote. They railroad the majority into being afraid, knowing that no good suggestion will go unpunished. And if you work in a large company, you know there's no shortage of those who are punching holes in the pails of anyone who offers an idea of how to double the sand in the box, fearful that the biggest share might not go to them. Those who can, do; those who can't, criticize.

The enemies of innovation do not attack the creation; they castrate the creator. They label the idea *generator* (nerd, nonanalytical, too out of the box, wrong background, not a team player, doesn't understand *our* product or *our* business). These corporate dinosaurs fear change, because they will no longer be experts. If they couldn't fix the wheel, you'd better not. After copying platinum, no one's going to oust their pet "big idea," which is going to be another color. And while the innovators spend time building perfect patentable products, the dinosaur builds perfect relationships with top brass, label dropping when appropriate. Eventually, due to the dinosaur, one label will finally fit the inventor: ineffective.

Learn from toxic big-business managers that good relationships are essential to getting best-selling products developed and marketed, whether you're in a large corporation or an entrepreneur. Then leave.

If you want to identify idea killers and idea generators quickly, count the questions. Attend a pitch or new proposal meeting where an idea is presented that hasn't been previously discussed. **Entrepreneurs and business builders will ask real questions in front of all their teammates. Idea killers and incompetents will not ask one!** Rest assured that within a few hours, the incompetent managers and saboteurs will have had several one-on-one meetings to slam the idea or the presenter. Anyone who asked a genuine question in the meeting is fodder for criticism too. Watch the deliberate eye rolling, exchanged sneers, flipping through papers, stonewalling, and avoiding when questions are asked by "brown-noses" who want to learn more or support idea generators. It's really the question killers who have their heads in the sand.

The ask-no-questions troops are at the top of the incompetence list. If they hear of a new idea that is going to be presented to a group, their office doors will open and close with such frequency, it'll feel like a hurricane. The rare questions that they belt out are prepared in advance, often with disruptive or negative intent, and it's obvious to everyone in the room. If they get wind of the idea before the presentation, they'll one on one before the presentation to ask for an immediate vote.

As sick as it sounds, some petty people even call clients to tell them not to purchase a new product from their own company, sabotaging the efforts of hundreds of workers who produced it, because they're so envious of the colleague who created the product. Most big companies have a Mr. Petty.

In one company, Victoria, a client services representative, had a dissatisfied client who demanded that she present some unique ideas for "campaign strategies." She and her boss asked Salvatore in the product development department for his help. The client was still awaiting a launch proposal for his new boat/outboard motor package after rejecting seven, yes, seven from Victoria that were "nothing new." In addition, the client, a leader in his field, was also seeking unique ideas to halt the declining revenue trend on an older product.

Salvatore's team spent two months analyzing data, developing proposals, doing ethnographic research (observing shopping behavior), and developing actual creative examples of consumer marketing materials, as asked. Victoria and the boss were aware of his progress at each stage and asked him to continue. She'd asked that Salvatore put his other clients on hold since her account work for her client was paramount, in her opinion.

After weeks of late evenings and overtime working at breakneck speed, Salvatore's team called a meeting to announce that they thought they had some never-done-before ideas that would drive sales and revenue sharply upward. Eight people arrived for the presentation, Victoria and her boss with crossed arms. They wanted to vet the ideas before the client saw them. Salvatore put up the presentation header slide with the client's name, the date, and "Campaign Strategies: Concepts," precisely what she'd asked for. When all were seated, he made introductions and moved to the second slide to begin discussion of the research findings.

"Could you move back to the first slide for a moment?" Victoria asked. Salvatore did. "Just what exactly do you mean by "Campaign Strategies?""

That was the last question she asked. Someone else started to ask a question, but she told him to wait until the end. At the end of the pitch, she rushed out, claiming she had another meeting, although Salvatore's presentation ended 15 minutes early.

Salvatore found out later that Victoria had been told by a few people that the ideas that were going to be presented were the best ever seen and would revolutionize the business. "You won't believe what he discovered about your client's business," they cooed. Immediately after the meeting, Victoria and the boss walked into his office and closed the door. She didn't speak to Salvatore and the ideas were never mentioned.

A few days later, Salvatore asked for feedback. "*We've* decided they're not exactly what *my* client wants," Victoria snapped. Sorry, wasn't it was the *company's* client?

"OK, can we set up a time to discuss what the client wants, how our proposal differs, and how we can deliver what they are looking for?"

"No!" Victoria stormed off in a huff.

Salvatore approached the head of sales, who was ultimately in charge of the account. Lyle was happy to see the proposals and voiced how, at last, somebody was delivering new, relevant ideas, exactly what they'd wanted for ages. He'd never seen anyone have such an in-depth understanding of the client's business and where they wanted to go. "When are we showing these to them?" Lyle asked.

A month later, Victoria and Salvatore were in the client's office. Salvatore pitched. Victoria sat silent with arms crossed and teeth clenched. At the end, the client and his team stood up and applauded. "Finally," he cheered. "When can we start?"

Victoria's face scrunched like a raisin. She sent Salvatore out so she could have a private conversation with the client. She returned to the head office and, in private meetings, told her colleagues that the client was uninterested. The client later said because he found out that Victoria's company was "just throwing around ideas" and since Victoria had misreported her company "operationally wasn't able to implement any of the ideas for the next three years," he was disappointed but would reluctantly launch with their existing lackluster program.

The launch was a bust; revenues never climbed. The client's receipts dropped by double digits over the next year. Victoria decided she didn't want to work anymore or perhaps the client helped her decide. Salvatore never knew because he was long gone. Victoria did not start her own business. Her supportive boss was promoted. Lyle the sales director left and went to a company that was number one for patents in its industry that year.

When you're dealing with people who don't ask questions, be certain never to ask *them* questions. Since the only time they ask a question is to attack, they'll assume that your motivations for asking questions are the same. You can always tell the new guy who's fresh out of college at the company town hall meeting. He's the one who puts up his hand when the CEO asks if there are any questions, in front of 1,000 employees. The minute he stands and opens his mouth, you can see the old-timers glaring at him with "asshole" written all over their faces. He's doomed. At college, he sought knowledge because he was taught that collecting information would improve his performance. It did, at college. Welcome to corporate America. Please insert your brain drain.

Tade had worked in a number of small companies, successfully developing a string of new products. When Company Y managed to sign him on as a group product manager, the CEO bragged about the coup and Tade's credentials. His manager told him to work with his secretary (who started two weeks prior) to arrange his own "meet and greet" schedule to introduce himself to other departments. It seemed that most people were too busy in meetings all day to spend time chatting to "the new guy." Used to short development cycles, Tade knew he had to acquire information quickly, to start making decisions. Eventually, his name was added to meeting lists. He asked questions such as: "Why did we choose to launch in November?" "Which of those products performed better?" "What other vendors are we using?"

Although everyone was polite to his face, it was evident that Tade had no support from his boss, and others were thwarting his work. He approached HR.

"I don't think this company is a good fit for me. It seems difficult to get things implemented here. It seems impossible to obtain information to make valid decisions."

HR had worked hard to sign Tade. The CEO had mandated that they get idea people in the company since they were scarce, and there had been an exodus recently of employees and clients. Plus, there was a hiring freeze and the departmental manager wouldn't be able to replace Tade and maintain the size of his empire. The HR manager might be moved to a process role again if she didn't keep Tade. "We're sending you to a career coach we typically use for our executive management. Perhaps he can find out why you've been successful in the past and have failed to replicate that success here."

The career coach spent hours with Tade. "I've got the answer," the coach promised, "which is questions."

"What?"

"You've probably asked me 100 questions. I don't mind your questions. They make me think. Problem is, you're asking all those people a lot of questions. About their jobs. You think they know the answers to those questions, because people in those jobs *should* have those answers. The truth is, they don't know the answers, and they know they should. They feel stupid. And they blame you, not their lack of expertise or lack of confidence, for making them feel stupid."

"Why don't they just say they don't know the answer, or say they'll get back to me?"

"Maybe they don't even know where to look for the answer. You came from the industry leader. You know the most up-to-date products. It's likely, since their company is so far behind its competitors, they don't understand your questions! Why do you think your boss avoids you? What's his pedigree? What's his experience? He's been in the same division of the same company for a decade and they're light-years behind the competition. Get it? What would happen if you didn't ask any more questions?"

"I'd make uninformed business decisions. It'd be more difficult to do my job."

"That's where you're wrong. It would be easier to do your job. They didn't hire you to make informed business decisions. From now on, don't ask any questions. See how it goes. You know what you really should be doing, with your smarts."

Tade never asked another business question again. After a few months, colleagues started inviting him to lunches and more meetings. More gossipers came to his office for one on ones. He did more of what his predecessor did—fill out charts, duplicate old ideas in different colors, recommend lots of fees, discounts, points, and coupons, and use the same yesteryear advertising for all products. The time he saved by not asking questions and by copying competitors, he spent setting up his own business. He got the idea for his company the day after he returned from the coaching session, during a meeting. He didn't tell them his idea, which they could have launched, because they didn't ask. Tade's company's revenue exceeded $1 million last year. That's $1 million that his former company could have had (plus more from economies of scale), if they'd only asked.

Tade's not the only one who's asking for the door. In a study of 1,100 workers from companies with more than 500 employees, 55 percent used negative terms such as exhausted, confused, and unsupported to describe their work lives. A third was intensely negative. They stated that they felt bad about work because their work made them feel bad about themselves. They reported low confidence in senior executives' abilities. They objected to incompetence.[12]

In a study by Leadership IQ of 70,305 employees at various levels, 87 percent said that "working with a low performer has made them want to change jobs" and 93 percent said their own productivity was negatively affected. Mark Murphy, Leadership IQ CEO, warned:

> It's one of the great management misnomers that low performers' major problem is technical incompetence. While some lack skills, most low performers are so identified because of a difficult attitude…. Leaders may have to remove their worst employees to keep their best employees…. Given that only 14 percent of senior executives think their company addresses this issue effectively, there's tremendous competitive advantage for companies that can turn this around.

> The five characteristics that defined a low performer were as follows…in order of importance:
> - Negative attitude
> - Stirs-up trouble
> - Blames others
> - Lacks initiative
> - Incompetence[13]

When managers are unable to create new ideas, you would think they could, or would, at least create an environment to encourage new ideas or hire those who can. They're incompetent to even do this. "...potentially successful innovations in mature organizations fail because they never find a marketplace inside the company that recognizes and supports their inherent value. How many times have we heard stories about great products or business concepts that failed to get internal buy in, only to have the innovators spin out and create a successful company?"[14]

The internal marketplace for innovation in big companies is the toughest. How many ideas do you know of that help corporate employees sell their ideas internally? If one problem is that the change averse have difficulty understanding new concepts because they can't visualize them, how can that be addressed? Would it make a difference? It's worth a try. Sparks Worldwide LLC has a presentation method that allows employees to show what consumers would see at an earlier stage in the sell-in process. There are countless corporate employees battling to market their ideas to internal audiences, an arduous process. New products (not processes) could be an aid to the sell in. Another opportunity for small businesses!

A study by the National Women's Business Council states that 42 percent of women-owned businesses and 61 percent of men-owned firms sell to large corporations or government agencies. A nice place to visit, but... Big business just keeps on giving. To be fair, many corporations have provided excellent training, knowledge, and experience to castoffs and deserters. They provided financial compensation that helped to fund start-ups in the form of salary savings, options, bonuses, and severance packages to would-be entrepreneurs prior to their departure. They provided a network of contacts for small-business people. They provide revenue to small businesses by buying their goods and services. If only they provided job opportunity.

The *Academy of Entrepreneurship Journal* reviews differences in personality characteristics and behaviors that differentiate entrepreneurs from corporate managers:

> ...the most critical factor distinguishing entrepreneurs from non-entrepreneurs is innovation.... Managers are motivated by typical rewards such as gaining power and promotion.

Entrepreneurs are motivated by opportunity and independence. Additionally, managers delegate tasks, while entrepreneurs prefer direct involvement....

[Business] founders were reported to be more stable emotionally, more independent, and more open to new experiences than heirs as well as managers.[15]

The data shows that not only are the entrepreneurial types producing more ideas, they're more open to *other's* ideas. They're more likely to roll up their sleeves than spend time talking.

Mediocre people can't make it as entrepreneurs. That's why most mediocre people work in big companies.

Based on the description of entrepreneurial qualities, you would think that big companies' HR departments would be banging down doors to offer entrepreneurs spots at the top of their command chains. You would be wrong. The current spot fillers are not leaving. Many don't possess the entrepreneurial qualities necessary to have the choice of leaving a heavily structured, resources instantly available environment. They are compensated for hiding failures or apathetic performance, whereas entrepreneurs starve for their failures. There aren't vacancies at the top because many are filled with comfortable people who keep the office the same temperature every day and fraternize within the same boys' club. Someone needs to have the guts to create open positions at the top. Rather than add chairs to the club room, it's time to kick out the ones who have been sitting the same way for so long that there's an indelible bum print on the seat. There are still some folks left in the club (men and women) who have leadership and innovative qualities, but most claim that to stay in the club, they've had to "dumb down" or abandon proposing most of their ideas because "you have to pick your battles." The rest chose early on not to fight and to become their own chairmen.

The corporate executives who lost their prized talent and finally turned to mergers and acquisitions to fill the void of creativity have had their chance to run large corporations. Without innovation, what we got back was corporate corruption, buyouts, parity, and price cutting to make the numbers. Perhaps we should stop labeling and stereotyping creative people as poor people managers and not tactical, and give them the chance to run the big corporations.

A McKinsey study concluded that employees were the number one source of competitive advantage. "Talented people, in the right kind of culture, have better ideas, execute those ideas better—and even develop other people better."[16] The right kind of culture is no longer in big companies. More than half of the U.S. workforce are in smaller companies, and the number is growing rapidly. What's more important than the number is the quality of talent moving to the smaller organizations to experience a better quality of life.

Onboard Entertainment

The increasing popularity of sushi trains is a case study in Japan's economic evolution. *Kaiten-zushi* eliminated substantial labor costs (the highest cost for sushi restaurants) with a simple conveyor belt and self-serve drink valves. At the same time, they provided a form of entertainment: chef and people watching, and sushi surfing.

Retailertainment (also called retailtainment) is the future. Mature Americans have more time and more disposable income than ever before. Compare the amount of time and money spent shopping when you were a teen to teens today. Retailertainment is what differentiates one restaurant or department store from another where most products are viewed as parity. Why else would anyone pay so much for food that is described as "just okay and occasionally inedible" after "long waits" with service from staff who are "inexperienced" and "even rude" at Rainforest Café? Because the "décor is just amazing" with "an artificial storm complete with thunder and lightning every 15 minutes or so" in this jungle setting complete with moving elephant and gorilla animatronics and a kaleidoscope of eye candy from the saltwater fishtanks.[17]

The sushi train was just as entertaining, less intrusive, and less expensive. The key to success is that the entertainment was directly related to the product. It was not an unrelated add-on. Businesses fail when they add "features and benefits" that have nothing to do with their products and services. Adding performers from Cirque du Soleil is not going to make me a loyal sushi customer. If I want to see Cirque du Soleil, I'll buy a ticket and go to a great sushi restaurant afterwards. But if the performers are making my sushi while doing contortions or swinging from the trapeze, well, maybe. Retailertainment that works has entertainment that is an integral part of the product/service or purchase transaction; it is not peripheral. More recorded or live music and dancers, mannequins and models that move, home and vacation settings, activities and learning experiences will become an integral part of shopping and eating out, as retailers search for ways to make their environments memorable and motivating among the advertising clutter. Me-too product offerings will start to be sold in a way that you remember the product rather than the entertainment. Instead of retail *and* entertainment, the two will be blended: retailertainment.

The desire for collecting new experiences is trumping the desire for hoarding more things. I view memories of my travels to 78 countries as far more valuable than any of the purchases I made along the way. The memory of experiences outlasts the threads of a new shirt. Just look at the growth in home improvement, even during recession. Americans clamor for backyard games, patios, and barbecue grills to serve as props for family experiences and memories. Why isn't advertising experiential? Would you be more likely to buy that new fancy grill, a dog obstacle course, or an outdoor stereo speaker setup if the stores that sell it were having a "backyard barbecue" in front of their stores, and everyone was invited? What if you were driving down the highway and billowing smoke caught your attention. You look up to see a billboard with a live family enjoying a cookout (with smoke coming out of the grill, and the family playing games around that terrific new patio set). The backboard of the billboard gives the name of the store and "exit 5" and some line that can be read in three to seven seconds about there being great outdoor fun stuff there with a verb included. (OK, Mr. Corporate Nonvisual Idea-killer: Yes, we would have insurance; yes, there would be a safety rail so the kids don't fall off catching the whiffle ball; no, the game doesn't have to be whiffle ball; no, the smoke is not "real"—it's a smoke machine; no, people won't think the grill burns things; no, they're not cooking real food; yes, it could be real food; no, it doesn't cost a lot; no, we won't be doing it in winter in the Northeast; yes, there's an alternative scene for bad weather days; yes, I worked in large companies long enough to know that you'd immediately focus on the problems rather than the opportunities and ideas to improve on it; help, get me out of here so I can start a company that does this.)

Live or living billboards are not new. In the U.K. on the Cromwell Road, a travel company put up a live billboard with a hammock, palm trees, and a bikini-clad, suntanned beauty who waved with one hand to the traffic from her hammock and held a fake (I think) cocktail in the other hand. In 2005, Target showcased a vertical fashion runway, with models walking Batman-style down the side of a New York City office building. Certainly won its share of attention, and sales.

Adults *and* children want to be entertained and will pay dearly for it. Many kid-targeted businesses prove that showing consumers a good time isn't child's play. American Girl, LLC, happily accepts $90 from parents each time they take home a character doll from the past for their present little darlings. Whether it's the dolls that are based on historical stories, or historical stories based on dolls, the world of pictures, scents, sounds, tastes, and touches has made the company a thriving playpen. Girls clamor for the magazine, engaging Web activities, enthralling games, and advice. They delight in the stories of other places at other times. Busloads of out of towners travel to Chicagoland with their daughters and dolls (dressed in matching outfits) specifically to visit American Girl Place, a shop, café, doll hospital, doll hair salon, and museum. Dressed as Kit from Cincinnati in 1934, Josefina (1824) of Santa Fe, or Philly's Addy (1864), young girls with moms in tow queue up around the block. American Girl Place's sales are $700 per square foot. Gap during its heyday was generating $400 per square foot[18] while department stores often struggle to break $200.

Pleasant Rowland is the entrepreneur who created the American Girls. Says her biographer, Chris Hansen:

> For a long time, I have said that positive dissatisfaction is the key to creating a business.... Pleasant Rowland is one of the best examples. For the most part, her success is based upon three things:
>
> 1. A compelling vision. (A market gap, the lack of educational dolls with historical stories)
>
> 2. A powerful mission. (To fill the market gap for a specific group. In Pleasant's case, this was girls ages 9 to 12.)

3. A passion to serve. (It was not the profit motive that drove her to do everything necessary to create her business. It was the absolute, unflagging belief that the dolls she made and sold would not reach the market unless she did it. She was right.)

But you may be wondering, how do all these things tie together? In Pleasant Rowland's case...it was her experience of history at Williamsburg and her dissatisfaction with traditional (lowest common denominator) toy offerings that led her to believe that there was a market for U.S. Historical dolls with a message and a story. The American Girl collection was born.

After leading her company to $287 million per year in sales, and creating jobs for over 850 employees, Pleasant Rowland sold the Pleasant Company to Mattel in June of 1998 for $700 million , making her the highest paid woman in the country.[19]

Build-a-Bear Workshop is another terrific example of nouveau business, combining entertainment with retail. Its tag line is: Where best friends are made. Wish I'd thought of that. Maxine Clark, the founder, spent most of her career working for large retailers, for whom she might have launched Build-a-Bear. Who knows? She might have suggested it.

For those who don't have a four- to 12-year-old, you actually "build" your own teddy bear or other stuffed animal. First, you pick the animal's limp shell, then you move to a machine full of swirling fluff. Next the hole in the shell is put over the feeding tube of the fluff machine and a touch of the pedal pumps fluffy stuffing into your animal, giving it form, making it huggable. You can place a heart inside (after making a wish by blowing on it) before the hole is sewn up or pick a Velcro bone for your dog's mouth. After combing your new companion, you choose to make a personalized storybook or birth certificate. There are tons of outfits and accessories to choose. To protect your furry friend from the elements, you get a bear box shaped like a house to carry him or her home in. Everything about this company is remarkable, from its happy-to-be-bear employees ("beary pawsitive") to the tiles on the floor ("pawfect"). This experience costs between $10 and $25: a deal. There's no doubt Clark will continue to innovate with "bearrific" ideas.

Retailertainment is a no-brainer. No high IQ required. "A well-thought-out store with an entertainment format sells 60 percent more per square foot than a similar-sized traditional store."[20] This isn't kids' stuff. How many places do you go that are this much fun?

If you sell a me-too product, you'll never stay profitable if you sell it in a me-too way. Entrepreneurs often trounce their former employers by buying the same items from the same wholesalers and selling them better. Processes, not just products, are patentable now and provide protection for unique methods of selling, not only things to sell. More about patents later.

Consumers are changing the way they buy. Despite our having more leisure time, the number of stores we shop in has dropped by 30 percent in just two years. "Americans simply have enough stuff," says Wendy Liebmann from WSL Strategic Retail, who authored *How America Shops*. "Previously, they always had to have the newest and latest—then they got it and realized that the latest wasn't much different from what they had before. So, enough already."[21]

Take the signage and colors out of stores, and most people probably couldn't discern the apparel department of Kohl's from JCPenncy's. Choose a product you'd like to buy, say a DVD player, and surf the net. Most of the sites are similar. Even virtual environments are boring. Excitement isn't about themed visual merchandising, or simply exciting the senses. It's about stimulating the mind, and the senses.

In 1986, I read a memorable article in *National Geographic* entitled "The Intimate Sense of Smell." Simulating the senses is an underused tactic in selling, although supermarkets, mostly a regional business, are among the strongest advocates. Smell is the "memory" sense. It triggers flashbacks of Nana's ravioli and love. For me, the smell of a mineral in sand conjures up a déjà vu of dust storms in Arizona with its joyful memories of grad school friendships and riding my trail motorbike through the desert. Notice that the sense of smell stimulates memories of the former smell *and* the emotions, people, and places.

The right smells drive us to blow our money and sniff at product prices. Often-edible smells infiltrate gas station convenience stores, bookstores, discount stores, properties for sale, and every other neighborhood corner, with impressive bottom-line impact. Some supermarkets have blowers in their bakery exhaust lines to fill the store with emotionally warming waves of baking bread. They experience increased sales of bakery products and other products. Go on, laugh, but scratch 'n' sniff works (except now it's pull 'n' sniff with encapsulated smells) to stimulate our appetite for all kinds of things. (Before you write, yes, I have heard about the August 1977 scratch 'n' sniff centerfold in *Hustler* and your recall supports the theory.) We've all heard that the smell of coffee or just-baked chocolate chip cookies can shorten the buy cycle and increase the offer price on residential real estate. Yet, how many of us, as home sellers, even took the 15 minutes to pop one blob of poppin' fresh prefab cookie dough on a piece of tin foil in the oven to make another $15,000. Or three minutes to make a pot of instant coffee for $5,000. Similarly, does Calphalon have scent blowers in department stores with cooking smells that remind potential purchasers of the end benefit of buying good cookware? How many packaged goods companies have pull 'n' sniff tab or Peel 'n Taste dissolving strip dispensers for grocery shoppers? Instead, they have automatic coupon dispensers to compete on price, the positioning that can never be sustained. With coupon redemptions at around 2 percent and steadily declining, you be the judge of which would be a greater motivator for the most people. When you smell food, can't you almost taste it too?

There's a scientific explanation why using scents and smells, particularly for food, increases the average sale. Insulin. Most of us think of insulin as the clear (or sometimes cloudy) liquid injected by people with diabetes. Since one in every 16 Americans has diabetes, it's easy to understand this generalization. However, insulin is a hormone produced naturally in most people, even most people with diabetes, in varying amounts. In a healthy person, insulin is produced to allow sugars (carbohydrates) to pass into the body's cells to provide energy. The carbs in bread, potatoes, and pasta can raise your blood sugar level almost as much as the sugar in that candy bar or soft drink. If you know someone with diabetes who is insulin dependent, you'll know that he or she injects insulin before eating. Our bodies naturally act the same way. If we eat meals on a strict schedule, our bodies may start releasing insulin automatically *before* the regular mealtime in anticipation of a carb attack. The sight of food often initiates insulin production, as will the smell of food. When insulin production increases, we get hungry. When we get hungry, we buy food, too much food.

If you tried the Atkins diet, er sorry, the Atkins Nutritional Approach, or any of the lower-carbohydrate diets, you'll now understand why you don't feel as hungry even though you're eating smaller portion sizes. If you've stayed on any diet for more than two days, congratulations. You didn't feel as hungry anymore once you'd retrained your body to stop overproducing insulin for the lower amount of carbs you were introducing. Yes, it's a simplified explanation so please don't try this at home. Ironically, Dr. Atkins died just as fellow scientists and the media recognized his methodology and results as valid. Upon announcement of his death, I overheard a discussion on his unfortunate timing.

"Ah," said the entrepreneur. "Can you believe it? Just as somebody gives the guy a little recognition for being right at saying something different, he slips on the ice, hits his head, and dies."

"That's just how the media are presenting it," said the corporation man. "It wasn't a blow to his head that killed him. He suffered cardiac arrest from doing his diet a year ago. He just had another heart attack as he walked across some icy path, collapsed from his heart stopping, and hit his head on the way down. It was the diet that killed him," he pooh-poohed.

"There was no evidence of cardiac arrest this time," argued the entrepreneur, basing his comments on facts.

"OK, OK," said the corporation man. "It might not have been a full-blown heart attack, but he was probably weak from not eating carbs or sugar, and passed out. The diet's a killer. Same result."

"Or maybe he lost his breath laughing so hard at the 25 million people following his quack diet," added the entrepreneur, giving in, sort of. Whenever there's a meaty success, there's bound to be a sudden outbreak of mad cows nearby. Where's the beef?

Perhaps it was the stress and worry
of fighting naysayers, to be tattered and torn
that mocked the Doctor, all forlorn
that attacked his heart
that tossed him down
that made him hit his head on the ground
that killed Dr. At

that suffered assault

that lay in the House that Atkins Built.

We all fall down. Atkins was right. At least for now. And that's what innovation is—"right" for now. Innovation is the fuel of entrepreneurs, producing the smell of fear for large companies. While Atkins lived, his approach changed and improved from a line of vitamins to a revolutionary mass lifestyle change that affected the fortunes of the orange, egg, and cattle industries, among others. At its peak, his company generated annually $200 million in revenue.[22] After his death, the flavor of the business changed from a medical-centric entrepreneurship (evolving) to an anti-carb-based packaged food business (limited and imitable). It was a rip-off of what was already on the shelves. There had been more than 400 low-carb products introduced in the three years prior.[23] Consumers soon lost their taste for this predictably short-lived corporate approach and Atkins's business went down the hatch (Chapter 11) while Americans' weight continued to escalate. The thrill is gone.

The thrill is in small businesses, and even big businesses are ramping up targeting their ex-employees as B2B customers. If you can't beat 'em, join 'em any way you can. Supermarkets aren't the only ones to smell a winner. Wholesale clubs aka warehouse clubs like Costco and Sam's Club initially catered to small businesses with just-right bulk buys for restaurateurs and office managers. As the number of small-business owners (SBOs) grows, so too does their expenditure on business supplies and raw goods. Business customers spend twice as much and shop three times as often as individual members.[24]

The majority of SBOs are sole proprietors (78 percent, and 87 percent for women-owned businesses), and they are consolidating their business and personal activities. Not only do they visit the same stores to buy office supplies and groceries, but they are paying for it on the same credit card. The Center for Women's Business Research says that 86 percent of women SBOs use the same products and services at home that they do in business, and two-thirds say this is a conscious decision. Two-thirds of all SBOs combine their business expenses on their personal credit cards wielding extraordinary power over the economy. Because we visit fewer stores, the businesses that cater to the growing army of sole proprietors are getting a bigger chunk of personal expenditures too. The very workers who could develop new, lucrative products and services for the self-employed have left, to become the self-employed. The self-employed are in the best position to create, produce, and market products and services for people just like them. They understand the market—it is they. As the number of self-employed continues to grow, the revenue of larger companies will continue to diminish as the ex-staff buy their small-business and personal products from people like themselves—providers with imagination who offer better products faster.

During a job interview, an interviewer asked me to complete certain tasks. "Let me write this down," I said while pulling out a pen. "I'm visual."

"So are 90 percent of the population," he sniped.

Excuuuuuussse meeeee. You mean I'm not special. Maybe he was upset because he was in the 10 percent minority, but I think he was just upset, about life in general. They have drugs for that now. I didn't get an offer; I have no regrets. I was visual enough to "see" what a great guy he'd be to work with.

If it's true that 90 percent of the population are visual, it would explain why about 90 percent of what you communicate isn't verbal.[25] Even when you're lying.

Dr. Phil McGraw lists the 13 ways to spot a liar, an action we think of as verbal. Only four are verbal.

- Pitch changes
- Answering questions that were never asked while avoiding a simple answer to the question that was. Defending themselves without being accused
- Providing excessive detail: Talking a lot about a peripheral topic while avoiding the central issue
- Stalling techniques such as umming, throat clearing
- Excessive or of lack of eye contact
- Fidgeting
- Touching the nose or rubbing the eye
- Pursing the lips

- Tick movements such as blinking or shrugging
- Dilated pupils
- Looking around[26]

If we learn the signs, we unfold the key to human behavior. When we understand behavior, we can identify those most likely to use a new product, or develop a new product leveraging behaviors and habits people already have.

When I studied international business at Thunderbird, where more than half the students were foreign nationals, I developed an interest in body language. While some body language was universal, some was not. The "OK" sign we make with thumb and index finger touching means "asshole" in some countries. Giving people the middle finger in Britain makes them snicker; their equivalent is the peace (or victory) sign with the palm inward. Victory, indeed. Is this why the expatriate boom has subsided and local nationals are managing foreign subsidiaries instead? Are entrepreneurs leaving because corporate management is failing to read the signs?

Ninety percent of us might be visual, but 90 percent are certainly not visionary. (Imagine if I'd said *that* during the interview: "Hold on a minute; I'm visionary!")

Gary Hamel of *Fast Company* magazine says that innovation is the only way companies can win today. He tells how to spot the visionaries (calling them "radical innovators") capable of generating corporate success. Radical innovators:

1. Challenge the status quo
2. Spot trends before they are widely adopted
3. See through the customer's eyes
4. See their companies as portfolios of assets and competencies

Hamel continues:

Most people who succeed at radical innovation inside large companies will tell you that they did it despite the system. What I find remarkable and disturbing is that so few senior executives seem to find that state of affairs to be remarkable and disturbing.[27]

Hamel goes on to relay his conversation with Nobuyuki Idei, Sony chairman, who commented on the success of Sony's most profitable business, PlayStation. (*BusinessWeek* magazine selected Idei as one of the worst managers of 2003.) Two years earlier, the inventor of PlayStation, Ken Kutaragi, told Hamel that he found it difficult to get support within the company. Kutaragi claims that Sony was so opposed to engaging in the video-game business that he moved his office to a different building on the outskirts of Tokyo. Ken eventually succeeded by selling a Sony sound chip to Nintendo, then finding one rare open-minded senior executive who supported him— the head of Sony Music in Japan, who envisioned a CD-playing PlayStation (another way to make it better). Concludes Hamel: "We've produced organizations that aren't much fun to work in. We've produced organizations that too often fail. And as they fail, so do the aspirations of the people who have devoted their lives to building them.... We should take revolutionary steps to achieve evolutionary goals."[28]

Despite the majority shrugging their shoulders, blinking, and clearing their throats, Sony won millions because a few visionaries decided to do something. Four in 10 adults and eight in 10 kids play video games. Think of all the other visionaries who left in the blink of an eye.

Loco Motives?

The courier pointed. My train had arrived. I hopped aboard, hoping that when I arrived in Nagoya, I could make the five-minute connection for my bullet train to Kyoto.

Like the sushi restaurant where the signs negated conversation, my assigned seat had everything I needed to be self-sufficient. There was a map of the train on the back of each seat so I never needed to ask anyone where anything was. I read *The Japan Times* and, out of the corner of my eye, watched two kids in Mickey Mouse ears wind down, stroking their treasures from their visit to Tokyo Disneyland. *The Japan Times* read:

Many of us have heard other foreigners remark how this place doesn't really seem like a real place at all, certainly not in terms of what we're familiar with from home.

It's kind of like what the creative geniuses at Disney would come up with if they were given "Japanland" specifications and told to go wild.[29]

In Nagoya, the train stopped at exactly 9:25 p.m., as scheduled, of course. A bright sign indicated that my connection to Kyoto would arrive on the adjacent platform, of course. I looked at the painted markers on the platform floor to find the correct place to stand and wait, so that the car with my assigned seat would stop directly in front of me, of course. One minute later, I saw the lights of my train coming, of course. The train schedules had been synchronized so that the customer would never have to wait, of course.

The sleek Shinkansen (bullet train) arrived looking like a proud, white platypus. The gleaming doors opened. At 9:30 p.m. exactly, the train's wheels rolled, as scheduled. I nestled into my assigned seat, opened my tour guide, and pulled out the outdated fortune I'd received at one of the temples. Although it was summer, it had been written last winter:

GREAT GOOD FORTUNE

When spring comes, the bare trees of winter blossom forth with flowers, and when the black clouds of midnight part, the moon shines brightly. In like manner, your lot will steadily improve and your happiness will increase. Your work and the fortunes of your house will prosper.

How ironic, I thought, wanting to believe in fortunes and fairy tales. When spring had come, I left corporate life and became a sole proprietor. How coincidentally accurate.

A well-dressed (everybody was, of course) man stood beside my seat and rechecked the seat assignment on his ticket. He did not have good fortune and was going to have to sit next to a *gaijin,* a foreigner. Although he probably felt the impulse to run from the train as if his suit was on fire, he never flinched or let on his discomfort.

Restless, I returned to *The Japan Times:*

Whenever I think this place may be getting to me I'm reminded of a tale once related by an old friend, who'd seen what can happen when a *gaijin* has had more than his fill of our gentle capital on the archipelago.

Seems his buddy was waiting for the train with him some day on some platform.... All of a sudden his friend, who'd seemed to my friend to be a bit on edge, for whatever reason, began screaming uncontrollably.

Not screaming as in: "Hey, Mac! Where's the fire?" or "Officer! That man took my purse."

No, it was, pure and simple, maniacal screaming.... After an unrelenting stream of hair-raising hollering...station masters and medical emergency personnel had to be called in to put an end to the outburst.

Needless to say, the unfortunate fellow was packed on a plane back to Britain within a matter of days, presumably never to return....

Just as there are, I'm sure, expats who lived in Japan for decades who get along just fine in their everyday lives, there are certainly others who've been here just a presidential administration or two too long.

Maybe they were that way when they got here, it's hard to say....

But one cannot live in a country and environment so alien from the one that formed their core.... We should feel for these fellow foreigners, if for no other reason than they are the harbingers of what we must not become.[30]

I couldn't help thinking of my friend Samira and a former boss, Roger. Samira worked crazy hours as a senior executive in the publishing business. Smart, vivacious, got along with everybody, steadily promoted, considered one of the business champions. Samira spent a decade at one of the icons of the industry.

"One day," she said, calmly sipping her tea, "I sat at my desk and starting thinking what the day was going to be like. Like all the others. And I thought, I'm afraid that someone is going to come and ask me a simple question, and I'm going to start screaming and I'm not going to be able to stop." No one at work knew she was unhappy, probably because everyone was self-absorbed with unhappiness too.

Samira left and started a children's creative crèche called Happily Ever After. Apropos. And she lived happily ever after.

Roger had a similar experience, but unfortunately, his unhappiness was more visible. He'd also spent a long time at his firm. In his key position as executive vice president of sales, his decisions and implementation of new ideas had driven the profitable growth of the firm. His hands started shaking during meetings. At first, many thought he had Parkinson's disease, but the intensity of the shaking progressed so rapidly, it became obvious it was stress related. He never stopped making good decisions, but he couldn't stop his hands from shaking. Rather than be supportive, most of his staff openly made fun of the shaking. Sadly, it was before psychotropic drugs were widely available to mask such symptoms. Soon, Roger had disappeared on medical leave. I was the only one to visit him during his leave. "I just couldn't handle being treated like I was stupid by my boss. Everything was an uphill battle. I'm sick of fighting every day." He moved to the Caribbean to sell time shares to vacationers. Seriously. His hands stopped shaking, except when he's dancing.

When in Tokyo, I took a subway trip to Kokugikan (the main sumo stadium) to see the sumo Grand Tournament. There are only three major tournaments each year in Tokyo, and the top sumo wrestlers would all be there. To my surprise, another *gaijin* got into my subway car. He was well-dressed (not a tourist). No one sat next to him either.

I got off the train and walked toward the stadium. A few wrestlers passed me on the sidewalk in their flip-flops, bathrobes, and shiny hair in updos (the hairstyle indicates rank and serves as head protection in case of falls). I no longer felt like an elephant. At Kokugikan, I bought the cheapest ticket possible and received the day's program (all in Japanese, of course) and for free, a comprehensive booklet in English explaining sumo wrestling (of course). Dream it, see it. Japan meets and exceeds expectations.

I was bursting to find out why no one sits next to *gaijin*. I saw two sitting alone in the back row of the stadium and approached them. The two blokes were Australian. One cited, "Japanese don't want to be embarrassed or offend by not speaking perfect English, so they avoid the opportunity to speak whenever possible." The other, "Naw.

They're just xenophobic—afraid of anyone who's not Japanese." A debate between the two ensued.

A few hours passed and I was still mesmerized by the wrestling matches. Why did they have different color belts? I looked for the answer in my booklet. Hmmmm. Not there. No question should go unanswered (the sign of an innovator). I approached a Japanese group of four: "Why are the belts different colors?"

They looked at each other for a few seconds, and a women answered, "There's no special reason. They just choose their favorite colors."

"Thanks," I replied, and added a compliment about her beautiful English.

Here was the paradox: In a place where people appeared to be timid or afraid of not attaining perfection, how could there be so many incredible people-friendly (for their culture) inventions. Among them:

- **Rent-a-dog:** Japanese apartments and housing rules often don't allow for pet ownership. At rent-a-dog places, there are more than 50 breeds to choose from. Rent by the hour or day.

- **"The Sound Princess":** It's a small sound machine on walls in stalls of public toilets. Press the button, and for 25 seconds, you'll hear the sound of flowing water. Japanese women, who are self-conscious about the sound of peeing, used to keep flushing the toilets. In an office with 400 female workers, this nifty device saves more than 10 million liters of water annually.

- **Combination toilet/bidet**, also available in public restrooms: Press the button on the side of the toilet bowl, and a little swing arm comes out to spray you clean. Don't worry. It only works when there's weight on the seat. Press the button with the girl icon to make the water stream move to a different angle. Some include a blow dryer. Yes, the water is heated to a "comfortable" temperature. Some even have a heated seat.

- **Attendant-free single parking spots** that guarantee payment: You drive over the raised bar to get into your spot. It triggers the timer. When you leave, just put the right number of coins in the meter to lower the barrier and drive out.

- **Free umbrella sleeves:** As you enter stores or restaurants, just dip your wet umbrella in this box, and out it comes with a plastic sheath around it. Your clothes don't get wet, and the floor doesn't get wet either, reducing the chance of slips and falls. Of course, there's a waste bin to discard used sleeves as you exit the store.

And there were thousands more great ideas in Japanland, the birthplace of Sony, Toyota, Fuji Photo Film, and Nintendo. The country that was physically and economically devastated after WWII, and had a reputation of uniformity, is delivering the world's greatest inventions. In the 2007 Top 25 list of U.S. patent assignee companies, "U.S. companies hold 7 spots, less than a third of the positions, while Japan leads with 13," according to IFI Patent Intelligence. The United States Patent and Trademark Office reports 41 percent of *all* U.S. patent applications (including those filed from non-U.S. companies) list a foreign national as inventor or co-inventor, with Japan the leader by far. The world is flatter.

But if ever there were a case for an American brain drain in big companies, the data on patent applications by U.S. companies is it. Out of patent applications filed in 2006 from only U.S. companies, 25.6 percent include a foreign national as inventor, triple the percentage from 1998. From large U.S. corporations, more than half list a foreign national.[32] More than half. A notable exception—Microsoft with 3 percent.

Why are Japan's big companies brewing big ideas, including those that amass profit and popularity in other cultures? Why is tenure at Japanese companies so much higher than at U.S. companies?

With big companies' titanic resources (including legal resources to process patents), one would expect them to have the most patents. Where do the entrepreneurs rank? Since they claim they're leaving to launch products and services, are they?

In the first chapter, we gave a couple of innovation facts. Here's a reminder:

- Small businesses produce 55 percent of innovations, twice as many per employee as large companies.
- More than half of innovations come from small firms.

- Sixty-seven percent of inventions and 95 percent of all radical innovations since World War II have come out of small businesses.

No surprise either that small businesses produce four times more innovations per R&D dollar spent than medium-sized firms and 24 times as many as large companies.[33] In the patent department, here's how small businesses measure up according to research from the Small Business Administration:

- Small firms received 71 percent of biotechnology patents, 68 percent of pharmaceutical patents, 80 percent of power generation and distribution patents, and 64 percent of medical electronics patents. According to the U.S. Small Business Administration, small businesses are the leaders in high-impact, leading-edge technology and are key creators in newer and science-intensive technologies.

- In addition to small businesses, individuals received another 20 percent of patents.

- Small businesses average 40 patents for every 1,000 workers; large business averages three per 1,000.

- In firms with 15 or more patents, the small firms had 13 to 14 times more patents per employee.

- Individuals' or small businesses' patents were twice as likely to be among the top 1 percent of most widely cited patents (citations for patents are a measure of their importance). Across the board, small companies are more likely to produce cited patents.

- Forty-one percent of the companies that have 15 or more patents are small businesses.

- Small-firm patents are twice as likely to be linked to scientific research.[34]

You would think that big companies would be busting down the doors of these inventors to make them job offers. Maybe they are. But unless large companies can prove that they'll be able to continue being serial innovators in a new home, no one's going to move.

Why aren't Americans leading innovation at mammoth American companies? Why did the best and brightest Americans leave?

Innovation in the U.S., which peaked in 1989, has been on the downslide ever since. The U.S. is falling behind as a leading innovator, lapped by Denmark, Switzerland, Finland, Germany and, of course, Japan.[35]

Earlier, there was a top-five list of why people *left* companies led by "job content" and "level of responsibility." Here's the top-five list of why people *started* companies according to *Inc. Magazine*:

Biggest reason for starting a business[36]	Overall	Among those who were successful
Identified a market opportunity	37%	33%
Autonomy and independence	32%	54%
To make more money	9%	8%
To use knowledge and experience	11%	0%
To show I could do it	2%	0%
Other (e.g., to learn, needed job, to be creative, to provide jobs, to avoid taxes, God's will)	9%	5%

For women, who are starting new businesses at double the rate of their male counterparts, the magnetism of filling a vacant market opportunity was even greater. Forty-four percent of women cited their reason for starting a business was identifying and wanting to develop an entrepreneurial idea, a "winning idea, or [they] came to realize they could do for themselves what they were doing for an employer." Coincidentally **entrepreneurial women are also more likely to state frustrations with their previous jobs in big businesses, listing this as their most frequently cited reason for going it alone.**[37] The fact that more women left primarily to pursue an "entrepreneurial idea" might also explain why women-owned start-ups have a much greater success rate compared to men's.[38]

Forget the glass ceiling cliché. It's simpler than that. People who left big companies and started their own businesses did it because they had great ideas and their former employers refused to listen, or do anything about it. Their frustration wasn't borne out of management blocking their ears when they occasionally asked for a promotion or flextime; it was because they were deaf to ideas. Totally. Their managers sat inside the glass solo cone of silence. Yelling and sign language only made it worse. Shut up to move up and eventually, you'll win the prize: your own cone of silence.

Fifty-nine percent of men and 41 percent of women started businesses related to their previous field.[39] That's a lot of people; that's a lot of ideas. Here's the math: 27 million small businesses divided by an average of 50 percent being started with an idea from a previous job equals 13.5 million ideas (or more, since entrepreneurs rarely have one idea) that were served up, ignored, and prompted the employee to leave.

It appears that, for large companies, change or innovation to fill market opportunities is even more frightening than 27 million people competing with them. But then, it's not the mathematical geniuses who stayed. It's the ones who are afraid. Very, very afraid.

The next highest reason stated for starting a business is "to be your own boss." This is linked with the first reason. If bosses allowed innovators to bring new ideas to market, many entrepreneurs wouldn't have sought autonomy. Studies show that the top factor that hampers implementation of big ideas is, you guessed it, management support.[40] There's nothing surer to stop an inventor from inventing than a boss who can't.

The truth is that big business promotes and hires management that is anti-change, and anti-change agent. Even when a change agent is hired, the person is so outnumbered that he soon leaves. When the masses are change averse, it doesn't matter whether the change agent is at the bottom, middle, or top of the corporate ladder. The rungs will be too weak to support him and he will crash. It's impossible to drag those with their feet cemented to the ground and their heads in the sand up a ladder to get a better view of the world. "In cases where executives were brought in as turnaround specialists, resentment sometimes breeds within the company's ranks, and it can be difficult for the change agent to assume a new role presiding over the company."[41]

Companies often hire "change agents" whose mission is to change their stagnant culture, without changing the stagnant people in top positions. Mission impossible. Labeling a new employee "change agent" is a death sentence. A change agent cannot change products or services offered without changing the people who have done nothing to change things in the past. A place that calls a worker a "change agent" is acknowledging that the company, as a whole, is averse to advancement and sees anyone who isn't as a freak. You can practically hear the screaming: "You're not going to change *me*."

Unfortunately, laws that protect some minorities in the workplace do not protect change agents. Among *themselves*, you'll rarely hear entrepreneurs or inventors labeling themselves "change agents" since they see improvement, evolution, and trial as natural. Fixing things and creating things are not change for them. It's the norm. Why wouldn't we want a lightbulb that never stops lighting, a car that never breaks down, and a bathtub that never needs cleaning, for the same cost of the inferior ones we buy today?

Not only do you have to change the roster of current employees who are supposed to implement change. You have to change the people filling their positions. Let's make it clearer. Fire them. Hiring a couple of "change agents" is the same as dumping a couple of hens into a pit of wolves and acting surprised when there are no eggs.

"Bain & Co., the management consulting firm, studied 21 recent corporate transformations.... The means were drastic: In almost every case, **the CEOs fired most of the top management**. Almost always, the companies enjoyed quick, tangible results, and their stock prices rose 250 percent a year on average as they revived."[42]

No one would expect a handful of Americans to move to Japan and change the culture.

When I created a telemarketing center at Citibank and hired mostly foreign nationals, several people complained to my manager. I hired a Gambian, Pakistani, Iranian, Frenchwomen, Indian, Jamaican, and others because they were the best candidates, they demonstrated a commitment to hard work, and they showed the greatest desire to learn new skills. Thank God my manager Jeff Goodwin wasn't prejudiced. He judged the people on their performance—just the way it should be—and our united nations continued to flourish and bring in business. (I've also had people complain to management when I had a department that was all men and, in the same company, when I ran another group that was all women. The people were obviously the right ones because we were extremely successful. Perhaps that's what the complainers were really complaining about. When some people can't attack the ideas anymore, they start to attack the idea generators.)

If you have to tell your employees to prize innovators and implement the best ideas regardless of whom they come from, it's clearly not happening today. If you give out little white cards that you want employees to carry in their wallets entitled "Our Commitment," which talk about "integrity" while senior management are cheating on their wives and their taxes, their commitment is going to be toward finding new jobs. When companies cover the walls with "meritocracy" signs and "diversity" posters, you should start wondering whom they're trying so hard to convince. More interesting would be to look at their employee attrition, number of arbitration claims, and EEOC claims—actual performance. If employees were not suing you, you'd have no reason to create arbitration processes, and no reason to force employees to sign binding arbitration agreements as a condition of employment. Employees don't engage in years of legal costs and wrangling with employers who treat them fairly. Arbitration processes (like many processes and processors) wave the red flag.

Diversity is about variety, not about color or sexual orientation. It's OK to be part of a legally protected minority, but to be in the minority who exhibit enormous creative energy in the work environment, watch out! The beacon of innovation won't find people "celebrating the differences" in most big companies.

In another company loaded with diversity posters, two employees in the elevator on their way to lunch were scolded to "speak English while you're in 'our' country" while having a conversation about their kids on which the third party who entered the elevator couldn't eavesdrop. In the same company, someone saw one Indian computer programmer (with a doctorate in computer science, but earning 25 percent as much as he) neglect to wash his hands after using the washroom on a floor that had many Indian workers. It wasn't his floor, yet he posted a nasty sign in the restroom and started running around the company telling everyone how "*none* of the Indians washes his hands." Guess what? Thirty-two percent of Americans don't wash their hands after using the toilet, and worse, three-quarters of *them* lie about it. The best indicator of future behavior is past behavior. Once a dirty liar...

Might makes right. Only if the Iraqis, Hispanics, or Japanese outnumbered Americans would we start to adopt their cultures. Why, then, do companies expect that by dropping in a couple of innovators, their cultures (their people) will suddenly become idea factories and new product launchers. What makes them believe that a lone *gaijin* can do it on his own? To bring the best and brightest back in droves, what has to change is that people who don't have a history of innovation become the minority. Anybody want to hire some anti-change agents?

Corporations have tried to put original thinkers in senior level positions, but they haven't stayed. It's not just an original thinker who's going to be thrown off the train. Anything or anybody new in a large corporation is likely to have a short lifespan. That's how averse to change organizations are. Thirty to 50 percent of newly hired senior executives "fail or are derailed" within three years. A study of recently "failed or derailed" executives found that 75 percent listed "culture" (surprise, surprise) as the biggest barrier to their assimilation. Eighty-two percent of the corporate executives said that the new leaders failed because they couldn't "build partnerships" within the organization.[43] Isn't it odd that those corporate executives expected the new people to have to "build partnerships." Wouldn't you assume that since you're now all working for the same company, you'd already be partners and wouldn't have to "build" partnerships? Why isn't the onus on the existing employees to welcome the new employee and build the relationship if one must be built? It's sort of tough for Johnny to build a house of blocks in a place where there are no blocks available. What it shows is that if you're new in a company, qualifications, expertise, and ideas are irrelevant. What's most surprising of all is when the "failed or derailed" executives start their own companies, they have little trouble "building partnerships" with new customers, vendors, and employees. It's obvious with whom the problem of building relationships lies. It's not with the entrepreneurial managers!

Studies show that in companies that have "a large number of long-term employees and a history of promoting from within, new leaders brought in from the outside often encounter the 'antibody problem.'"[44] It's a reaction by those who felt entitled, for just being there, to get the new guy's or gal's job. Or sometimes, the attacker is the manager faced with a new employee who recommends changes.

Corporations have tried to incorporate forward-thinking new employees. It hasn't worked. They haven't been able to accomplish much. And being results driven, therefore, they haven't stayed. Here's how to get innovators to be effective and stay:

Five Practices to Keep and Attract Original Thinkers

1. **The original thinkers must be substitutions, not additions**.
   Businesses must remove senior management and other staff who have not proposed and produced groundbreaking business solutions. Yes, really. The original thinkers are not going to stay as long as they have to compete with Mr. Negative or Ms. Neutral. To keep status quo managers is to tell your organization that you approve of their behavior and that way of doing (no new) business. **If you want innovation, whom you fire matters much more than whom you hire.**

   Adding positions and people to jump-start innovation is counterproductive. Studies show that the larger an organization is, the more difficult it is to innovate. Businesses cross the threshold at 200 employees. Once you have more than 200 employees, you move from a company of entrepreneurs and "intrapreneurs," where each person is committed to *and* controlling ideas, time, and emotional resources, to a bureaucracy where the only battle is for control for power.[45] (The *American Heritage Dictionary* definition of intrapreneur is "an employee of a corporation allowed to exercise some independent entrepreneurial initiative.")

   It's the "antibody" issue. New people and new ideas are treated like poison in large corporations, and the majority will quietly, but fiercely, attack any unfamiliar, foreign cell. Add a few more ideas that are new or new people, and the white corpuscles multiply their forces. Should they not be able to destroy the unfamiliar element on their own, they'll go to someone with more power (a doctor) who'll prescribe antibiotics to quell the disturbance. The body is programmed to maintain the status quo, even when the unfamiliar part will save its life. In the case of a kidney transplant, the system that pre-existed will do everything possible to destroy the kidney, although its destruction may spell the end for all. The more transplants that have occurred, the higher the chance is that the latest one will be rejected. In fact, in cases where several transplants have failed, it's best not attempt another. Immunosuppressive agents have to be used at an early stage so that the first transplant is successful.

If you claim you want innovation in your company and you have continued to allow the antibodies to destroy what's new, you're simply all talk, no action. Here's the talk: Companies say that their target is 35 or 40 percent of their sales from new products. Here's the action: Less than 5 percent of their staff costs are allocated to new product development.[46]

2. **The original thinkers should not just be in senior roles; they must be in the most powerful roles.**
   Usually new employees are layered under the old-school boys or in a process role. They aren't in the P&L ownership roles. They don't have the power to fire nonproducers. The first step is to give the entrepreneurial newcomers the authority to change and the power to fire, even your best friends. And let the organization know the minute they walk in the door that they have complete authority. Empower new ways of doing business, and you'll have new products and services. The old "build partnerships" method hasn't worked to advance the business, so why continue doing it that way?

3. **The original thinkers must comprise the vast majority, at every level.**

4. **The original thinkers should do all the hiring and managing.**
   It *does* need to start at the top.

5. **Product-failure postmortems need to eliminate the people who caused the failure through negligence and poor business practices, rather than kill original thinking.**

If a large company were to instill the five original thinking practices, who do you think would be lining up to get inside? The pension seekers or the perfection seekers? Where are the top college grads going to seek jobs? At the idea labs or the companies with the "antibody" problem? Would the entrepreneurs come back? For the resources *and* the opportunity to build and manage *more* entrepreneurial businesses, sure!

Why can't we just send existing managers to get training to make them innovators? Haven't we been doing that for ages? The results show that, when it comes to being entrepreneurial or innovative, leopards do not change their spots. Seminars, training, mentoring, and other "leadership" development programs trying to get sleepy or change-averse corporations to embrace new ideas are a total waste of time and money. People who are creative compulsively create. Those who are afraid of change will never overcome their fears, particularly because they have been rewarded for so long for smothering ideas and the people who mention them.

The number of entrepreneurs with their own businesses is increasing in direct proportion to the increase in the number of courses on change "facilitation" and change leadership. What a farce. Most of these courses focus on politicking, butt kissing, and bartering support from nonvisual, anti-change old-timers regardless of whether the ideas are right or wrong for the business. Companies who employ these types of courses and training are making a statement that they refuse to hire people who are proven innovators and that they support bureaucracy and politics as the chief decision-making tools. More important, they are saying they refuse to fire the blockers and tacklers of good ideas and expect good people to have to "deal with it." Remember, the only way to effective "change management" is literally to change (replace) the managers.

The biggest howler is the "How to Deal with Difficult People" course that companies have their employees queuing to attend. How idiotic do you have to be to spend money endorsing courses like this rather than solving the problem by firing difficult people? What better way to reinforce antagonism at work by making the people who are *not* the problem go to training as if *they* need to be fixed to deal with the people who are the problem. Obviously, the company feels it's a total waste of time attempting to train the difficult people to not be, well, difficult. So it tries to fix the "normal" people. And you wonder why people quit!

As luck would have it, my mailbox this week contained an invitation to attend a "Program on Negotiation for Senior Executives" offered by Harvard Law School. The seminar schedule, which also offered a "special 3-day session including 'Dealing With Difficult People,'" promised you would be able to apply these concepts by taking the training:

1. Identifying the symptoms of a poor working relationship

2. Negotiating with subordinates who have their own interests, understandings, and sources of support

3. Learning how to organize a work environment that can better cope with conflict

   Learning how to organize a work environment that can better cope with conflict

   Learning how to organize a work environment that can better cope with conflict

Yes, I also had to read that last concept three times because I just couldn't believe my eyes.

Man, corporate America really is in trouble if they have senior executives who need help identifying whether or not they have poor working relationships and they think a course is going to solve that. And "learning how to organize a work environment that can better cope with conflict" is like training your two-year-old to learn to organize his crib environment to better cope with soiled diapers rather than potty train him.

Has it really come to this? America's companies stink so badly that they are training managers to cope with crap rather than removing the crap. And this course was for senior executives! Gee, I can't wait to work for another big company where the senior leadership team is going to teach me how to cope with all its conflict. Surely I'm not the only one flabbergasted at this corporate mentality. Have we lost our minds? Brain drain? It's more like a big flush. You don't see small-business owners lined up for the "Difficult People" courses or attending training courses to help them better organize their environments to cope with conflict. Because they've already coped by leaving big companies.

What it comes down to in big companies is that ideas are irrelevant. Work has become just a game. Playing the game has become more important than winning the game. After the team sacks its own quarterback enough times or neglects to defend him, he'll stop running thc ball, go to another team, or quit. Eventually, you think they'd sort out that the majority of players just can't cut it, and trade some players. Same players, same results. How many coaches have come and gone? Everyone's so engrossed in parading his uniform (padding his résumé) that he's hardly aware of the other team. So there are more and more training sessions that only the few decent players show up for and listen to. They learn that everything would improve if they took more time to befriend and build relationships with the lousy players, and to "build acceptance" and "gain support" for not throwing the ball to the other team or fumbling. The team keeps losing, but who cares? They're still hauling in the big bucks. And that is precisely why we get a Bear market.

A company that wants real "change leadership" needs to change its leaders. **The best predicator of future behavior is past behavior**. Cheerleaders don't suddenly make good linebackers, and linebackers don't suddenly make good cheerleaders. Of course, you could have a rare individual who's a great cheerleader and a great linebacker. Let your imagination run wild. But if a mature adult has never been a cheerleader and excels as a linebacker, it's unlikely that he or she is suddenly going to wake up the next morning and be a great cheerleader. Yet, this is how people are promoted into top jobs in companies. The guy who has never put his left shoe on first is suddenly beamed up from planet finance to lead the marketing team. The women from the quality galaxy is expected to be a star as head of new product development. You know companies where this is true, and just to prove they haven't changed, you'll see they've repeated this over and over despite never having launched unique products while their market share is plummeting.

If your car needs repair, you bring it to a seasoned mechanic. When seriously ill, you seek the advice of a doctor or, better still, a specialist. And you don't ask the human resources training manager to address IT network issues. So when companies need new products or innovation, you would think they'd draft innovation experts: those with a history of generating unique ideas that significantly boosted market share.

Who's in your brainstorming meetings? Who's your leader for product development? Who's the grand poobah of your marketing department?

"Past behavior is the top indicator of future behavior" is the mantra of risk management. And it works. So Mr. Mortgage, you lend a ton of money to people with low credit scores, no proof of sustained income (e.g., bank statements), and no history of paying a mortgage; please stop crying when your sub-prime mortgage business collapses. America, please don't endorse government officials who use the government's money (that's *our* taxes) to bail bad lenders out. Why should the citizens who pay their bills have to bail out big banks? How ironic that the country that claims that businesses thrive in a democracy (and that all the world should work in democracies) is constantly crawling to the Emiratis and Saudis for a bailout.

If your key managers haven't had a history of unique, patentable ideas delivered with success in the marketplace, most likely, history will repeat. Credit cardholders who pay late continue to pay late. Those who pay the bill in full each month continue to pay in full each month. People who exceed the speed limit continue to speed. Drunk drivers drink and drive all the time. People who have habits that have made them overweight will tend to be overweight the rest of their lives (that's why famous diets become fads). Even people who divorce are more likely to divorce again. People who commit crimes commit many crimes. And people in mid-life who have never invented a thing in their lives probably won't. While people who have invented a lot of things will continue to do so.

Police Commissioner William J. Bratton was appointed by Mayor Rudy Giuliani in 1994. Bratton (or Giuliani, depending upon who's telling the story) is largely responsible for reducing crime by 60 percent in New York City in a two-year period. He did this by changing two things. First, he implemented the best-predictor-of-future-behavior-is-past-behavior rule. He knew that criminals will continue to commit crimes. Destroyers continue to destroy. He ordered petty thieves and lawbreakers to be picked up and fingerprinted. Guess what? Turns out that the fingerprints of purse snatchers and subway fare evaders also happened to match those who committed unsolved multiple homicides, burglaries, rapes, and car thefts. Lock 'em up.

Second, Bratton changed the structure to precinct based rather than headquarters-centric. Bratton expected each precinct commander to know the fact patterns of crimes through new software called

Compstat and develop "innovative means" to drive ways to fight crimes. He demanded innovation, competence, and results. In return, he also gave them full authority to make decisions without prior approval for tactics and strategies, which was a 360 from how it was done before.[47] In other words, he treated them as small-business owners, giving them incredible autonomy. Read this book review of *The Turnaround: How America's Top Cop Reversed the Crime Epidemic* by Jeffrey S. Reed:

> This book is interesting, further, because Bratton...details the infighting that often happens between the old guard and the new guard. As Bratton explains it, members of the old guard do not take well to newer officers who are advancing quickly, and try to thwart their progress.[48]

The massive reduction in crime couldn't have happened if the same people who had permitted its rampage stayed in place. "Resistance was so high to Compstat that in its first year, *75 percent* of the city's precinct commanders had to be replaced, for either failing to work with the system or ignoring what Compstat analyses showed about crime in individual precincts."[49]

After reported run-ins with Giuliani over publicity and who was getting it, Bratton left the NYPD to become a consultant. In 2002, he became chief of the LAPD. On *60 Minutes* aired on February 23, 2003, Ed Bradley asked Bratton what motivated him to keep battling against the anti-change guard. Bratton replied, "This is the culmination of a lifetime of wanting to create change."

Yes, Bratton had to remove, change, 75 percent of his directors to change the NYPD. He quickly accepted that taking years training, cajoling, begging, and stroking people who hadn't gotten a grip on crime was not going to serve the city's residents best. The change made New York City a much better place to live. I lived there during his tenure so I benefited from his (or Giuliani's, depending upon who's telling the story) management. Companies that really want people who can make a difference to be in their ranks may have to replace, not add, 75 percent of their directors. Are they willing to do that? Do they really want change?

We covered some of this earlier, but it's worth restating because it's the single most important thing corporations can do to stop the brain drain, and get the best and brightest to come back: Companies that want to sustain industry leadership need to put senior managers with a history of successful innovation implementation into <u>all</u> their key, top P&L roles. They've got to eliminate those "process" roles or departments entitled "new product development" because product enhancement and development, i.e., change, is *everybody's* job. They need to stop putting new ideas through processes that were designed to improve service quality or correct manufacturing defects. Give the person who's proven he can innovate and deliver in other organizations the head role of a division or group of products, and watch him light up the world.

The best way to sustain industry leadership is to put people who have experience in producing supersellers in the most powerful functional P&L spots, so that driving and implementing innovation is part of the culture—shared in everyone's job.

Progressive Group of Insurance Companies was one of the pioneers in an aversion category. An aversion category includes products or services that are not fun to buy and you'd like to avoid shopping for them, but you have them in the event that something bad happens or because having them is the lesser of two evils.

You don't want to think about getting in a car wreck. The thought of buying or shopping for car insurance is a reminder of the possibility. Checking accounts are also an aversion category for most people. And obtaining and managing credit cards are too (although using them is not). (Why else would Capital One have been so successful selling the "No Hassle Card"?) We tend not to change our providers of these services often because it's unpleasant to shop for them. Even when they increase their rates, we pay up rather than shop for a better deal. A study by Progressive found that one in three drivers doesn't know how much he pays for auto insurance. We stay rather than switch to switch off—not deal with it—not because we're "loyal," which is one of the most incorrectly applied marketing terms.

Progressive was brilliant. The company analyzed carefully what was the most profitable way to run a car insurance business. Bad drivers tend to stay bad drivers. Teen drivers are more likely to get in an accident. And, coincidentally, people who have low credit card scores (based upon late payment history, number of cards, etc.) are more apt to make a car insurance claim. The type of car and its color make a difference. The neighborhood you live in may have more fender benders or auto thefts. Teachers and members of some other professions are less likely to make claims (hence, Farmers' Insurance Group, and Teachers Insurance and Annuity Association). Behavior doesn't generally change. So, after capturing information about you, statistically, Progressive will be able to tell with a high level of confidence how much it would have to charge you for you to contribute to its overall profitability based upon your likelihood of making a claim.

Progressive was the first to offer an "apples to apples" comparison of rates to auto insurance shoppers, for free. Call Progressive for a rate, and it does the comparison shopping for you, providing up to three competitors' rates instantly.

The ingenuity wasn't simply taking the aversion of shopping for rates out of the aversion category to attract new customers. It was that providing the comparison allowed the company to maximize its profitability on every customer. How? The auto insurance industry became cutthroat on prices. Prices got so low that, on average, claims exceeded premiums collected by 3 percent. The insurance business made its profit on cash management—getting six months of premiums up front or charging a fee to pay in monthly or quarterly installments, and investing the premiums.

What Progressive is not selling is lowest price. It sells an anti-aversion package: a shopping comparison service, easier sign-up, easier claims. Instead of setting a rock-bottom price, and hoping that it's lower than another quote the prospective customer already has, the prospect comes to Progressive first for its anti-aversion shopping comparison service. If the customer is statistically a "good" driver and good risk, it can undercut the best competitive quote it provides by only a few dollars. Because the prospect has already provided his or her details to get access to the shopping service and has an aversion to going through the process again, he or she will be likely to sign up with Progressive even if the price is slightly higher. Without the comparison shop, the insurer might have given away $100 in premium revenue in the hope that its price was lowest. Progressive can bag the customer for a few dollars. It maximizes profitability on best potential drivers.

When a driver who is a poor risk arrives, you can be certain that Progressive will not have the lowest quote. The large rate difference will encourage the "bad" driver to go to a named competitor. Progressive ends up with all the most profitable, low-claim customers, while steering the worst customers to competitors.

No wonder it's named Progressive. It operates like a small company with big ideas. It was the first insurance company to go online with a Web site. Progressive was first with its own drive-in claims service in 1937. It was the first to have its own fleet of accident response claims agent vehicles that could arrive at the scene of the accident, assess the amount of damage immediately, and even cut a claim check on the spot. You can see the win-win of this system for both company and consumer, not the least of which is reduction of fraud—one of the industry's highest costs that drives premiums sky high. Progressive is now the third-largest auto insurance group in the country despite years of ferocious attacks for changing the middleman commission system of insurance agents. In 2002, it grew three times faster than the industry average. Consumers were voting with their feet, while Allstate and State Farm dug their heels in further, trying to convince people that the old-fashioned product with the old-fashioned commission-based intermediary way is best with "You're in Good Hands" and "Like a Good Neighbor, State Farm Is There." In the past few years, Progressive added agents, who now produce two-thirds of its new business. I hope this doesn't spell the beginning of the end.

Before 1994, when Progressive launched its comparison service, I'll bet that that same idea had been suggested dozens of times by mavericks or "radical" innovators at other auto insurance companies. Can't you just picture it? Most of the top people in the industry are finance guys, and most of the profit comes from investing premiums. But it's 1992/1993 and the country's in recession. Investment income has crashed. Profits are down. So the CEO says we have to come up with new ideas. A financier or risk management expert who's also an innovator is a tremendous asset. The people who thought how to maximize customer profitability on Progressive's shopper comparison service understood risk management. But this is an old-fashioned auto insurance company. It recently got a spanking-new marketing group because it needs better brochures and advertising. Let's all get together and have a, no, no, help, help, not that. Yes, a brainstorming session.

Are "brainstorming" sessions great or a great waste of time? Do brainstorming sessions satiate entrepreneurial hunger? The truth about brainstorming can change the way your company approaches innovation, with dramatic results.

Travel Forecast: Brainstorming Is All Wet

I arrived in Kyoto on time. The sky was a dull, gray blanket. The forecast for the next three days: rain. I wasn't going to let a little rain slow me down....

Most big companies use brainstorming to create a team approach to develop new products. Is brainstorming all wet? It helps if you start in a favorable climate, get expert advice, and know the patterns. Here are six reasons why brainstorming is predictable as the weather:

Brainstorming Truth One: The decision maker of the output of brainstorming is not usually an innovation expert.
Most brainstorming ideas that make it to market fail. Take a moment and list every product idea initiated in a brainstorming session that was a blockbuster in the marketplace. Bet you didn't need more than a moment.

Here's the standard brainstorming session:

1. Write a flurry of ideas on board quickly.

2. Don't discuss ideas on board in detail.

3. Ideas on board are given to decision maker.

4. Decision maker doesn't make further enquiries about ideas on board.

5. Decision maker picks favorite idea on board to implement.

Even if you have a few seasoned inventors in the group, on average, 90 percent of your "new" products will fail. It's because the person who is *choosing* which ideas on the brainstorming list to implement typically has never created a unique product. He has no track record of success and refuses to give the decision-making power to someone who does. The person with the deciding vote typically has a history of implementing me-too programs and products, copied from competitors after market saturation, which the company refers to as "new" products.

The idea that is chosen was already going to be implemented before the brainstorming session took place. Usually, the person with the power called the session believing that if other departments had a "chance to participate" or "had their say," they would support the mediocre plan already in place. When asked, the decision maker is usually unable to describe the benefits of the unique ideas put on the board because he didn't fully understand them and didn't investigate further or ask questions to obtain an understanding, because he doesn't care about anyone's opinion anyway. But he's labeled a team player for calling lots of brainstorming sessions, voting on his own ideas, and ignoring everyone else's. The same exclusionary process is used for deciding which ideas make it into research. And which don't.

The Product Development Institute, Inc., surmises that the wrong products are developed because "decisions are not based on facts and objective criteria, but rather on politics, opinion, and emotions (i.e., manager's pet projects)." Here's an example:

Shawn is a senior manager in a large conglomerate. His last job was heading a division that supplied products to Store XYZ. Store XYZ tried to chase its competitors by copying their strategy and lost. Shawn's division sales plummeted as Store XYZ descended into bankruptcy.

Unfortunately, if Store XYZ doesn't pull out of Chapter 11, Shawn's massive inventory will be written off, a huge blow to the conglomerate's bottom line. Shawn eagerly convinces his conglomerate cronies to buy Store XYZ to try to turn it around, although they have no expertise in running that type of retail business. Not surprising, Shawn is put in charge of the turnaround (integration) effort, although he had been sending shipments of inventory to exceed his sales quota and get a bonus, even though he knew the retailer couldn't pay. Shawn has no prior experience in Store XYZ's industry, but he's a buddy of the cronies.

Shawn hires Patrick from the quality group to manage the paperwork.

A project leader, Kim, from Store XYZ who had been analyzing data now reports to Shawn. She recognizes and develops a detailed strategy and tactical proposal for turning the business around, and presents this to Shawn. He never criticizes the proposal but tells her to present it to other business "stakeholders" to get their buy-in. The stakeholders are junior staff with no decision-making power. Each stakeholder agrees that this proposal will not only save the store, but make it profitable within a year. Each time Kim comes back with the good news, Shawn creates an updated list of more inconsequential "stakeholders" who must all vet and approve the concept. Just one "no" will kill the idea. To Shawn's dismay, all stakeholders agree that the proposal will work and insist that the proposal needs to go immediately to the CEO of the holding company.

Shawn never shows Kim's proposal to his superiors. He's busy getting celebrities as spokespeople and other high-profile publicity stunts. He wants to spend big bucks on a sweepstakes. There have been only minor changes to the store or merchandise.

He can't afford to hire the celebrity, do the sweepstakes, *and* implement Kim's idea, and he's certainly not going to cut the sweepstakes or celebrity budget. So he tells Kim to prepare all costs for implementing her proposal. Upon receiving the requested budget breakdown, Shawn asks Kim to lower the budget to implement the solution. No matter how much Kim cuts the budget, it's got to be lower, although Shawn refuses to say how much he is willing to spend to go forward with the idea. Kim finally proposes a bare-bones program that can be tested *and* rolled out for half the original quote— half the amount of his celebrity and sweepstakes promotions.

Four months have passed. Shawn continues to provide a list of higher hoops for Kim to jump through. Kim hears that the quality guy, Patrick, is involved in the project. Although she's been warned not to discuss the idea "for confidentiality reasons" with anyone who's not on Shawn's growing list, she presents the case to her colleague Patrick, who she knows has the CEO's ear.

Patrick tells her, "This is exactly what the executive leadership team have been looking for. Why didn't you present this sooner? The bad news is that last week, we decided to close the store."

Two months later, Store XYZ closed, resulting in an exorbitant multi-million-dollar write-off.

Patrick really was a quality person, and after finding out how politics prevented him from finding the solution, he resigned despite several attractive counteroffers. Shawn was promoted by the cronies to "manage" another turnaround situation that turned into another round of financial calamity. Kim left and started her own company.

There's no shortage of new ideas that have been presented at big companies. Unique ideas are forever being put on the board. Mostly, imitations are being chosen over inventions. Few of the "innovative assets" of a company are implemented—"the most common barrier to innovation is that it has to pass the cultural test, though not necessarily the money test."[50] Ninety percent of the ones that are implemented, fail. Either the wrong person is doing the picking or *most* of the ideas to choose from are garbage. Which is it? Take your pick.

Brainstorming Truth Two: Most of the participants are not innovation experts.
Look around the brainstorming table. How many of the participants have patents? How many launched unique products that were successful? How many have worked for the industry leader and led a profitable new-to-market product there? How many are also customers? How many know their company's market share *and* their competitors'? How many have bought their competitors' products in the past few months. How many have listened to their customers in the past week? How many have run a successful business before? How many would lose their jobs if a better product were launched at their own company?

Let's be honest. Most of the people are in the brainstorming session for political reasons—to get their department's buy-in, or because they'll go along with whatever the decision maker chooses at the end. The majority of participants aren't there because they're original thinkers or inventors; they're there because they are "team players." They are popular (and rewarded with camaraderie) because they haven't pushed change. The worst thing that can happen is that this group of people, who don't understand half the ideas on the board and have no clue why their customers buy their products and, more important, why their competitors' customers don't, will take a vote (or rank) to decide where to place the company's resources, or rank the ideas. They aren't in tune with their industry's new technology or software because they rarely speak with anyone in their industry who doesn't work for their company. The most popular, not best, idea will win. That popular "new" idea is the one they've all been discussing for months, and their competitors have been doing for years. If the competitor launched a platinum one and then a red one, why they'll do a green or plum one, 'cause that's really different. They'll give 1 percent more cash back, twice as many points, double the discount, and more money to charity, because more of the same thing is so unique.

The most popular idea is going to be the one they're familiar with, the one they've done before, so they can remain an expert at something, even if it's not innovation.

I've participated in a creative day facilitated by Ideas to Go, Inc. The company provides the "voice of the consumer" with a group of Creative Consumers. The BrainStore uses a similar method, often involving kids. The room is infiltrated with people who have a track record of coming up with relevant, profitable business ideas. If you believe that it takes a group of people to come up with innovative ideas, at least be sure that the room is loaded with *proven* successful inventors. Unfortunately, the stack of phenomenal business thinking that comes out of these sessions, in most cases, is a waste. Because it never gets implemented.

Brainstorming Truth Three: Brainstorming is not a process.
Here's reality: *Processes do not invent. People do.*

The objective should be to create business and customer solutions, not to engage in more processes. We've already seen how Six Sigma has failed to increase the number or success of new products. Before Six Sigma and now, there are tons of processes designed to develop profitable ideas. None of them works. What works is people who invent solutions as part of their everyday job, because they understand what the customer wants and can't yet have.

Years ago, McKinsey & Company came to a financial services company where I was a consultant. This client loved having lots of meetings. It even had a session in its new employee initiation course (loaded with meetings) about etiquette in meetings. Instead of harnessing the phenomenal resources that this giant had, the employees spent all day in meetings posing and jockeying. They stunk at innovation, but they were masters at attending meetings that accomplished nothing except a lot of writing on boards, and agreeing to do what people might have been doing anyway, had they not been in meetings all day.

The McKinsey consultants did a presentation about three phases or "horizons" for sustained business growth and said that companies needed to be engaged concurrently in all three. They were:

Horizon One: Defend/Extend Core Businesses

Horizon Two: Build Emerging Businesses

Horizon Three: Create Options for Future Businesses

The McKinsey speakers were engaging and inspiring. I was inspired that they could get paid so much to do this presentation, the same one, to so many companies (who obviously highly valued repetitive concepts and ideas that were given to their competitors). The aftermath assignment was for the product development team to brainstorm and come up with its top strategy for each horizon. The Three Horizon method was now our new process for making business growth decisions.

The Horizon One and Two ideas were entirely predictable, since I'd seen them in dozens of meetings. The ones a few people were already working on were voted tops, so they got to keep their jobs doing the same things. Now it was time to come up with dazzling "options for future businesses"—Horizon Three!

Ideas were frantically scribbled up on the board. Some of the suggestions were launching competitors' financial products. One was to make a bold leap into corporate financing, a growing market. Ideas aimed at ethnic markets cropped up. The winning big idea, after the vote, was a sweepstakes on the existing product. Yes, really. Another sweepstakes at another company. The rationale was that, on the *current product*, we had never done a sweepstakes. "Haven't we done a sweepstakes before?" somebody asked.

"No idea is a bad idea. We're not here to criticize. And yes, we've done sweepstakes for existing customers, but not as a way to attract new customers. The sweepstakes is truly a Horizon Three idea; it's an option for future businesses," was the reply from the popular meeting organizer. And that is precisely what was implemented as the great leap forward in revolutionizing their company.

Processes do nothing to create new worlds or new horizons. To see a new horizon or a new world, *you* have to move. The new world and new horizon don't come to you. You can perform as many rituals as you want, fill out as much paperwork as you please, and have as many meetings as you can muster, but if you're still in the same place, the view of the world is not going to change.

Companies who have brainstorming meetings (or have another euphemism for idea "sessions") are reinforcing that they don't have empowered employees who innovate as an integral part of their daily work. Just the process of calling a brainstorming meeting shows utter ignorance in how great ideas are developed, and lack and rejection of people with naturally innovative personalities who are made subject to majority rule by people who aren't. Gee, we don't have people who *normally* come up with good ideas, so let's all get in a room once a month and come up with solutions. Then everybody who couldn't do it on his own can share the credit or share the blame. Brainstorming is really blamestorming.

Brainstorming Truth Four: Every idea is not a good idea.
So it's the big day. Everyone gingerly enters the brainstorming den to "throw up" ideas to build revenue or net income. The facilitator now announces the rules:

1. Come up with as many ideas as possible.

2. Criticism is not allowed.

3. No idea is a bad idea.

Come on. You know that most ideas *are* bad ideas, for two simple reasons: Someone else is already doing it (or worst, your competitor is doing it), or the idea is not based upon data.

At nearly every one of the 50-plus credit card brainstormings that I've participated in during the past 15 years, an idea scribbled on the board was "Let's make it a platinum card." According to BAIGlobal, 79 percent of direct mail credit card offers are for platinum cards. Obviously, this was the "winner" in the brainstorming sessions—all of them. However, the average direct mail response rate has not improved in 15 years. In fact, it has dropped, now at about 0.3 percent (yes, that's less than half a percent). Points, anyone?

On the other side of the coin, my pilot of a co-branded MasterCard received a 6 percent direct mail response rate, plus another 4 percent on the follow-up six weeks later, in the midst of the summer vacation season. The word "platinum" was not included. Its promise was based upon data. There was no brainstorming session.

So how do you start to ferment a great idea? Copy an industry with a long-term record of strong earnings (remember, everything is relative). Pharmaceutical product development starts with data. The majority of data is not about the company's current products; **it's about people.** Compare this with the last time you joined to create ideas that would deliver more profit from prospects. It seems obvious, but did everyone in the room know the following?

- Why prospects *aren't* buying your product in their own words (customer verbatim, not research manager "pick one" verbatim)

- What end result (not product) prospects want *that no one offers*

- What the competition is doing, right and wrong, so that you don't copy either (recall Audi's super tagline "Never follow," because follow the leader is forever)

- What the prevalent consumer trends are

- What are existing prospects' habits and how you can leverage their existing behavior

Compare the disastrous launch of New Coke (vs. Classic Coke) to the launch of Mobil's transponder Speedpass.

Decline the invitation to brainstorming sessions that don't require that every participant study all the prospects and competitive data beforehand. The people who haven't read the data are usually the ones suggesting points programs and sweepstakes without knowing if their prospective customers are players, or recommending sales, rebates, and discounts because they know nothing about the customers or the competition.

So the brainstorming session continues. Besides the overenthusiastic few, there are uncomfortable pauses, because no one is allowed to criticize. You keep to yourself the 25 reasons why Joe's idea will never work, and Kathy's and Billy's. And as hard as you try, you can't stop thinking why most of the ideas are dogs. It's stifling, realizing your colleagues will be doing the same should you dare to contribute. Why?

Because critical thinking is a habit. And results are produced by leveraging habits, not changing them. Best ideational sessions *can* be driven by criticism, when the participants have a proven record of creating and implementing patentable products or programs. That's right. Critical Exchange is an "intrapreneurial" process where a neutral party (a nonemployee) who has a history of designing successful new products in that industry synthesizes all the relevant data and presents short, written, bulleted concepts of a unique, new product and the essential elements that achieve the company's stated goals and maximize the company's resources. Participants, who have also reviewed the data, then delete or substitute bullets, but *never add*. Most important, they are encouraged to discuss in detail why they are deleting or substituting.

Criticism (of ideas, not people) is the stated objective and is encouraged. There are several other guidelines (like re-substituting), but this type of forum rewards employees for making an idea better, rather than labeling people as "negative" for having natural, critical thoughts or tactical concerns, or asking questions. In the same meeting, another two or three alternative, but very different, unique product ideas are presented and the critical approach is repeated.

In Critical Exchange, the final ideas were improved by a group of innovative people—not voted on. In typical brainstorming sessions, a huge list of ideas is culled by one or two managers (usually with no history of product launch success), destroying any harvested team spirit, or voted on. As we discussed, voting ensures that the best idea never comes to fruition. In voting, the top idea may only have the support of 30 percent of the group (yes, that means 70 percent stated they didn't want it). Voting and culling are certain ways to encourage back-office conversations and create pools of "losers" who feel mute. Their dragging heels and whispers will inevitably turn into "I told you so's."

Prepare to have Critical Exchange proposals morph into totally new ones, or to see brilliant sparks for new products become even brighter. At the last Exchange session I attended, a group of seven men and two women emerged from the room whispering about the fun they had tearing a concept to pieces to reconstruct it into something better, and the new marketing program they had just created for their best customers that blew the mercury out of the profit thermometer. A simple idea made better, it generated a 600 percent increase in sales. And it was patentable. With a patent, they'll be the leader, and there won't be any followers.

Brainstorming Truth Five: Seeing is believing.
We've already talked about the impact of the sense of smell and its link to memory.

Read Paco Underhill's study of the "butt brush" in his book *The Science of Selling* if you need proof of how the sense of touch can make or break a sale. (Underhill warns against narrow aisles in retail stores, where women will drop merchandise and move away if someone squeezes by them.) Or you may feel more comfortable with the concept of "The Touch Campaign," designed for a clothing retailer after in-store observation showed that shoppers touched everything they passed in that particular store, and their purchase decisions were based upon touch. You won't be surprised that its catalog and Internet sales were weak. Can you guess the retailer? Can you imagine the increase in sales by adding swatches to their catalogs and mailings?

Fascinating then, that brainstorming depends upon the weakest sense—hearing. It's not surprising that in traditional brainstorming, most find it impossible not to focus on the ideas that they see written on the board, rather than thinking up the next inspiring gem or listening to the next concept offered. And what else would most participants suggest as ideas than what they have already seen?

If hearing is the weakest sense, then how can brainstorming be productive? If you choose to adopt Critical Exchange, you'll see the team focusing on *altering an existing written concept* they can already see.

If you are an inventor or interview one, you will find that as people are speaking, or as they read data, or as they observe prospects in action, inventors actually "see" pictures of the invention and how it would be marketed to prospects. Inventors are able to quickly modify these imaginary pictures as colleagues or clients offer improvements or obstacles. I've often added a copywriter and art director to my team to visualize ideas so they can be sold to noninventors. This is why advertising and marketing agencies present storyboards and comps to win business. In one case, when presented with visuals for a new product concept, the marketing director of a large home fashions company leapt across the table, grasped the visualized concepts, and dashed down the hall. Now everyone would see what a great idea this really was. Why do people go to see a Web site for confirmation of something interesting they hear about. An essential part of selling in big ideas in big companies is having professional visuals at the earliest stage—and that is when the idea is mentioned for the first time. It is interesting how the focus will shift from criticizing the idea to criticizing the copy or artwork. This is a breakthrough in getting to market. Because seeing is believing.

In numerous direct marketing agencies, I've been surrounded by bevies of integrated individuals. *Their* traditional "brainstorming" sessions are invigorating and exciting. They aren't planned meetings. Their brainstorming is their everyday conversation, passing in the hall or while drinking a cup of coffee. Their output is a choice of original, data-based, profit-making solutions that are even more wondrous when brought to life by art directors and copywriters. How can they, day after day, delight in authentic life improvements?

With their strategic planners, research hounds who are also visual, these integrated individuals share a long history of innovating. Pioneers in the direct marketing agency world are openly rewarded and widely admired for their creativity, particularly when the agency has fewer than 200 staff. Their company leaders are those who not only support this culture, but are innovators themselves. However, most of their brilliant ideas are never implemented by the clients they design them for.

Truth be told, ideas generated in brainstorming haven't taken the world by storm. **Individuals rather than groups in meetings invented most of the great ideas of the past two centuries**. Looking at corporate patents that list multiple inventors is unreliable since anyone who suggests that the new widget can be sold in blue or platinum often gets his name added to the patent as an inventor. The politics of insisting on being the lone inventor on a patent in a large corporation can make you a loner for life. You add friends in the hope that the idea will be implemented, because inventors create for the joy of seeing the idea available to customers.

Brainstorming and other committee-based processes do more to drive entrepreneurs out of corporations than give them an outlet for their creativity. When a creative individual is pouring out dozens of never-done-before-strategies and recommendations to drive the business, and the group or senior decision maker keeps picking a sweepstakes or discount as a revolutionary leap forward, he realizes they're not in the same league or the same planet. The *outcome* of brainstorming in corporate America reinforces the sea of difference between the can-dos and can't-dos. It reinforces that the most popular idea is chosen over the best idea. It proves that the most popular person will be promoted before the best person. It solidifies that innovation and innovators are not popular. It explains why those with the greatest potential to nurture organic growth in big companies can't wait to leave and start their own.

When brainstorming is a company's chief idea-generation tool, individual ingenuity is frowned upon, and individual proposals will be rejected. It signals a company full of intellectually weak individuals who will only approve ideas if they can take part of the credit for them, since they are incapable of generating unique ideas themselves. If the company were chock-a-block with employees offering brilliant ideas, brainstorming wouldn't be necessary. If business managers produced unique, blockbuster solutions as part of their everyday jobs, brainstorming meetings (aka we-don't-have-any-decent-ideas-now meetings) would be history. Only companies devoid of original thinkers or with managers who are too threatened to accept original thinkers' ideas that are based on data have brainstorming sessions. Entrepreneurs will tell you their former companies had regular brainstorming meetings. They will also tell you how none of the original ideas was ever selected or implemented. Brainstorming assumes that one person can never have a great idea. When you find a company that lauds brainstorming, you may assume that it suppresses or doesn't hire inventors. Since no one person has the variety of skills to invent, maybe 10 people together can put all their one-dimensional skills together and get lucky.

Individuals, not brainstorming, generate life-changing products and services. Even when supported by the resources of a large corporation, sole inventors, not groups, are responsible for most significant inventions:

- Phonograph, incandescent light bulb, telephone transmitter, movie projector, improved stock ticker machine (Thomas Edison, telegraph operator, then entrepreneur)

- Masking tape and cellophane tape (Richard Drew working for 3M), tape dispenser (John A. Borden, another 3M employee)

- Basketball game (James Naismith, physical education teacher)

- Internet (J. C. R. Licklider, psychologist and computer system designer), sorry, Al

- Microwave oven (Dr. Percy LeBaron Spencer working for Raytheon)

- Coca-Cola (Dr. John Stith Pemberton, pharmacist, to replace his own concoction, French Wine of Coca, during Atlanta's prohibition period)

- Blue jeans (Levi Strauss, a tailor), rivets for blue jeans (Jacob Davis, Strauss's friend, also a tailor)

- Potato chips (George Crum, chef, to satisfy a customer complaint about his French fries)

- Bar code readers, automatic teller machines and cordless phones, cassette players and camcorders, fax machines and 550 more patented inventions (Jerome Lemelson, former employee of an aircraft manufacturer, a metal refiner, and a weather balloon company, then full-time inventor)

- Cat's-eyes road reflectors (Percy Shaw, road repairman and wire-making mill engineer)

- Plastic (Leo Baekeland, a chemist, and millionaire who sold his photogenic paper idea to Eastman of Eastman Kodak in 1898)

- Ballpoint pen (László Jozsef Bíró, journalist and newspaper editor)

- Band-Aids (Earle Dickson, a cotton buyer at the Johnson & Johnson company)

- Gyroscope (Jean Bernard Léon Foucault, a French physicist)

- Segway Human Transporter, iBot (the wheelchair that climbs stairs) (Dean Kamen, entrepreneur of a business that creates solutions for large corporations, worked with gyroscopes and tilt sensors)

- Dual cyclone bagless vacuum cleaner (James Dyson, who built 5,000 prototypes before he perfected his machine and whose idea was rejected by several major manufacturers to whom he offered the technology including a Hotpoint executive who said, "This project is dead from the neck up," Dyson now has 30 percent market share in the U.S.)[51]

Like most groundbreaking ideas, none of these came out of a brainstorming session. They weren't team efforts. They were **one person's brainchild**, properly nurtured. Corporations can produce more brainchildren by trusting and supporting inventors' and entrepreneurs' ideas, rather than by subjecting them to majority rule.

One thing you should notice about most inventions, including those listed above, is that the invention was discovered while trying to solve a human problem, not while trying to solve a product problem or company problem. Dean Kamen owned a business that produced medical devices such as insulin pumps and dialysis machines after hearing his brother, a doctor, complain about the limitations of current machines. After seeing a man trying to negotiate a curb in a wheelchair, he invented the wheelchair that could climb stairs and maneuver on two wheels by making an analogy to a gyroscope.

Richard Drew invented masking tape while trying to help painters paint straight lines. Although his job was in paint, he didn't invent a new type of paint or new paint can. He invented something to help the painter do a better job. Earle Dickson made his first Band-Aid for his wife, who had cut herself again in the kitchen. He was trying to help his wife, not find another use for cotton. Dr. Percy Spencer developed the microwave oven after a candy bar in his pocket melted while he was passing vacuum tubes. They weren't sitting in brainstorming meetings saying, "Let's create another vacuum tube," or "Let's run a sweepstakes to sell more vacuum tubes."

Inventors make analogies. That's what sets them apart. They see life as a bowl full of cherries and wonder if the cherries can be made into wood stain for a fading table or lipstick for bleeding lip waxes. They are on the third horizon already. To make them sit on the first horizon and pretend to imagine what the third horizon is like when they've already been there is agony. Their businesses start on the third horizon.

On the third horizon, innovators and mavericks are developing new businesses by thinking of *people*. It just happens. It's spontaneous. They see gyroscopes when looking at wheelchairs, and cat's-eyes when they're having trouble making out the lines on the road at night. They don't do well in brainstorming because everybody thinks they're not "team playing." Brainstorming is a linear process. Inventors are not linear thinkers. The chocolate bar melting in Spencer's pocket didn't make him think of the problems of working near vacuum tubes. It reminded him of cooking—fast.

Get back on track. Get back on track. How often does a creative individual hear this in a meeting? Getting back on track means thinking linearly. It inhibits innovation, which is borne of analogy, parallels, correlations, connections.

In Britain, ballpoint pens are still called "biros" after the inventor, László Jozsef Bíró. Bíró was frustrated with smudges and clothing stains from fountain pens, like all consumers in the 1940s. As a journalist and editor at a newspaper, Bíró observed that ink used in newspaper printing didn't blob and dried faster. Newspaper ink was thicker and wouldn't work in a fountain pen, so he fitted a ball in the tip.

Bíró's job was writing and editing. It was not creating writing instruments. His parallel between newspaper ink and the creation of a ballpoint pen was to create a solution to make his and other people's lives easier, not to improve the newspaper articles.

Brainstorming normally starts with fixing a *product*, rather than solving people's problems. How many vacuum tube brainstorming sessions do you think Spencer sat through? No matter how many Spencer attended, in a group setting, the idea might never have been proposed. If it had, you can bet it would have been nuked.

Inventors make connections constantly that seem illogical. They synthesize and convert data instantly. To make a connection between a metal ball and fountain pen smudges is normal for inventors, and not standard operating procedure for most adults. To think of marbles to prevent auto accidents is not accidental for inventors. They ask questions that seem off track to the point of irritation to those stuck "in the box," but they're making parallels of what could make life better. You cannot train or create inventors. They are an unusual breed, and their unorthodox way of seeing all objects in the world as somehow correlated into one big picture makes them a breed apart. This is why they are capable of being strategic and tactical. They see each element connecting with all elements in the universe. Their minds connect the dots as quickly as our nerves' synapses respond, within milliseconds. They are a diverse crowd and they know that seeing is believing—most people can accept diversity of looks, but not diversity of thinking. They make people who don't have their ability uncomfortable, because it can't be learned. Imagination is innate. It is organic. So Bill Gates ends up labeled a "nerd," working in a garage with another diverse friend. As his business grows, he collects all the diverse thinkers whose synapses also fire in all directions continuously. And his business grows primarily through organic innovation, not acquisition.

Let's pretend. Today's make-believe brainstorming session features Percy Shaw, who invented cat's-eyes. Let's join him for a brainstorming meeting in 1934 with seven of his colleagues at the road repair company where he works.

Meeting moderator: We're meeting today to brainstorm on how to get more business. As you know, we've already repaired most of the roads around here and put in the new asphalt and concrete. Our terrific workmanship and the new materials mean that roads no longer need to be re-repaired, ha ha, as often. So work orders from the government are way down. We need to find ways to generate new business. So everybody give me ideas and I'll just write them down.

Lateral thinker one: Let's convince the government that the roads need to be wider.

Lateral thinker two: Let's convince the government that each road needs more layers on it.

Lateral thinker three: Hmmm. Problem is that the new study shows that newer rubber tires on cars will cause less wear and tear to the roads.

Percy: Why don't we start installing gutters and curbstones like they're doing in other places.

Lateral thinker four: Then the roads will never fall apart and never have to be repaired. We're in road repair, not gutter and curb construction.

Percy: Then we could partner with the gutter and curb companies, and after they put in the gutters and curbs, we could fix the damage they've done.

Lateral thinker five: Hell, no. We're not working with them. They'll figure out what we do and steal our business.

Lateral thinker six: We could offer a discount. How about two repairs for the price of one?

Lateral thinker three: A sweepstakes, a sweepstakes! Every new job for the next six months goes into a barrel and the mayor who wins gets a prize.

Lateral thinker two: Let's put more advertising in the newspaper and talk about the high quality of our road repairs.

Lateral thinker one: In the ads, we could get a movie star to kiss our asphalt or press in her handprints, just like in Hollywood.

Percy: Actually, I was driving home last night. Normally it's hard to see. But it was foggy, and the moisture in the air mixed with the headlamps made the tram tracks really bright.

Moderator: Percy, get back on track.

Lateral thinker five: What about if we offer free line painting with every road repair?

Percy: This is relevant. Last week, while I was driving home at night, I spotted these two bright flashes on the horizon. It turned out to be a cat's eyes. The headlamps were reflecting off its retinas. And I was thinking how we could duplicate that idea to help drivers stay on the road and prevent accidents.

Moderator: Percy, if the idea isn't simple enough to say in one sentence, then it's not a good idea. If you need to explain an idea, it won't work. Try to stay focused.

Percy: OK, here's the line. Why don't we put these clear marbles, half lined with reflective silver, in the middle and on the edges of the road, so the headlamps will reflect off them, and people won't have accidents.

Lateral thinker six: Typical Percy. Goes off on some tangent about cats and a game of marbles because he can't think of an idea to increase road repairs.

Lateral thinker two: Yeah, but when the cars run over them, we'll have to replace the marbles. Do you want us to be in the marble repair business? (Laughing.)

Percy: Look, I made one so you can see it. When car tires press on them, the marbles dip into this rubber housing that cleans them with rainwater. See, embed the mirror marbles in this casing that fills with rainwater. The weight of a passing car will depress the spheres and clean them, like eyelids or wipers. We make money by tearing up and repairing the roads to put the housings in. I've done estimates and this would give us more business than we've had in years. Plus the profits from the cat's-eyes production. I named them "catseyes."

Lateral thinker one: We're not going to make any stupid marble boxes. Man, you drive me crazy. We're trying to get more business repairing roads, and you're off building Chinese checkers sets.

Lateral thinker two: If people wanted marbles in the road, there'd already be some there. We're not making no cat's-eyes here. (Doing a movement like Moe poking out Curly's eyes with his two fingers.) Nyuck, nyuck, nyuck.

Moderator: Percy, we'll have to ask you to leave if you can't be a team player. You're being disruptive.

Lateral thinker four: Let's get back to the main subject. We should create a points program where the city governments earn points every time we repair a road for them, and after they get so many points, they can redeem them for free stuff.

Moderator: Everyone, thanks for your great ideas. We got a lot accomplished today. I'll discuss these with Mr. Schnauzer and we'll get back to you with our decision.

Let's pretend you've never been in a brainstorming session like this. Let's pretend you've never worked in a big company. Let's pretend Percy didn't leave and start his own company and call it "Catseye."

Brainstorming Truth Six: Brainstorming produces old features on old products, not new products.

The average credit card has 26 "features and benefits" (i.e., rewards programs, shopper discounts, rental car insurance, concierge services). The average consumer can recall *correctly and accurately* two. I say "correctly" because consumers make up what they think researchers want to hear so they don't sound stupid. In one round of credit card research I reviewed, hundreds of consumers were asked their top reason why they had chosen a certain credit card. The third most popular reason was the points program. That card did not have, and never did have, a points program.

So consumers can only accurately describe two features of their credit card, and almost all consumers remember the same top feature. Typically, after the top feature, less than 4 percent of consumers will use another feature offered. Conclusion: Ninety-six percent of benefits offered on credit cards are not useful or wanted by consumers or prospects. Yet, they cost the credit card companies money to manage and increase the price of the basic product (through either fees or interest rates or discount rates). So why do credit card companies keep adding useless benefits that make no difference to consumers?

Because the result of most brainstorming meetings is not to create new solutions that customers want or need. The objective of most brainstorming meetings is to sell more of the existing product regardless of what the customer wants. Therefore, most of the suggestions that will be thrown up on the board will be how to try to make people interested in a product they don't need or don't want, rather than produce a new product that people need or want. If you've already tried cutting the price through sales, discounts, cash back, and rebates, and people still don't want it, the next eureka to fix a mediocre product is going to be: Add a feature!

The feature is usually something of little cost to the company and equally little value to the consumer. But if you can't come up with a decent new product, keep adding features that customers won't use anyway will keep you employed for a while. And in a big company, your main objective is to stay employed. Most of the features that are added don't improve the core product in any way because they're not related to the reason why the core product was selected. In other words, people have credit vehicles to pay for items without cash. They can book a vacation, purchase car rental insurance, and get discounts on TVs without your credit vehicle. And about half of consumers believe that adding features equals overcharging.

I call these additional features "slap-ons." (Analogy time: It's like a huge Subway sandwich with layers of meat, cheese, all kinds of stuff. You can slap on another piece of anything, and nobody's going to taste that one more piece. Cutting the price or adding one more piece of bologna doesn't produce a massive queue of new customers. But offering a choice of yummy new-to-the-sub-market rolls or a multimini sub flight, now you're talking.)

Slap-on features are products that usually come from some company that is also having trouble selling its product because it isn't innovative and no longer uniquely solves a consumer problem. The sequence of events is usually that a company wholesales its slap-on product to another company, at a discount, because it's not worth very much anyway. And your company slaps it on its product thinking that combining two weak products makes a good one. Two wrongs...

Gevalia Kaffe gets an award for this one. Owned by Kraft, the product is really good. I tried it when an agency friend was pitching its retention marketing account. It's a membership coffee retailer. It's like the record clubs, where you sign up and they'll send you another shipment each month until you cancel your membership. In the marketing business, this is called a "continuity program."

The coffee is marketed as "extraordinary, smooth, rich, and delectable." You would have to really love coffee to sign up. Good coffee is important to drinkers who join. That would be me.

Gevalia has historically had trouble retaining members. Gee, why would people go to all the trouble of becoming a member of a coffee club only to quit a few months later? Because Gevalia Kaffe's membership incentive is a coffeemaker. It has tested several membership incentives over the years—mugs, a regular coffeemaker in three exciting colors, a programmable coffeemaker in stainless steal, a thermal carafe. The latest offer is a coffeemaker, carafe, *and* travel mug. Since none of the three was retaining members, someone decided that all three together would. Gulp. At least the premium is related to coffee.

Think about this. If you are nuts about coffee, enough to join a club to get "special" coffee that costs more than premium coffees available at the supermarket or Starbucks, don't you already have a good coffeemaker? A coffee connoisseur probably has a $300 grinder/cappacino/expresso coffeemaker combination. Who is most likely to sign up for Gevalia's offer: someone who wants exquisite, expensive coffee mailed to her home every month, or someone who needs a thermal carafe coffeemaker? Once you get the coffeemaker, carafe, and mug, you cancel your membership.

Gevalia's membership acquisition response rates are good because there are a lot of people out there who want a good carafe for a very low introductory-offer price, particularly when the sign-up deal is two boxes of coffee with the three goodies for a "total approximate retail value" of $168, all for just $22.95.

Gevalia's retention rates would suggest it attracts the coffeemaker needy, rather than the premium coffee klatch.

Its slap-on fails to attract people who want its core product, the coffee (since I assume Gevalia doesn't manufacture the carafes). Yet, it believes its acquisition efforts are successful.

If you have a product that is sold through a continuity program, shouldn't your incentive be continuous too? Shouldn't you receive the incentive for continuing membership each month? For example, how about if Gevalia hitched onto the customizing/menu trend and let customers build their own coffee blend—strength, spiciness, origin mix, etc. What if Gevalia sent every three months a free sample of an exotic (not flavored) or organic coffee from new plantations in faraway locations not typically known for plantations? What if it engaged customers by asking them to become tasters in selecting new beans and blends for the next Gevalia product by sending three samples to test and e-mail their opinions back?

If Gevalia perceives its problem is a retention one, and not an acquisition issue, it may never win. The problem is an acquisition one: Gevalia is not attracting the *right* customers—coffee drinkers who want to be in a continuity program for incredible coffee. Its solution is a slap-on one. Since the company might think the direct marketing agency handling acquisition is doing great (just look at the numbers), it separates out the retention part of the business. Gevalia hired a separate advertising agency whose job was to keep members who don't want Gevalia coffee, just a coffeemaker with a Gevalia logo (the people who signed up and immediately quit).

The slap-on coffeemaker offer actually deflects good coffee buyers from signing up. I drink loads of coffee, but I don't want another coffeemaker (already have two), thermal coffee carafes (already have two of those, also), or travel mug (four of those). And I certainly don't want to pay $22.95 to sign up because I only want the coffee, not the "free" gifts that I feel are built into inflated prices. So the retention agency is bound to fail, because the best potential customers never signed up, and the ones who need a coffeemaker have to be kept although they now have the only thing they wanted.

The revolving door of retention agencies should have given Gevalia a clue, and you can imagine that there might be a correlation to the longevity of the retention managers at Gevalia headquarters. Have they been branded as failures for being unable to keep coffeemaker collectors? Have acquisition managers been promoted?

Someday, all companies will figure out that acquisition and retention go hand in hand, and hire the same one internal person and one agency to be responsible for profitability on the coffee business, not the membership acquisition *or* cancellation numbers.

The basic principles of direct marketing teach lifetime value of customers as a basis for advertising cost. It's easy to figure out that, without the coffeemaker offer, Gevalia would get fewer members, but that each member would stay longer, paying more into the company's coffers, dynamically increasing profitability. Again, it's a great product, and, as a coffee addict who purchases premium coffee, I can't see any reason why they can't increase sales, particularly with the trends for gourmet products.

Before you add a feature, consider this: **If the feature is such a great idea, you should develop it as a new separate product.** If it wouldn't be successful as a separate product offered by your business, then your customers don't want it, not as an add-on, not at all!

In 2007, Xerox was issued 517 patents. Anne Mulcahy, Xerox's chairperson and CEO, has this advice and insight:

- License ideas that don't fit the core business.
- Forget bells and whistles if they don't save customers' time or money.

- Research by nature does not create specific products. It tends to be more broad based and often results in ideas that are best used outside the traditional business.[52]

Try to recall all the brainstorming meetings you've attended. How many generated completely new product solutions for consumers? How many generated another price initiative or me-too add-on? Now recall the entrepreneurs you know. How many left to start a business with a new concept? How many gave up their corporate salaries to take a chance on an add-on?

Mulcahy doesn't recommend curbing innovation of ideas that don't fit the business model or that the company has the right resources to develop. Keep creating, and license them out, creating another source of income, is her message.

At one corporation where I worked, there were tons of creative individuals who developed patentable ideas that the company either didn't want to put resources behind, the timing wasn't right, didn't neatly fit into one of the current business cells, or was blocked. If launched by a competitor, many of these product ideas wouldn't affect the corporation's current product sales. But the ideas would bedazzle other companies who had the ideal set of resources to produce and market them. I asked to start a new division that would collect or create products ideas from colleagues throughout the corporation with the primary purpose of licensing the ideas or assigning the rights to noncompetitive companies. I estimated that the rights to some patentable ideas we'd already created were worth half a million dollars, each.

From the funky looks I got when I made this suggestion, you'd have thought I was standing on the boardroom table doing the chicken dance. Maybe they were chicken, so I flew the coop. Years later, I started a company that does just that—creating and selling patentable ideas. I'm still dancing. Perhaps they're still crying, "The sky is falling."

Entrepreneurs who start their own businesses can fail or find roadblocks even with substantial venture capital and an eye-opening, jaw-dropping idea meticulously developed. Some industries are so "closed" that a majority of professionals will douse any new fiery product introduction. Not all the self-employed are innovators. Lawyers perform to precedent. You don't need a marketable, *unique* idea or mega idea to start a business. But it doesn't hurt. But a whole lot of people who introduced marketable, unique ideas and mega ideas in conglomerates suffered for it. And left.

Round Trip—Faster Than a Speeding Bullet

The next morning, in Kyoto, I woke up early. My room was miniscule but had a TV with CNN, a tea kettle, and the usual two pairs of slippers (one for in the room and the other for only in the bathroom— never to be confused). Home away from home. I remembered the tightened look on the porter's face the night before when I took four steps into the room without taking off my shoes. This is Japan. No one tells you when you screw up. Not even when you screw up badly. No one looks shocked or horrified. The worst thing you can do in Japan is blow your nose during a meal. It's bad enough to make any bodily noise, but blowing your nose is never an accident and is never to be done in public. At a meal, it's so revolting to Japanese, they'll gag. Yet, they'll never openly reveal that you've embarrassed them or yourself. It's all very, very subtle.

I guess they don't have employee appraisals. They don't need them. You just know if you've screwed up, or not. You know how fair those employee appraisals are anyway—as fair as your boss. In a fair company, appraisals are unnecessary, because if you don't know whether you've done a good job or not, you haven't.

My hotel was directly across from JR Kyoto Station. I scoped out the neighborhood. Great. An Internet café, a ton of vending machines, and a Pachinko parlor right next door. What a terrific location! The vending machines sell porno magazines, gum, CDs, videos, beer, milk, umbrellas, disposable cameras, batteries, you name it. There was already a queue outside the closest Pachinko parlor, waiting for it to open. Gambling junkies. Well, not legally.

The parlors look a lot like our amusement park arcades. Pachinko is a combination of a vertical pinball machine and a slot machine. If the silver ball drops through the maze of metal pins into the right holes, the slot machine feature kicks in. Get three of the same icons, and you win lots of...silver balls. You can't exchange the silver balls for cash because gambling is technically illegal in Japan. But you can trade the silver balls for stuff in the gift shop, like cigarettes, or a gold icon thingy. Just outside the front door of the parlor is usually a kiosk or window in a back alley where you can exchange that stuff, like cigarettes or the gold thingy, for cash. Selling cigarettes or gold thingies for cash is not illegal.

A block away, I stopped into a little convenience store, like a 7-11. I bought some Pocky white-chocolate-covered cookie sticks (my favorite Japanese snack), bottled water, and a pot of instant ramen noodles. The cashier gave me chopsticks. Back in my room, I boiled some water in the tea kettle, enjoyed my ramen noodles, put my Pocky sticks in my knapsack while admiring the cartoony box, and crossed the road to Kyoto Station to hop the subway.

I was off to Gion, the old *geisha* district. I felt like a kid going to DisneyWorld for the first time. I wanted to get there first and be there when the doors opened. Although I am not a voracious reader of novels, I was overwhelmed by *Memoirs of a Geisha*. I had to see some for myself.

The world of the *geisha* is in decline. Exclusive, available only through introduction, elite, the epitome of prestige and status, the company of *geisha* is unattainable to most of Japanese society and foreigners. Numbering more than 100,000 before World War II, there are fewer than 500 left in Kyoto.

I got off the subway, crossed the river, and passed the famous Kabuki Minamiza Theatre. Gion, at last. But there was nothing there. Gion comes alive at night and stays awake until the wee hours. Everyone in Gion was still asleep. The bamboo shutters had been rolled down on the tiny two-story *Machinya* wooden town houses. The occupants were still asleep concealed behind the wood-latticed facades. There was not a sound, not even a wind to teeter the red paper lanterns outside the teahouses. Everything was still. There were no *geisha* or citizens roaming the narrow roads—only me. I had arrived too early.

Fiona had arrived too early. The recruiter misinformed her that this business was "ready for a big change." Fiona was brought in as president to turn around a stuck-in-the-mud corporation. Her credentials were impressive. The board paid her a large bonus to start right away even though they knew eight weeks after her initiation, she'd be going on a long-planned vacation for a fortnight. A true pro, within a month, Fi had assessed the company's ills (her background was in the industry) and laid out a recovery plan. Before leaving on vacation, she called the senior "leadership" team together to talk about the reorganization and intertwined product developments required to bring the company back to good health. The team agreed that they would implement the reorganization three weeks after her return.

Upon returning from vacation, Fiona learned that the team, in her absence, had reorganized the entire company in a way that thwarted the product development and growth plans. Employees had been "misinformed" by the team that their changes were Fiona's bidding. When Fiona questioned the team members about the reorganization, they claimed they "misunderstood" her directives and wanted to "surprise" her by implementing the plan early to show how proactive they were. Their reorganization gave more power to the "leadership" team members who were responsible for poisoning the company over the past few years.

Fiona quit immediately. Once again, to their delight, they were a leaderless team. The company slumped onto its deathbed. Chunk by chunk, the leaderless dissected groups of employees in a series of layoffs while in a morphinelike state of euphoria, because they were still standing and doing the operating. Ahhh, control. The wonder drug. The diagnosis shows it's terminal, but the E.R. is still happy as long as there are still a few patients left to cut up.

Fiona became a self-employed consultant, helping their competitors, using the knowledge she acquired while being stitched, leaving the malpractice behind.

As we've discussed, "change agents" are not brought in to "turn around" companies that are doing great. Rather than face change (something many managers are incompetent to handle), senior managers will sabotage leaders who are trying to save jobs—theirs. The average tenure of a CEO is now five years.[53]

Entrepreneurs at all levels have taken their big ideas and vowed never to return. A recent survey by the National Association for the Self-Employed found that only 4 percent of the self-employed would say "yes" if called with a job offer from a former employer or business contact. **When asked if they would go back to work for**

someone else after the job market improves, only 3 percent said they would.[54] They didn't start businesses because they couldn't get another job. They're not in a hurry to go back. More money is not going to do it because it's not why they're leaving. Points, days off, and trading cards, neither. A fancy title won't crack it since they can have any title they want in their own companies. A great health care plan, no.

Employee points programs, days off, trading cards, employee-of-the-month awards, company picnics, corporate rah-rah meetings, training, mentoring, bigger desks/offices, money, pension plans, or health care plans have not kept America's leaders and business builders in big companies.

It is utter nonsense that people stay in crummy jobs or start new businesses because of health insurance. This excuse is propagated by those who don't have the skills or the confidence to leave a rotten job that's affecting their health.

According to the U.S. Census Bureau, there are 47 million U.S. residents (15.8 percent) without health insurance. And that's why people say we need a national health plan. This solution is the only solution to people who have never lived in a country with a large population that has national health care. I have lived in a national health care country. Trust me, you do *not* want this. When there are no incentives for someone to study to become a medical specialist to earn meager wages and work 18 hours a day, when you have to wait four years for minor outpatient surgery, when the hospital waiting room (because it's free) is overrun with people with flu and indigestion and the walls are covered with blood and puke because no one cleans them, when the shortage of nurses gets twice as bad as it is now, when companies offer additional private health insurance to their employees anyway so they can get privileged (non-national) service (where the best doctors will be), you'll wish you knew more about national health plans before you voted "yes."

You always read about those poor, poor people who can't afford health insurance. Some are poor. Immigrants tend to have lower incomes. About a quarter of uninsured are foreign born. Let's talk about the "free" ride of national health insurance that people with jobs are going to have to pay for in the form of higher taxes. The highest annual increase in uninsured is among those with an average U.S.

household income exceeding $75,000 per annum.[52] Young adults ages 19 to 29 comprise the largest group of uninsured—30 percent of the total. Yes, I know I'll get hate mail from the few young adults (or their enabling, helicopter parents) who really can't get a job and afford health insurance. However, 100 percent of the 19- to 29-year-olds I've met so far who have told me they didn't have health insurance were healthy and capable of working but too special to take a job at McDonalds with their $80,000 bachelor's degrees so they could buy health insurance with their salary (like I do), spent $150+ per weekend on rounds of cocktails and premium vodka for their friends while dining out, spent $2,000 a year on a fancy health club, believed they would never get injured just because they were texting while driving, had a pure breed pet accessory (called a dog) with designer outfits, purchased a $4 extra-rich latte every day, took several beach vacations a year, or habitually bought new apparel and shoes although they already had enough to clothe all the uninsured people in their zip codes. They had enough debt on their credit cards (which they used to buy things they didn't need) to pay years of health insurance premiums while they chatted on their $100-per-month cell phones about how health costs are out of control, due to people like themselves who don't pay their medical bills when they wind up in the hospital. They are not in the news. Their stories are not newsworthy because they represent the norm. They are not turned away at hospitals. They receive the same health care as the premium payers who are subsidizing them. Yet, the above people who choose to let others pay for their hospital care by being uninsured are the same ones lambasting others for not giving back to the community, criticizing others for not being "green" enough, and complaining about the crime rate. Stealing comes in many different forms.

In the 2004 presidential election, only 47 percent of 18–24 year old citizens voted (probably those with health insurance), while 66 percent of citizens 25 and older voted. Those who couldn't be bothered to vote deserve the economy they got. The best excuse award goes to Josh, who told me, "Like, I didn't vote because I like didn't register in time." But like Josh is always like on time to like line up for concert tickets and the new iPhone because that stuff is *really* important.

And while I'm sure you'll tell me about the case that warrants getting out the violin, the point is that many (not all) people *choose not* to have health insurance. Whether it's holding out for the strategy chief job offer or opting for the Prada handbag, health insurance is not their priority. That SUV is. Most of us are happy to find a way to provide health coverage for people who truly can't pay for health insurance. But to denigrate the entire health care system because a majority of uninsured choose not to be insured—balderdash.

One-third of the U.S. workers without health insurance are employed by large companies and that percentage continues to grow, while the proportion of uninsured in small and midsized companies is shrinking.[56]

The decision to have health insurance or start a business has nothing to do with money; it is about priorities. It is about choice. Health care coverage has almost no impact on someone's decision to start his own company. In fact, it's not even mentioned on the list of why people *don't* start their own businesses. Top reason for staying where you are: 63 percent say they want stability.[57] In other words, they don't want change, they don't like change, they don't like people who like change, and therefore, where they are offers the opportunity to avoid change. And that's why people who are bright, creative, and progressive leave.

Why should you be up in arms about people who don't want to pay for health insurance when they can afford it and then don't pay their medical bills when they have an accident? We're subsidizing them! As a self-employed couple, my friends paid more than $12,000 last year on health insurance premiums. As a self-employed person, I paid *only* about $4,000 in health insurance premiums to my big, big, big health insurance company last year. With that generous policy, I paid $10,000 out of pocket in medical expenses last year after a ski accident. If you think your deductible is "it," there's also that "co-insurance" thing, which is actually another deductible, but not called that. I spent another $30,000 in time on the phone sorting out the claims. The best one was when they called me to ask me if my ski accident happened while I was at work, so it could be covered by workmen's comp and not their insurance. If I get in a car accident and bust the same knee, they'll probably say it's not covered because it's a pre-existing condition. That's why we hate big companies.

The second highest reason people stated for not starting a new business was "financial risk."[58] The deserters see market "opportunity." The people who are staying are doing so because of perceived "risk." They criticize entrepreneurs and innovators as frivolous high-risk takers when studies show that entrepreneurs take only moderate levels of risk.[59] The same people think riding in a car is safer than flying in a plane. "Flying is risky," they say. Fear of change is seldom based upon data, unless it's only *your* data from your experience. If you've failed at making changes in your life, it's easier to blame "making changes" than to blame your own incompetence. To the anti-change agent, any amount of risk would seem excessive. Sleepy companies would rather cater to those who dream up nonexistent risks than to those who assess situations and find growth opportunities. What a nightmare.

To the change agents, going to the same office with the same anti-change group of people and working with the same (albeit dwindling) customers on the same outdated products seems like a big risk. Why do corporate loyalists see "risk" as a negative? (Risk-averse automatons also play the stock market. Some even put 100 percent of their 401(k) savings into their own company stock, placing all their eggs in one fragile basket.) To the change-the-world agents, it seems risky not to exercise your brain to maintain its good health. Change involves risk. The level of risk is often perception. As long as inventors and change agents are viewed as the devil and their output as hell, the angels will continue to defect to avoid being burnt and to reap the rewards of a higher ground. Amen.

Although entrepreneurs don't venture on their own primarily for wealth, there's more financial risk by staying in corporate America. Two-thirds of millionaires in the U.S. are self-employed.[60] Of the population earning $200,000 per year, 46 percent own their own business, 29 percent have their own professional practice, while only 33 percent work for a public/private corporation (there's some overlap).[61] But let's get down to the average Joe. "Self-employed independent workers average $58,000 a year, compared to $45,000 for those with regular wage jobs. Small-business owners are often the most successful, averaging more than $110,000 a year, and they report more job creativity and satisfaction in life."[62] What was that you said about financial *risk*?

You can judge a company's tolerance for change by how it treats its "change agents," and how often the saying "outside the box" is used. You never hear inventors or creative businesspeople calling ideas "outside the box" because their thoughts aren't constrained by concrete parameters. To those who use this saying, please explain, what is "the box"? And how do you confirm which things are outside it? Whose subjective opinion is gospel? Someone who has always been inside a box?

The phrase "outside the box" is indicative of corporate idea generation. The people who think up good ideas are outsiders; they are outside the box, the corporate walls. For them, new ideas will never exist inside the box. Most people who use this phrase, when asked what a box is, would describe a six-sided container with no windows. Those who claim to seek outside-the-box thinking are contained inside their own worlds, unable to see the competitors, the customers' needs, or gaps in the marketplace. They are insular. There's usually a correlation between the narrowness of one's "box" (and how much original thinking will fall outside it) and the number of times someone uses this term multiplied by his or her seniority level.

Most large companies have no idea what their competitors are doing and claim to be surprised by industry new product launches despite the fact that the competitors' plans have been splattered across the press for ages, often revealed by egomaniacs who couldn't wait to see a quote from themselves in print (usually attempting to assume credit for the idea). Almost none have an up-to-date competitive chart showing differences and similarities. They only look at industry data that provides market share or revenue. This is the "what." What about the "how"? How did they get there? How did they do it?

The purpose of competitive info is to see the niche that is unfulfilled in the market—what entrepreneurs are calling the "market opportunity." It isn't so that you can copy what your competitors have done. Corporations follow (or acquire); entrepreneurs find new opportunity.

Follow the leader is forever. As long as you are copying the industry leader, the leader will be spending its time coming up with the next innovation, filling the upcoming consumer needs. The leader is smelling the sweet air of success, while the follower is smelling the behind of the leader. Forget copying your competitors; it's ensuring that you will always be in the back picking up the crumbs left by customers whose hunger has already been satisfied. Be the leader.

In most large companies, you will find drawers and shelves full of research. Dig deep and you will find that they've re-commissioned the exact same research studies every few years, unaware of the duplication because they never did anything with the previous ones. (They can be found in the abandoned office of someone who left to start her own business with information gleaned from the research reports, who tried to act on that data and was ignored.) This research isn't cheap, ranging from $40,000 to $100,000 for qualitative or quantitative research consisting of a few hundred questionnaires, a handful of focus groups, or two dozen in-depth interviews.

While there are libraries of useful research that's gone unused, the research studies that often do get used in big companies are loaded with bias. If I queried you, and asked if you would rather eat crap, spit, or puke, crap might win. But it doesn't mean you want to eat crap, and it definitely does not indicate whether you will eat crap and pay for the privilege of doing so, particularly if tomorrow a competitor offers you chocolate. Yet, countless products have been based upon the lukewarm or cold choices that Employee X chose to put in front of the interviewees, in the language that Employee X wanted to use. And you know where most of those choices came from—the board in the brainstorming room that was a rehash of all the old ideas. Not only has Employee X, the choice chooser, never created a unique idea that was profitable in the market; Employee X has never studied copywriting to know the science of motivational and biasing words and language. Meanwhile, Employee Y offered 10 new ideas, none of which made it to research. Employee X, who can't envision anything that doesn't exist today (but only sees what the competitors are doing), didn't understand any of Employee Y's ideas, and didn't bother to ask. So the consumer ends up with crap because 65 percent preferred it to spit or puke.

There are as many ways to skew research results as there are people inside the box. I've seen research where products that were created specifically for teens were researched among older shoppers, so that the results would show poorly. At another company, one jack-in-the-box called the research firm to change the questionnaire eliminating ideas that were not his, circumventing the research director and product manager. At other times, parts of the description of new products were intentionally eliminated, so prospects would be confused. The two most frequent research errors are that:

1. the multiple choices are crap (garbage in, garbage out), and

2. when a good idea does get through the myriad of research hurdles and prospective consumers clamor for it, the research (like the inventor) is nailed shut in a small box by opinionated mismanagers who have nothing in common with the consumer so that the idea will never see the light of day.

I've been involved in the aftermath of several $50,000 research sessions where managers scrambled to come up with viable excuses why they couldn't (read, didn't want to) launch a product concept that customers chose five to one over others presented. When forced to move forward, they'll sabotage or alter the concept so that by the time it launches, you'd never recognize it. Then, of course, they blame the inventor when it fails.

The problem with research is often that researchers ask consumers to predict (conjecture) how they will behave rather than look at how people habitually behaved (fact) in similar situations. Using a correlation based upon fact is stronger than asking people (who lie) what they will do. Yet, most research and the actions resulting are based on conjecture, not fact.

On two product launches, I worked with ACNielsen Vantis, which used to be The BASES Group and is now Ipsos Novaction & Vantis.

This is the company's blurb:

> Ipsos-Vantis provides a comprehensive market research system that integrates consumer behavior intentions with advanced marketing models and statistical methods to forecast demand and optimize product configurations.

Here's my blurb about Ipsos: It is one of the only firms I've worked with that accurately calculated what the consumer would really do. Its "marketing models and statistical methods" analyze correlations between what consumers have actually done and what they say they will do. It works. Most research just asks consumers what they say they will do, and don't have mathematical accuracy on what I call the "lie factor."

One of my clients wanted to understand the behavior of credit cardholders who were revolvers, that is, they don't pay their outstanding balances in full each month (thereby typically incurring interest charges). All the interviewees in the research focus group were selected because they had one of the bank's other credit cards and had revolved every month.

In the warm-up session, the moderator asked the folks in the focus group to introduce themselves and talk about their credit payment behavior. Six of the 10 cardholders told us they *never* revolved although they were revolving every month on our card, used our card every month, and had substantial balances. During open discussion, we asked more about revolving behavior. As the most opinionated talked about interest rates, the others, one by one, started admitting to being revolvers. At the beginning, they wanted the approval of the interviewer, whom they assumed would be negatively predisposed against people in debt. Toward the end, they tried to win the approval of the strongest personality in the group to join the popular complaint about high interest rates. Had these been one-on-one interviews, 60 percent of our sample would have been misleading—the majority. Most companies would base high-cost decisions on this "data."

For another card issuer, I observed research about fees; in particular, late fees. Most credit cards currently charge $35–$39 per month (in addition to interest) for failure to pay the minimum amount due by the "due date." This time, we selected only customers who had paid late fees several times in the past year on our card. Eight of the 11 told us they *never* paid their bills late. By the end of the hour, all admitted they paid late on most of their cards, most months. Rather than say they compulsively purchased items they could not afford, or overspent and needed another paycheck to cover the minimum payment, or were irresponsible about all their bills, they told stories about how they just "forgot" about the credit card bills "just once or twice." The conversation changed to a heated discussion about interest rate "rips-offs" (as late payers, they were also revolvers). It's interesting that most were paying more in late charges than in interest.

Asking what people are willing to pay for something in research doesn't work either. Late-paying credit cardholders will react with outrage when hearing they will be charged higher late fees and claim they'll move their card accounts. But they won't because if they are too lazy or disorganized to pay bills on time, they certainly are too lazy or disorganized to close one account and open another. Or they are maxed out on all their cards, unable to get approved for another card with lower fees. When you're inside the box, that's typically why this type of research is commissioned. The result would have been nothing—to keep late fees the same, because most of the focus group would have lied and said they wouldn't stand for higher fees (they have).

The smarter companies did the same research in the early 1980s and compared fact (actual late-pay statistics) and consumer perception. They learned that consumers are less sensitive to fees than to interest. The mavericks, *early on*, dropped interest rates (temporarily) and gave zero-percent introductory offers on balance transfers (moving your outstanding debt balance from another credit card to theirs). Initially, they compensated for the early-stage loss on the interest income line by whacking up the interest to higher-than-average rates on the combined transferred balances after the introductory period expired. Then came the rest of the crowd. The followers copied. You see the same copy on most of the marketing pitches (probably because some companies only hire people who have done exactly the same job for somebody else, and it's the same people doing the copywriting and agency briefings):

- No annual fee
- 0 percent APR on balance transfers
- Up to X percent cash back
- Worldwide acceptance
- No preset spending limit
- Online information and bill pay
- Annual account summary
- Concierge service
- Purchase security
- Privacy protection
- Bonus miles

- Yawn

- Yawn

- Yawn

- ZZZZZZZZZZZZZZZ...

It's the same people in the same brainstorming.

The two lame reasons I hear for copying competitors are: First, **we copied the competitors because, in the research, people said they wanted it.** Are the people you researched inventors? Can people articulate and describe a product that does not exist? Since the idea chosen is usually the most popular one, what's the chance they'll all invent the same new product idea? If they did, would the researchers understand their idea? Were consumers asked to say what they liked about existing products, to invent new products, or asked what problems they needed solved? Twenty-five years ago, did people say they wanted tiny cell phones or wi-fi? You'll never get a majority vote from the public on a single item that is nonexistent or new. In market research, customers keep saying they want credit card rewards programs, because they were asked about credit card rewards programs. In 2001, fewer than half of cardholders had a rewards card. Now, it's 84 percent.[63] A rewards program is no longer a competitive advantage. It's a given, like having your name embossed on the card.

Second, **we copied the competitors because everybody's buying it today.** Everybody's not *buying* it. By the time you offer it, everybody's *bought* it. How does "Gee, the market leader is the leader because it keeps offering new groundbreaking products," translate to "Gee, if we do everything they've done, we'll be market leader." Once someone has that Gevalia coffeepot, even if he wants the coffee, he's not going to sign up with a competitor to get another coffeepot. If I just bought a super-duper outdoor grill, I'm probably not going to buy another one.

The banks have created the fee-free monster. The car industry has no one but itself to blame for making drivers rebate sensitive. E-marketers have made purchasers shipping-and-handling sensitive and produced promo-code googlers. The lack of innovative products is making consumers price sensitive. Mothers of little girls clutching their American Girl dolls or Build-a-Bears aren't complaining about the prices, rebates, or fees. They're talking about the product.

Lack of innovation is a key driver of America's corporate brain drain. Entrepreneurs have said loud and clear they left to plant new seeds and make them grow. Smart people don't want to work for dumb companies. Creative people don't want to be in a crypt. How do you get the smart people back? Innovate. What's the proof of innovations? Patents.

Herbert M. Baum, the chairman, CEO, and president of Dial Corp., believes in "First, Fast, and Fresh to Market." He says the reason he "embarked upon this strategy of being a first to market versus a fast follower is that **if you are first to market you get higher pricing, higher margins, and larger market share. And that's pretty much axiomatic in brand marketing**."[64]

Baum not only rewarded innovation; he made it a requirement. Each scientist was required to develop two new patentable ideas each year. The patentable idea didn't have to be linear—it could be a product, packaging, promotional, anything. Under Baum, Dial went from producing four or five patent applications per year up to 30 to or 40. I'll bet lots of entrepreneurs got a welcome back there.

Never judge a book by its cover. I go out of my way for Mobil, not because its employees welcomed me as brethren the moment they found out I was an inventor, but because Mobil made a great invention come to market to make life better.

In 2000, shortly after the ExxonMobil merger, I visited Mobil headquarters in Fairfax, Virginia, to discuss ways to expand transponder opportunities. The transponder is the little Speedpass wand that hangs from your key chain. You just wave it in front of the gas pump, and your gas purchase is automatically charged to the credit card of your choice. It's great, particularly if you're a motorcyclist (which I am), since you don't need to pull off your gloves to dig out your wallet. It works on the same technology as E-ZPass and I-Pass systems on the tollway—radio frequency signals. Yup, it's free.

After going through three security checkpoints, I was in a meeting room with six Mobilatrons from the same cookie cutter. They walked, talked, dressed, and even looked alike. It looked like same the brand of vanilla. This is supposed to be a bad thing in the days of diversity.

These dudes were smart and I really didn't care what they looked like and what flavor they were as long as they had a taste for change.

Mobil developed Speedpass (way before people used contactless credit cards) by working with Texas Instruments and the Wayne Division of Dresser Industries. It was part of the company's strategy to push its premium products and additional station services (like the convenience stores). Mobil didn't create the patented transponder, but it was instrumental in coming up with ties to products and services (including its own) to put it on people's key rings. It was a conduit for patented innovation.

The 6 million drivers waving their wands gave Mobil a 20 percent boost in gas sales and a 100 percent increase in convenience store purchases. Not bad. The company sees it as a "Horizon Three" idea, a separate business. Speedpass purchasers spend twice as much at McDonald's and cut the transaction time significantly, one of the highest sensitivity components for profit at drive-in windows.

Conglomerates that nurture innovation attract and retain the best and brightest. Those who don't can rest assured that those who can innovate will depart for new horizons.

Japan was full of contradictions. The *geisha* in her traditional kimono clickity-clacking by the computer store. Kyoto residents who say they are not religious in a city of 1,800 temples. They are "born Shintoist, marry Christian, and are buried Buddist."[65] The colossal sumo wrestlers and petite everybody-elses. A language made up of three alphabets. Among work colleagues, the guarded etiquette of the boardroom vs. anything goes in the bar after hours.

The greatest paradox of all was how a country whose people prize "harmony, achieved through conformity and consensus,"[66] could literally rise from the ashes to one that is turning world markets upside down through innovation.

The American view of consensus is giving up and giving in. People are unwilling to share a rung on the corporate ladder, or to move aside so someone else can pass. Our corporate culture says there aren't enough rungs at the top. The American corporate ladder is narrowing and vertical. By hopping off the ladder and starting your own company, you are at the top of the ladder. America's corporations need to change their perception of what the corporate ladder looks like.

In Japan, the ladder is generally horizontal and very wide. "'Compared to the U.S., this society is not a competitive society,' said Daijiro Hashimoto, brother of the former prime minister. 'We don't want winners and losers. As a society, we help each other.'"[67]

Here, we brainstorm because left-brain thinkers want to stay on top of the right-brain thinkers. As long as we believe the best way to the top is to operate with half a brain, we shall never succeed. There are right/left whole brains out there, mostly running their own businesses. When the individuals are whole, they have no need to compete with each other—only for customers. Then, there is conformity. From Absolut Innovation:

> Companies are made of individuals.
> Innovation is based on individuals' ideas.
> Therefore, a company's ability to innovate depends on individual ability to innovate.[68]

Japan was beginning to make sense. Despite years working for a Japanese company with Japanese management, I was blind to why and how their motorcycles were technically superior and had captured the greatest world market share. I only understood once I was in *their* culture, where *they* were the majority.

There was **consensus to innovate**. Japan is a comparatively tiny country. The Japanese had decided to compete against other nations, not each other. They had decided that the way to win in the world market was to be the best and the brightest, universally—for each individual to contribute toward invention, differentiation, and improvement. They recognized that offering superior, innovative products and services would take them from a source of cheap toy widgets for American children of the sixties to America's number one auto manufacturer in first quarter 2007, the leader in electronics, and a leader in technology. There was conformity in using the entire brain to make decisions. It was not a team effort; it was grand efforts of individuals who believed that good was never good enough. More important than salaries, bonuses, or promotions, motivating people to innovate is at the core of Japanese culture.[69]

In the U.S., 8.5 percent of adults are currently working to start a new business. The number one reason for leaving corporate America is to market an "entrepreneurial idea," to be able to innovate. In Japan, a mere 1.6 percent want to go it alone.[70] That's because in corporate Japan, innovators are not alone. They are the majority.

I stood on the platform waiting for my train to return to Tokyo, where I would board my flight to Korea. Faster than a speeding bullet, the white platypus arrived and opened its doors to welcome me. What a journey it had been! Now I was on the same tracks but looking in a different direction. Should entrepreneurs get on a track that takes them back to corporate America? Will they ever be able to leap tall buildings in a single bound? If corporations take a new direction, perhaps. That'd be super, man.

Navigating the Minefield:
Coworkers—Watch Your Step

uly 23, 2002. Seconds after crossing the Thailand/Cambodian border at Poipet, I saw the first of many dismembered beggars. A pretty girl with doe eyes looked like an eight-year-old but was probably 12. I'd been warned to watch my valuables here, since pretty beggars are often decoys for pickpockets. Just like Manhattan.

I was lucky. My Cambodian driver and his assistant were waiting for me in a minivan that used to be white. Most tourists fly directly to Siem Reap, township of the mysterious ruins among twisted trees of Angkor Wat, which Americans remember as the filming site for *Indiana Jones*.

From the Thai border to Siem Reap is 160 kilometers, about 100 miles. Travel time: 10 to 12 hours. Road conditions were appalling. The road was mostly unpaved and loaded with deep potholes.

Every kilometer or so by the side of the road, there was a "no" sign—you know, the ones with the red circle and a red line across the diameter. The drawing of the little man on those signs looked a lot like Kokopelli stepping on hot coals. How ironic that Kokopelli is a Native American symbol of life and these signs were warnings of death and destruction—land mines. Directly behind the Kokopellis were partitioned, groomed farmlands, making one wonder who or what (e.g., a cow) had been unfortunate enough to determine that there were mines in the area. There are still thousands of land mines scattered throughout Cambodia, evidenced by tens of thousands of young (and old) amputees.

For women who needed to "spend a penny" during the rough ride, the decision was an easy one. Signal everyone to look the other way and drop your drawers. Your choice was literally to lose your pride or leave the dirt road to find a bush and possibly lose your legs. Yes, I knew I would probably never see these folks again, so why should I care if they saw my butt?

Crossing the numerous bridges along the way was a combination of luck and goodwill. Many of the bridges over irrigation streams were a few moveable boards. You exited your vehicle to move the boards to the correct width of your axle track. Then you tipped a passerby or farmer to direct you to steer left or right to stay on the boards as you drove across so that your vehicle didn't plunge between the supports. An error spelled disaster not only for you, but for any other traffic using the road for the remainder of the day. This was not some side road to a holiday resort; it was the main road between Thailand and Cambodia's third-largest city and primary tourist attraction.

Barely 15 kilometers into the Kingdom of Cambodia, we encountered a military police roadblock. One of the three officials approached the driver's window and began scrutinizing my clothing and luggage (a single backpack). It was obvious that the purpose of this examination was to determine my value—how much the driver and his assistant were paid for their travel services. With a tourist, there were more dollars to extort. Not many Westerners traveled overland by this route due to its reputation. The official was delighted to see me. It was his lucky day.

Although I didn't know a word of Khmer, the banter between the driver and the officer was obviously about me and money. But I could easily read the emotions of the uniformed dude and the driver and it wasn't making me feel very comfortable. You can hear fear.

It was getting ugly. Like a deaf man reading lips, I was reading their tones, faces, and body language and translating:

"Where are you going?" asked the official, who was deliberately stroking his firearm.

"We're bringing the tourist to Siem Reap," replied the driver.

"What country is the tourist from?" This question is also value related. If you're a savvy traveler, you know that obtaining your nationality is used to determine the asking price of goods, what you are willing to pay, and whether you know how to bargain. Most Asians cannot detect which country an English speaker is from any better than most Americans can decipher whether someone is from northern England, Wales, South Africa, New Zealand (Kiwi), or Australia (Aussie), although particular words are dead giveaways. So if anyone without a weapon asks you where you hail from, the worst reply you can give is "America" because you will pay top dollar. Every backpacking Canadian has figured this out and sews his national flag to his rucksack so that he won't be perceived to be "ugly" or rich, even if he is. Aussies and Kiwis, in general, have traveled more and for longer periods, making them careful to stretch their dollars further. They haggle in a lighthearted way so the completed sale is a win-win. Asians will tell you that most Americans are terrible bargainers because they think it's about the Yank winning and the other party losing. The bartering process and interaction with the merchant are supposed to be part of the enjoyment of the shopping experience, not an opportunity for one party to "get one over" on the other. Bartering in the U.S. is taking on an Asian flavor. eBay has forever changed American buyer/seller relationships.

"She's from England," says my driver. The sort-of jolly-good news is that I'm traveling in Cambodia on my British passport.

Here it comes. "How much did she pay you to drive her to Siem Reap?"

"Nothing. She paid my travel company employer directly."

"Surely she's given you a tip, some money."

"No, nothing."

"How long did you wait for her at the border?"

"Maybe an hour."

"Well, did you pay the parking fee for waiting in Poipet?"

"There is no parking fee."

"Of course there is! You parked and waited, didn't you? The parking fee is $20! You must pay now!"

Twenty dollars to avoid a confrontation with Mr. Thug and the Thugettes may sound like nothing to you, but the average annual salary in Cambodia was $249. In the most recent census (1998), 36 percent of people were below the dollar-a-day poverty line. Twenty bucks was probably a month's salary for the driver, whom the travel company may not have fully reimbursed for "tollgate" expenses. I'm certain Mr. Thug didn't give receipts.

As you'd expect, the driver did what came naturally and started to haggle in a jovial manner. "Aw, c'mon. Surely the parking fee is much lower...say $5."

He picked the wrong number. Mr. Thug was insulted. His eyes squinted, arms straightened, hands clenched, and he waved his loaded weapon. His voice was shrill: "Get out of the van. Get out! Get out!"

The driver's assistant was terrified. I wasn't too thrilled either. In a hushed voice, the assistant stuttered, "Ju..ju...just give them what they want. Don't argue. It's n...n...not worth it."

The Thugettes, the official's two gunslinging buddies, who were watching from their little checkpoint table by the side of road, snickered. Mr. Thug was having a larger-than-usual power trip today and knew that $20 was extortionate—literally.

The driver was escorted to the table of Thugettes. After the exchange of a few soft words, the driver emptied his pockets, and the officials helped themselves to his family's grocery money. We went on our merry way toward Angkor Wat, in silence.

In 1986, Angkor Wat and the surrounding ancient city of crumbling temples and monuments attracted a whopping 565 tourists. The year after Pol Pot died (1998), 85,460 tourists scoured the towers and hallways of this enigmatic village of ruins. About 500,000 made the trip the year I did.[1] In 2007, more than 2 million.

Most of the carvings of celestial dancers that graced the temples are gone, reliefs have been chopped from the walls, and heads of statues decapitated. A single pilfered Khmer objet d'art gets between $30,000 and $300,000 once over the Thai border.[2] Despite UNESCO's best efforts to prevent the destruction, it's hard to protect this sprawling outdoor natural museum, particularly when the people hired to protect it are the thieves or accessories. In 1996, 26 soldiers were caught looting one temple.[3] In 2000, "military officers using power tools and heavy equipment" were caught burglarizing others.[4] Imagine how many times they had been successful before becoming so brazen that they were caught.

As the local people constantly reminded us, one out of every three Cambodians was killed during the years of upheaval. Every family has mourned for parents, children, and best friends. Those who did most of the killing are now the neighbors of the mourners. Others are military officers, politicians, corporate leaders. The Khmer Rouge by any other name would smell just as...

A few bad apples ruining it for the rest. People destroying their own people, their own culture, their own environment. Corrupt, damaging behavior is sanctioned or ignored by those in power. Extorting or looting and driving away tourism (the greatest source of revenue and national rejuvination) continue while those with the ability to stop it see no evil, hear no evil, speak no evil. Land mines intended to destroy one's compatriots who might create a better place were laid by those unable to succeed through competency, intelligence, or valuable skills.

Bullies. Anyone who has the ability to leave to avoid them will.

Remember the *Harvard Business Review* study listing the most common reasons for people leaving jobs? After "job content" and "level of responsibility" (covered in the last chapter), the next two reasons were "company culture" and "caliber of colleagues."

I doubt that mediocre or incompetent quitters claimed they left because the caliber of colleagues was too *high*. Therefore, you can assume that the best employees left because of the *poor* quality of their so-called teammates. So-so or lousy employees wouldn't say they resigned because of "job content" either. Since colleague caliber and job content are among the top reasons why people quit, you can easily deduce that the highest-quality people are the ones who are quitting. Brain drain.

There are plenty more surveys listing top reasons for quitters. Careerwomen.com found that 66 percent of women said their colleagues were responsible for their unhappiness at work.[5] In a 2007 study on retention, Teresa J. Rothausen-Vange, Ph.D., found the top reasons for leaving among high performers who had received positive appraisals from companies with positive public images were:

1. Executive team leadership

2. Executive ethics

3. Facilitation of their careers

4. Company culture

Say Dr. Rothausen-Vange, "A stunning finding of this research is that the top two facets employees cited as reasons for leaving—executive leadership competence and executive ethics—didn't even register in research done 10 or 20 years ago. The latter was especially important for women and for younger workers in this sample. Employees cited a lack of upper management communication about decisions and changes, executives' poor general management skills, a sense that executives weren't employee advocates, as well as a belief that upper management could not be relied upon and trusted and that upper management wasn't consistent and stable." When those surveyed were asked if they'd go back, she found "disillusionment about a company's culture, strategy, respect for human beings and lack of a sense of accomplishment are the most permanently damaging to the employment relationship"[6] Ouch!

This is a trend. With consumers getting greener about the environment and redder about corporate malfeasance, management behavior will soon become more important than job content and responsibility across the board in choosing where to work. In fact, studies are showing that Americans want less responsibility at work.

The *Human Resource Management Guide* lists another recent study that found that "90 percent of the 109 surveyed executives say they are finding it difficult to attract and keep the best people in their organizations. Respondents cited corporate turmoil and limited career opportunity as the key reasons for unwanted turnover."[7]

Departures resulting from "corporate turmoil" and "company culture"? Ironically, these terms were chosen specifically for their ambiguity. "Culture" comes from the Latin word "cultūra," which means to "promote growth" or "care for." The antonym is "barbaria," which means "rudeness" or "savagery." Let's look at the facts on rudeness and savagery in the workplace:

- Each year, almost 2 million workers are assaulted verbally or physically at work.

- Homicide is the number two cause of death at work and number one cause for women. Fourteen percent of workplace deaths are due to homicide.

- "Workplace violence has become so prevalent that in 1998, the U.S. Centers for Disease Control and Prevention classified it as a national epidemic and public hazard."[8]

The violence begins with bullying. **Thirty-five percent of corporate employees admit to having been bullied at work at some time compared to 13 percent of those from a small or family-run business.[9] And owning your own business means your chances of being bullied by a colleague are almost nil.**

If you don't enter the minefield of corporate bullies, you won't be maimed. If you've been in the corporate minefield, you won't go back and take a chance that one "positive" step will result in physical or emotional injury. How many companies have cleared and disabled the mines, so there's no longer any potential risk?

For each incident reported, how many went untold? How many men (or women) would happily admit that a corporate bully targeted them or caused their dismissal or resignation? When quitters go because of "company culture or corporate turmoil," HR departments don't probe what that means because they already know. In fact, "only 3 percent of bullied or berated employees ever file a formal complaint because they often feel buried in layers of corporate hierarchy and figure that such treatment is part of life in modern organizations."[10]

MBA programs now include courses called "Business Ethics." Amusing because it assumes that one's morals change from 8 a.m. to 5 p.m. The press's assault has been where the demise of business ethics is tied with fraud. Yet, for the fourth year in a row, workplace violence is the number one security concern in American companies. Fraud ranks sixth.[11] The press were all over corporate collapses for a while. The "Whistle-blowers," Cynthia Cooper of Worldcom, Coleen Rowley of the FBI, and Sherron Watkins of Enron, were *Time* magazine's 2002 Persons of the Year. Profits lost through bullying (i.e., departure of high-potential employees, health care costs, impact on job performance and revenue delivery) far exceed corporate fraud losses. A University of North Carolina study "showed that, in response to hostile treatment, 24 percent of workers decreased the quality and quantity of their work, 28 percent lost work time avoiding the bully, and 52 percent lost time worrying about the unresolved situation. They take 50 percent more sick days and incur 26 percent more chronic illnesses than their coworkers. **Eighty-two percent left their jobs as a result.**"[12] In short, the bullies are winning; companies are losing. There aren't many whistle-blowers. For the few who are blowing the whistle, management continues to play deaf.

The loss of good employees is a fraction of the cost. Added together, bullying costs dollars and cents—unnecessary dollars and cents. "Employers and insurers pay an estimated $250 billion yearly for direct employee health care costs, turnover, and retraining costs, accidents related to stress-induced fatigue, litigation and settlements, and resistance to top-down change initiatives."[13] The average cost to "lose an employee and retrain a new one is $100,000."[14] Where are they on the balance sheet? Are they hidden? Or, it is it worth $250 billion for the bosses to keep the bullies. Just what do the bullies have on those managers?

Bullying is a top reason why change agents, rainmakers, visionaries, mid-level leaders, and the smartest businesspeople are leaving big companies. These are the people whom bullies most often target. The top four reasons people bully are the following:

- Independent target refused to be subservient (58 percent)
- Bully envied target's competence (56 percent)
- Bully envied target's social skills (49 percent)
- Target displayed ethical behavior; bully retaliated (42 percent)[15]

Thirty-three percent of those surveyed said that in their company culture, bullying led to promotion.

In fact, studies show that you are most vulnerable to being a bully target at work if you have a higher educational degree, greater job skill, greater ethicality, or greater passion about your job and greater commitment to work than most coworkers.

Who's the number one bully? The boss (81 percent)![16]

The excuse used to keep bully bosses is that they've achieved results. Believe me, they haven't. The people they bullied achieved the results, and when it looked as if they might get the credit due for improving the bottom line, they were bullied right out of the company so the bully boss could claim the credit—over and over again. If the worker bees aren't in the hive anymore, they can't claim the credit. The queen bee will live as long as there are worker bees—it doesn't matter which ones they are—as long as they spend all their time feeding the ego of the queen bee. There will always be more worker bees to keep the queen alive. Should anyone be recognized as royalty, the queen bee will quickly destroy her and replace her with another anonymous worker bee. Should the worker bee inadvertently recognize a weakness in the queen bee, it spells instant death. Recognition is everything to the queen bee; honey production is irrelevant.

The word "bully" makes people uncomfortable. The first reaction is to hear: "Well, I wouldn't really call them 'bullies.' But there are some people who certainly are harder to work for than others. And they do make life difficult for the people who work with them."

Call them "difficult, critical, blockers, nitpickers, gossipers, liars, hard-asses, toughies, aggressive, naysayers, politicians, backstabbers." Most guys just call them "assholes." They *are* bullies.

Why would companies retain employment of and promote people who are universally known to be "hard to work for" and who "make life difficult" for others? This type of person is incompetent—at working with others. A "difficult" person lacks interpersonal skills and should never be allowed to affect other staff. If there are jobs they are "uniquely" qualified to do (which is unusual) where they will never be in situations that display their lack of people skills, let them work off-site and send their work without any interpersonal correspondence. Otherwise, fire them.

Why? People who make it difficult for others to do their jobs make their companies miserable places to be. It's causing the best people (who can get other jobs or start companies) to leave. There is no reason to retain difficult people who make others miserable. Retain the losers and lose the winners. Your best employees will go to the corporations or small businesses where these bullies are not tolerated, or start their own companies.

Tolerance of inept people managers says loud and clear that people are the lowest priority in your organization. It's reinforcing to your employees that your company is not attractive enough to retain technically competent managers of people. The presence of even one "difficult" manager is equivalent to having a town crier herald daily that everyone is in a loser organization.

There are tons of technically competent people-positive managers in every industry. HR can find them running their own companies. Of course, not every entrepreneur and small-business owner has exceptional people skills. In fact, many left corporate America because of their poor interpersonal skills or their inability to fit within a highly structured environment. But there are plenty of others who just couldn't put up with the "company culture" and "corporate environment" (most guys just call it "bullshit") that not only tolerates, but promotes, people who lack the ability to treat others with respect.

The reputation of corporations as business boxing rings is changing goals of youth and young adults who will shape the country's future. As we discussed in Chapter One, the number of under-40 executives who started businesses climbed by 36 percent in one year. Not only will America's corporations continue to face a brain drain as younger top talent leave in droves, but the withering brain will be starved of oxygen and blood by the refusal of new blood to enter corporations at all.

While baby boomers have turned a blind eye toward "hazing" in the workplace, the majority of younger workers are not willing to accept counterproductive, unnecessary crap at work. Thirty-eight percent of college students said that owning a business is the best road to success. "Major business schools report that one-third of their students plan to start their own businesses, up from roughly 10 percent five years ago."[17] Remember that twice as many respondents said they'd rather be a founder of a start-up company (top response) than CEO of a Fortune 1000 company, and 56 percent said that it's likely they would start their own business or work for themselves someday. Working with "inspiring colleagues" was an important component of future careers to 96 percent of grads.[18] Tomorrow's best and brightest execs won't enter or stay in corporations that reward and support mediocrity, low-caliber staffing, and mismanagement. Today's executives need to stop acting as if someone passed wind whenever the word "bully" is mentioned. Let's stop making excuses for people-bashing people and label them exactly what they are: bullies.

Illegal discrimination (e.g., sexual harassment, race-related issues) prompts knee-jerk reactions from management and human resources staff to stop the assailants, but bullying, which happens four times as often, finds management and human resources reaching for the reflex hammer to strike the bullies' targets again.

You're not more likely to be targeted if you're an ethnic minority, but if you're a highly educated, competent newcomer with a track record of success, who also happens to be female, look out. Women and men are equally aggressors, but women bullies target other women 84 percent of the time; men bullies choose to nail women 69 percent of the time.[19]

Perhaps it's not coincidental that the U.S. Small Business Administration reports that women are starting businesses at twice the national average. More than half of women business owners (58 percent) say *nothing* could attract them back to the corporate world. Only 11 percent reported that greater flexibility at a corporate job would entice them to return. The percent of women who claimed they fled the corporate village because of their work "environment" is steadily increasing. Even though women entrepreneurs were mostly likely to come from management positions, they stated that the greatest reward of entrepreneurship is "being one's own boss."[20] Any wonder?

If you're still laughing or dismissing bullying as no big deal (or a women issue when it's a competency issue), you either haven't worked in many large companies, are a bully, are living in a cocoon (since facts show that coworkers are aware of the bullying), or have been encouraging bullying by your actions or inaction.

Shame on you if you've asked: "Why don't they just leave?" They do, eventually—after about 17 months of being picked on for being competent.[21]

Have you ever been in an auto accident where it was clearly the other person's fault? According to the National Safety Council, your lifetime odds of being killed in a car accident are one in 244. Three out of 10 of us will be involved in an alcohol-related traffic accident. Knowing that there are barrels of drunk drivers out there causing accidents, and that your chance of dying is astronomically high if you sit in a car, how can you be stupid enough to ride in a car? Why don't you just "leave" the roadways, so that no one hits you? *It's your fault* when a drunk driver, or any other careless or negligent driver, hits you if you "stay" on the roads.

Seriously, only the drunk drivers and their enablers believe that the problem is the sober drivers who ought not to drive. Only bullies and their enablers believe the bullied should leave their livelihoods.

This same logic is applied between domestic abusers and workplace bullies. Penalizing those being hit by asking why *they* didn't leave their homes or jobs is the same as insisting that good drivers shouldn't be on the roads. If you remove drunk and road-raging drivers from the roads, spouse beaters from homes, and bullies from jobs, the best people will thrive and can continue to contribute to society. Stop blaming targets by asking, "Why don't they just leave?" and start asking why the incompetent, emotionally unwell, and dysfunctional aren't *removed* from roads, homes, jobs, and society.

Every year, $5 billion to $6 billion is lost in the United States economy because of employee abuse[22]—clearly not enough for managers to remove the bullies. If tens of thousands of top-class employees' resignations haven't incited action, why would intentional work injuries or a few billion dollars make a difference?

What do bullies, domestic abusers, and drunk drivers have in common? They are **repetitive** offenders who, despite warnings and penalties, are unwilling to stop destructive behavior, and unless they are harshly punished, the severity and frequency of their antisocial behavior escalates. Mothers Against Drunk Driving (MADD) states that one-third of DUI arrests are drunk drivers who have been *caught* before. DUI offenders drove while smashed an average of 87 times before the first time they were caught! MADD says that drunk drivers are more aggressive and hostile than other drivers and don't see drunk driving as a serious problem. They lose their licenses, and drive again, drunk, anyway. Bullies are also more aggressive and hostile than other workers and don't view bullying as a serious issue.

The "cure" rate for domestic abusers is negligible. Two-thirds of domestic batterers assault an average of six times within one year of being arrested.[23]

Corporate bullies act the same way as domestic abusers by

- creating lies or stories to manipulate others' impressions (most common),
- humiliating in public or private,
- constantly criticizing (particularly never-ending nitpicking of irrelevant details),
- minimizing or laughing about the abuse (i.e., she just can't take a joke),
- sabotaging work,
- giving false accounts of actual events or misrepresenting facts,
- taking away job responsibility,
- encouraging others to betray or abuse the target,
- misusing label "insubordinate,"
- stealing credit for others' work,
- abusing performance evaluations by distorting data,
- screaming,
- name-calling,
- denying the abuse,
- personally insulting (often about looks, clothing, or hygiene),
- threatening,
- concealing or vandalizing property (e.g., cars, computers, computer data),
- gaslighting,
- excluding or isolating,
- withholding information,
- changing rules,
- staging public battles or provoking arguments,
- setting unreasonable deadlines,
- unfairly assigning duties, and
- controlling or withholding resources.

Although both workplace bullies and domestic abusers repeat their criminal assaults and/or psychological attacks continually throughout their lives, usually focusing on one target at a time, abusers insist that each target caused them to act, seeing themselves as "victims." If you're not a target but see that a coworker is "difficult" through personal observation, image what that mismanager is doing when out of the public eye!

Domestic bullies have recidivism rates paralleled by workplace bullies. In 99 percent of cases reported, the bullying was a series of incidents. The majority of targets had never been bullied before. **But 77 percent of those who reported being abused at work knew other people these Attila the Huns had harassed at the same company!**[24] Like that Cambodian guard, bullies' actions are fairly overt because they know there will be no retribution for their actions. Corporate bullies, from experience, learn that abusing "A" players causes A to exit. If you're a "B" player, you learn by observing that the best way to get to the top in Corporate USA is to make life unbearable for more-experienced or smarter colleagues, because there's no downside! If you weren't aggressive when you joined a big corporation, you'll witness the rewards of becoming Attila II or joining a team of Huns.

When talented executives are bullied:

- 44 percent leave the company involuntarily (remember that the bully is most often the boss),
- 38 percent quit,
- 11 percent are banished to another department/division,
- **in only 7 percent of cases is the bully punished,** and
- **in only 1 percent of cases is the bully terminated.**[25]

Just in case you missed anything, here's a summary. **In 93 percent of cases that targets have the courage to report, <u>nothing</u> happens to the few corporate bullies who continually behave in a blatantly abusive and dysfunctional manner impacting 35 percent of the corporate workforce, causing the exodus of the best employees and damaging their companies' profitability.**

That translates into one bully harassing an average of 35 workers to the point where they report it. The rest, seeing that big companies have condoned the abusive behavior toward the previous 35, don't bother to report it, and leave. This is one of the greatest causes of employee dissatisfaction and attrition, and I've never heard it mentioned *once* in an employee retention meeting! In Workplace Violence seminars, the word "bully" is rarely mentioned!

In every big company, it seems there's always (at least) one. Just like going on a group trip abroad, there's always "one." If there's not one, it's probably you.

Experts are calling bullying "America's silent epidemic." An International Labor Organization survey concluded that bullying is the fastest growing complaint of employees. And lawsuits against employers began with bullying.

The University of Manchester Institute of Science and Technology conducted research on employee health issues. Their findings: Up to one-half of all stress-related illness is caused by bullying.

> One of the most crucial aspects of creating a healthy workplace is what an organization does when it finds it has a problem employee or manager. The instigator should be made aware that the behavior is inappropriate and not given further responsibility over others. *To do so would be to institutionalize the inappropriate behavior.*[26]

Where criminal vandalism (for example, in the company parking lot) occurs, corporations often keep data. Those who have had their cars keyed, tires slashed, or gas tanks contaminated have a good idea who the vandal is. Some large companies don't ask who the suspect is because they'd rather do nothing, and want to avoid a negligence claim. When they do ask (or are told), the same few names keep coming up. Yet, after a deluge of complaints, companies might employ only minimal security methods designed to cover the company (not the victim or future victims) against negligence claims—methods they know won't catch or stop the vandals. It's quite clear that the objective is to silence the complainants, rather than prosecute or terminate criminal coworkers.

Mark Braverman, a psychologist at Crisis Management Group, says, "Bullying and intimidation can't happen unless there is a climate that allows it." And he explains that the climate that allows it is the one that discourages employees from reporting the potentially violent offenders.[27] Corporations discourage reporting by promoting bullies, firing targets, and ensuring that every employee knows the

HR and top management mantra: The person who *mentions* the problem *is* the problem.

In fact, when workers tell HR (63 percent) and the bully's boss (73 percent) about the problem, HR and the bully's boss are predominantly "destructive, not supportive." Since most employees witness the brat boss detonating several other golden geese without intervention, it's surprising anyone bothers to tell anyone. Targets are least likely to go to HR because they believe HR will back management, proven by the statistically significant correlation between HR and bullies' bosses support levels ($r=.496$, $p<.0001$) (U.S. Hostile Workplace Survey 2000).[28]

Fast Company magazine ruffled feathers when its cover article was "Why We Hate HR." One reason we hate 'em: "HR isn't working for *you*."[29] Gee, ya *think*?

Study after study show how most big company human resources departments dump more poison in the corporate fish tank.

"Statistically, at least once in your career everyone will be in a no-win situation," said Damien Brinkel, director of the Winston-Salem, N.C.-based nonprofit Professionals in Transition. "If it hasn't happened to you yet, it will."

Ben Leichtling, a Denver psychotherapist and specialist in workplace dynamics, claims that efforts to engage support in human resources departments usually fail or make matters worse.[30]

Isn't it ironic that human resources staff and senior management attend all kinds of courses and read mountains of memos about high-value employee retention, while they actively and passively cause the top guns to desert! Human resources staff took **negative** actions against the target 32 percent of the time, and did nothing (51 percent) most often, encouraging the bully. In only 17 percent of cases did the HR rep do **anything** to help the target or discourage the bully.[31]

In a corporate culture that fosters bullying, most often by inaction, HR departments also have their own bullies. When a killjoy is rampaging unfettered through your own department, hearing others' problems strikes an uncomfortably familiar chord. But do nothing?

It's understandable why HR would do nothing, because in most cases, its ability to change things is nothing. In big businesses, most HR executives are in powerless process roles looking after only one of the following: benefits, recruiting, employment, policies, training, compensation, regulatory compliance; but not people. When department or division had its own HR leader who had all the skills above, it had some influence over what happened to people because their job was about people, not things. Now a lot of those functions are outsourced. Today, many are largely ignored by senior management in power positions, except to complete tasks and provide order-taker roles. They've become big business burger flippers.

What would make you feel worse in HR than having the 10th disgruntled employee show up complaining about the same bully, knowing that the bully's manager is going to tell you in a "nice" way to shut up and get lost? It's a reminder that you're impotent in your job, the management stinks, and that you should have left ages ago because the company's going downhill. Nothing like the 10th victim appearing at your office door to make you feel bad about the fact that you've done nothing to get out of a loser organization where you have a meaningless job. That 10th target is like a neon light flashing: "Your job sucks.... Your job sucks.... Your job sucks." If you're really bitter about your inability to leave, you might as well knock out the whiner's lights by siding with the bully. Eliminate the reminder of the problem if you can't eliminate the problem. To stop the ringing in your ears of "your job sucks...your job sucks," you can either block your ears until your arms get sore or, much easier, eliminate the noisemaker. The person who mentions the problem becomes the problem. *You're* not going to mention the problem again to the bully's boss and risk being her next target. Destroy the complainant, no problem.

Lata worked hard for her MBA and soon afterward found her dream job. A popular woman, Lata made friends at all her old stomping grounds, and a former colleague told her about the opening. During the interview, Lata asked why the job opening existed. "It's a newly created position," replied the HR representative. "Meet the boss, Bradlee." Lata took the job, her first management position, after confirming with Bradlee the vacation dates for her pre-booked trip to Hawaii in the summer. It was the best position at this level in the company, working with the newly launched products.

Soon Lata discovered that the person who held her job previously had transferred to another department due to problems with Bradlee's "management style." (Ding, ding, ding. Alarm bells. "Management style" usually equals bullying in big companies.) Lata soon found that Bradlee would scream at her for not completing tasks that had never been asked for. "You must have deleted the e-mail," Bradlee would accuse, regarding her imaginary request. Of course, when Bradlee didn't give *her* boss required items in a timely way, she'd lie and claim Lata hadn't completed them, although Lata had never been asked for them. Projects were typically assigned to Lata at 5 p.m. with delivery demanded by 9 a.m. the next morning, or a few minutes before noon with delivery in two hours on a four-hour project. Bradlee insisted that Lata was insubordinate for leaving the building for lunch. E-mails that were forwarded would show that Bradlee sat on the requests for days before making the demands on Lata. Lata became terrified to go to lunch, knowing that if she did, a project would be e-mailed to her the moment she left her desk with her purse. She was belittled for missing calls while in the ladies' room.

A week before Lata's vacation, she was told to cancel it because things were too busy. "I've had this booked for a year!" Lata pleaded. Oh, dear, refusing to be subordinate. "I had these dates agreed as vacation when I interviewed for this job!" Oh, heavens, harassing a supervisor.

Lata's coworker, Dana, entered the room. "I just want to make this clear," boomed Bradlee. "Everyone is going to suffer because Lata just decided to take a vacation and dump all her work on her staff. Neither of you better get pregnant. And if you do, don't think you're going to take all your maternity leave, because we're busy."

Lata made her fourth trip to HR to report this. Predictably, nothing happened. Lata said to her HR rep, "I know that Bradlee has been abusive to employees before. I know about the guy who transferred, and the truth about why the position became available. I also know about two other good people who quit because of Bradlee. I know other employees have reported the abuse to HR."

"Yes, there have been others who have quit because of Bradlee, but none have been at *your level*."

Which of the following is the HR rep really thinking?

A. It's OK to bully good people as long as they're not the same level.

B. It's OK for Bradlee to bully people.

C. What's the big deal? At least Bradlee's consistent.

D. Good employees don't matter to us. We're interested in keeping bullies.

E. I've tried to do something about this before, but I'm not empowered to do anything in my job, so get lost.

F. I'm sick of all you people complaining.

G. Please resign. I didn't do anything the last three times you complained, so why are you stupid enough to think I'll do anything this time.

H. Oh, oh. Bradlee said something illegal about the maternity leave. I have to cover my ass somehow.

I. I hope the other woman doesn't complain about what Bradlee said, or denies it, so I don't have to deal with a class action suit or EEOC claim.

J. Stop complaining. You're lucky to have a job. It's better to work for an incompetent bully and get abused every day than not have a paycheck.

K. We all work for incompetent bullies. You're in the in-crowd.

L. If I confront Bradlee, she'll target me.

M. Which is more difficult? Me having to actually do something (like deal with Bradlee), or me doing nothing (and you resigning). The choice seems simple to me.

N. Bradlee's manager doesn't care so why should I.

O. The fact that Bradlee has bullied lots of other people means this is normal. Just resign; that's normal here.

P. I wish Bradlee only threatened people when there weren't witnesses.

Q. Boy, I wish I had Lata's skills and could leave this stinkhole and get a job in a decent place.

R. She makes a lot more money than I do. How dare she complain.

S. I don't handle recruitment anymore, so who cares if another leaves.

T. Shit rolls downhill. Bradlee attacks her, now she's attacking me for doing nothing. I'm going to nail her.

U. I'd better dig up some dirt on Lata, so we can stop her from complaining.

V. I always wanted a job in Lata's department. If Lata leaves, perhaps I'll get her job.

W. It's just a personality conflict, management style.

X. Lata isn't black, disabled, or gay, so it's not illegal.

Y. The job market is really bad out there. I'd better get Lata to quit, because if I raise the issue of Bradlee's attack on another employee, I'll be seen as a complainer, not a problem solver. The person who has the problem, is the problem.

Z. Lata is the problem because she mentioned the problem.

I'm out of letters. But human resources will never run out of excuses to do nothing about the problem while spending money on retention seminars.

Similar to what happens in most companies, Bradlee will attack a new employee as soon as Lata leaves and will be applauded while taking the credit for the work performed by the recently departed target. It's easier to deal with an exiting employee every 17 months (the average length of time before the bully succeeds in removing the target) than deal with the problem. **Because lousy companies love having popular, repetitive processes.** People don't like change. And in a lousy company, the exit process for good people is normal. Exiting long-term bullies is not.

When Lata returned from a week's vacation in Hawaii, she had 127 e-mails to read through. Friends came by to ask about her trip, and she plunged into the mass of memos. At 10 a.m., Bradlee appeared at her desk, smirking. "And why have you not completed the project I e-mailed you about five days ago. I needed it by 10 this morning. I'll bet you haven't even started it!"

Of course, Bradlee hadn't forgotten that Lata was on vacation and she certainly hadn't forgotten to figure out a way to get even with Lata for having a happy life, good marriage, and restful vacation. Bradlee the Bulldog was going to make Lata pay for her happiness and popularity. "I told everyone that I e-mailed you five days ago and you've done nothing. You're incompetent. And you have the nerve to stand around chatting when there's so much work to be done."

Whereupon, Lata walked into HR, resigned, and walked out. Success. Another brightest and best leaves the company.

Once again, Bradlee was rewarded for bullying and the company punished an employee for being popular and competent. Whereupon, the remaining employees promised themselves that they would never appear popular or competent to avoid becoming targets, and decided to become bullies as managers knowing that was the quickest route to the top.

HR, concerned about a lawsuit, contacted Bradlee's boss. Bradlee's boss claimed she was unaware that there was any problem although every time Bradlee failed to deliver, she'd blamed Lata. Bradlee's boss claimed to be unaware or forgot that there had been other complaints about Bradlee. Bradlee's boss never examined the cause of regular turnover. Bradlee's boss never spoke to Lata. Bradlee's boss is therefore incompetent.

Within days, Bradlee started attacking and insulting Lata's best subordinate, since Lata was no longer there to do Bradlee's job. Bullies usually select new targets between two and 14 days after the departure of the last victim.[32] Soon there will be another "personality conflict" due to Bradlee's "management style" with a carefully selected popular, top-performing employee. The cycle repeats itself.

A week later, Bradlee's company placed a recruitment ad looking for "individuals" with "excellent communication skills" and "the ability to interact well with others"—particularly bullies. In other words, they're looking for several Latas, since she was doing the work of two (hers and her boss's). Chances are they'll be placing the ad again in 17 months.

Lata is self-employed, running a home-based business in the same field as the company she left. As a well-liked business builder, she had all the skills to lead and manage a profitable company. The cycle is repeating itself. Bullied women are getting even by starting their own companies, competing with the corporations that drove them out to keep the losers. The best revenge is a successful, happy life.

A few months later, Lata ran into a neighbor shopping downtown on a weekday. "I quit my job because I couldn't stand that the key competency of the management was politics," Lata explained.

"Politics? I love it," gloated the neighbor, who'd worked for Worldcom forever. A few months later, Worldcom orbited out of control and, in line with the planets, the neighbor was laid off. After several exotic vacations to the far corners of the world, a bout with depression, returning to college, etc., the neighbor is still unemployed four years later. There are fewer big companies recruiting VPs of politics.

It's not HR, but bullies' *bosses* who make the greatest contribution to perpetuating bullying. They are "bully breeders." While 40 percent ignored complaints against their incompetent staff, 42 percent "directly helped the bully or punished the complaining target!"[33] Hey, remove that exclamation point; this is not surprising at all.

The person who chooses or mismanages a bully is mediocre at best. Great managers don't retain bad people managers. It's like choosing ugly friends to make yourself look prettier. CEOs can easily identify a bully: They have chronic, one-at-a-time employee turnover. CEOs can easily identify a bully breeder: They have chronic two-at-a-time employee turnover, one with the bully's subordinates, and one with the bully's peers. The manager who has one bully in the group has a retention problem among the entire team of subordinates. Bright, competent businesspeople will not stay in groups with bully peers. If you're surrounded by dogs, eventually you'll step in their shit, and everybody inside and outside the pound is going to smell it on you. If you're in a minefield, eventually you'll step on one, and your livelihood will come to an abrupt end. Better to leave while you've still got two legs to stand on.

Waring & LaRosa was a small Manhattan advertising agency famous for its groundbreaking work on Fisher-Price and Perrier. I worked for Saul Waring, heading his direct marketing division. I asked Saul the secret of his success—not just producing great work, but being surrounded by great people who loved working for him and terrific clients. He was obviously proud, happy, and content. He replied, "We only work with people we like." Being competent was an ingredient of being liked.

A large, long-standing flooring company asked the agency to produce an integrated marketing campaign for its tile product lines. The flooring company requested we produce three solutions to choose from. We thoroughly researched the market and discovered that it took a full year between the time someone decided to replace the kitchen floor and the happy event. Delving deeper into why the process took so long, we learned that most consumers are not visual—that is, they cannot picture how the pattern on the 12-square-inch sample will look laid out in their own kitchen. This is also true of wall paint. However, women (the principle decision makers) feel that if they make a mistake with paint color, it's not a catastrophe. Simply repaint. Make a mistake with flooring, and the decision makers felt they'd have to live with that mistake forever.

The solution we developed was to transform the 12-*inch*-square tile sample into a 12-*foot*-square poster sample. The actual square tile was on top and a poster-style sheet was attached, folded underneath with the same pattern and texture. You simply folded out the giant poster and placed it on your floor. You could trim it with scissors to fit around islands, appliances, etc. and see it *in your home*, not on a PC screen. Yes, it was more expensive to produce than a single tile, but it was far more profitable because of the conversion rate from enquiry to sale. The competitors didn't do this. The company probably could have patented the idea and won significant market share. We even designed ads for home magazines so that, for a small fee, customers could check the color samples that they wanted beside the photos, and the company would mail them to their home with a list of local retailers. This type of advertising on the Web is common now, but at the time, home computer penetration was 17 percent.

We knew, based upon the research, this would change the dynamics of tile purchasing, shortening the buy cycle and building the company's reputation as customer focused. The client had asked for three solutions, so we also developed two other programs to build the business. We excitedly pitched our groundbreaking ideas. The reaction we received had us floored. The group of clients sat stone-faced, shifting their eyes back and forth like cat clocks on a wall, trying to catch a glimpse of a reaction from one of their colleagues. "We'll get back to you," one said in a monotone voice as they shuffled out the door like robots.

A week later, the client called to say he wanted three more ideas. He said there was no feedback about the first three ideas; he just needed to see more to be sure if the originals were any good. "We just want to see how many ideas are out there."

We learned that they were never happy with any of their many previous agencies' ideas either. In fact, this client was never happy about anything. If one of the clients liked the idea, that was enough for his colleague to eradicate it—hence the poker faces. The objective of the company jerks was to atrophy the company—to find any reason to prevent administering a cure, looking for side effects that didn't exist, spreading fear of germs from any change. The management wouldn't eliminate the virus and provide a healthy environment so that great ideas could grow.

Despite the potential loss to forecast revenue, Saul called an agency meeting and asked us to decide whether these were the kind of people we wanted to continue working with. The best way to prevent catching a virus is to avoid exposure to those who have it. The vote was unanimous. In his professional and polite fashion, Saul explained to the client that he didn't think we had what it took to make them feel good. What he didn't say is that we'd agreed that a few mutated cells had spread cancer throughout their organization and it was beyond recovery.

The disease was terminal for the flooring giant. The company later filed for bankruptcy under Chapter 11.

Saul was an inspiring manager. "You should begin thinking about starting your own business," he coaxed me. "You have all the qualities needed to be happily successful on your own." Saul wanted the best for his people. He believed that encouraging them to move to bigger and better things would eventually benefit all. He put people first.

Small businesses and sole proprietorships have become the places where people come first. "'Corporate' has become a dirty word because it lacks human values," says Foote, Cone & Belding's director of brand equities (obviously a process job).[34]

Note the differences between how Saul worked with his people and how the flooring company interacted. What makes employees want to stay is working with others they admire.

If you've worked in several large companies, you can easily predict the merry-go-round of typical tactics that whiz by when the best employees are leaving in droves. None of these tactics includes removing the people that caused the good people to leave. The bullies, incompetents, and people in process roles go round and round, bobbing up and down to dodge any interference by faster racehorses or carriages that are more beautiful. Mediocre corporations happily spin out of control, believing they are winning because they always stay in front of the horse in back. In fact, the horses behind have lapped them, and they are actually in last place.

The worst employee retention tactics are points programs, employee recognition programs, and formal employee surveys. Companies that don't have pervasive morale problems don't have most of these, because they make the problem worse. Top talent is motivated by working with equally talented comrades. Good employees are motivated by seeing their innovative ideas succeed in the marketplace. Good companies have ongoing dialog with employees and integrate their suggestions on a regular basis. Good managers empower their staff to make decisions and credit them with success, so people are enabled to implement best practices rather than request them on an anonymous survey. Good businesses maintain the ship's hull rather than conduct an opinion poll or distribute thimbles to bail out the ship after it is sinking and the people in the engine room have drowned.

Employee surveys are moot. Companies treat employee surveys like advice from McKinsey or other organizational consulting firms. They laud the advice that confirms what they planned to do anyway and ignore everything else. When "everything else" is mentioned too much for them to ignore, they hold internal focus groups to "delve deeper," knowing that they are mixing the very people who are the problem with the ones who are complaining about them. This practice fuels intimidation by the problem people, exactly what the company's problem-management want. In other words, managers stifle what they don't want to hear, which is that people, many of whom are their friends, should be removed along with the process silos that were created to cope with their lack of business skills.

After an employee survey, companies implement the same flavor-of-the-month "improvements" bought from or recommended by some outside employee retention consulting firm. The improvements simply improve the ability of managers to claim they addressed the issue but don't impact morale or curb attrition. What improves employee morale and retention is exiting the bullies and incompetents, not a program. Retailers with the best products do not need programs. Exceptional employees design and deliver exceptional products. Companies with the best employees do not need programs. But as sure as the sun rises in the morning, a company full of bullies and buddies will launch a program to dole out more rewards and recognition to the "right" people.

I had the opportunity to review the verbatim results of several large companywide employee satisfaction surveys. Employees reported that not receiving recognition or rewards had far less negative impact on them than watching a bully or the boss's buddy receive unsubstantiated or undeserved recognition or rewards. Employees expressed highest levels of intention to leave when they watched incompetent employees be promoted or stay promoted, and stated that it nullified any positive effect from their own promotions, recognition, bonuses, and rewards. In other words, as long as managers reward bullies, the best people will always go elsewhere, no matter what incentives you give them.

A survey of 5,000 U.S. households published by CareerBuilder confirmed that more than half of employees were dissatisfied with their jobs. The greatest source of job dissatisfaction was the promotion policy (46.4 percent) with wages far behind at 33.9 percent. It's surprising, then, that the result of employee retention strategies never includes removing the incompetent people who were promoted—the primary source of attrition from the company. This study was not difficult to find, and the results of other employee surveys reinforce this conclusion. So why do companies refuse to acknowledge and address the main cause of turnover of the brightest candidates: the promotion of the not so bright? The quickest plug for the brain drain is obvious. It's not about giving more rewards and recognition to a handful of good people; it's about *removing permanently* the people who have been promoted unfairly, and thereby the rewards and recognition *they* receive. When is the last time you heard of any large company doing this en masse? If you want to reverse the flow and get the best and brightest back, simply replace incompetents. It's impossible to believe that the reading comprehension level of CEOs is so low that they can't decipher from all the published surveys and studies that the highest-potential employees simply do not want to work with jerks. High pots don't want big-title process roles or to be promoted, only not to work alongside the jerks. They don't want to work in the same company as jerks, at any level, at all. By starting their own businesses, they don't have to work with jerks.

When staff request that the "right" staff get rewards and recognition, they want you to stop giving rewards and recognition to undeserving staff. This never happens. Managers treat staff as idiots with "employee of the day/week/month" bulletins, thanking masses of people at meetings, and handing out certificates or paperweights to every breathing body in the room. The bullies and buddies of managers still get the largest percentage of these.

Since employees already know that the company penalizes the person who mentions the problem and rewards the problem people, most employees who need their paychecks won't mention the real issues (what's the point?) since they believe the company is tracking who makes the comments and will retaliate on those employee surveys. If you can't trust your company not to dismiss bullies at work, why would you trust it not to retaliate if you name names.

In one employee survey in a manufacturing plant, all four staff members detailed abuses and attacks by the three managers of their department, including withheld pay without cause, personal comments about speech patterns and dress style, and demeaning nicknames. (The first question is why does the company need three people co-managing four staff who all do the same job?) The company's response was to lay off all four and outsource the entire department while keeping all three bully managers (who now manage no one).

No one else in the company had complained about the four staff except for their incompetent, inexperienced managers. Of course, there were stacks of complaints from other departments about the three bully managers, several involving lawyers and security due to severity. The department was one of those process departments listed in the earlier chapter, which never should have existed in the first place, and the three managers got the jobs because of their social skills with senior vice presidents. The three bully managers are still there, managing no one, and have all selected new targets to pick on, now that their staff are gone.

This company also launched an employee recognition program— no doubt, to recognize the bullies and their buddies. Whoopie.

Sooner or later, a points program (where employees earn points redeemable for products or prizes as a reward for good deeds or favors) will be launched with an exciting logo, free water bottles, baseball caps, T-shirts, and other paraphernalia certain to attract the most intelligent people who need clothes, or who desperately need a water bottle or desk toy to play with when bored.

Employee points programs are rarely related to contributions to net income, revenue generation, or new business dollars. Points programs favor those with the most friends. The most productive, farsighted, original thinkers and collaborative employees rarely have the most friends at work since they are busy doing their jobs rather than doing the social circuit. Being bright, they question the status quo, threatening existing jobs and making enemies. They work when they could be schmoozing or gossiping about coworkers. The key reason points programs don't work is that the person who has final say in the number of points and who gets them is usually the reason for the morale problem in the first place—inept departmental management and mediocre peers.

No one asks for an "employee recognition" program. When employees say they haven't been recognized for their contributions, they aren't saying no one at the company has been recognized. They mean that the allotment of recognition has not been fair. Same managers, same allotment. Stinky employees don't complain about lack of recognition. But everyone complains when stinky employees do continually get rewarded and recognized. When they get sick of complaining, they leave.

Here comes the quota system, where the bottom 10 percent of employees of each department will be asked to leave while the top 10 percent get huge rewards. Problem is that flies are attracted to shit. In other words, only lousy staff are left working for lousy bosses. So the bully bosses and bully breeders who have driven out good people lose 10 percent of their staff (usually the one good employee left who poses a competence threat), and the brilliant managers who have only top talent in their group lose 10 percent of the company's future leaders while demoralizing another 80 percent. We all know this system is subjective hogwash. Companies that treat people in percentages are giving garbage managers an opportunity to exit somebody who doesn't fit in. And that's typically the entrepreneurial genius. Companies that need to provide a percentage quota for how many incompetent people need to be fired under each manager are clearly saying their leaders haven't made decisions on who is incompetent and who should no longer work at the company because they're trying to keep the relative size of each empire even. Imagine telling a people manager that he must get rid of 10 percent of staff at each review, whether 90 percent of his staff are losers or 100 percent are brilliant. If it's not literal and there are exceptions, then why establish a standard that no one intends to implement, except where it suits him? In every company, a superior business manager is a superior people manager because part of every business is managing people, whether they are staff, colleagues, clients, vendors, or customers. Having to set quotas is an indication that your businesspeople cannot make intelligent and profitable decisions.

The other butt-covering scheme in companies overridden with incompetents is the everybody-has-to-reapply-for-the-open-positions tactics, typically occurring immediately before an employee uncovers gross misconduct by management. Guess who's writing the new job descriptions? Usually the gross "misconduit."

If you've got a morale problem, you've got a management problem. If you don't *remove* people, you won't *remove* the morale issue. Management who *add* points, programs, and surveys should be subtracted.

Reducing stress programs? Why not remove the source of stress—you know who they are. Companies that create programs to keep good employees are like a husband who buys flowers for his wife right before beating her or only after cheating on her. The greatest source of job stress is office politics according to 43 percent of white-collar workers.[35]

Not only do reward programs encourage bullies, but inaction is the greatest contributor to abuse in the workplace. Bully breeders reward bullies just by keeping them in jobs they don't deserve. A bully never deserves a management position. Neither does the bully breeder.

Why do bully breeders defend their offspring?

1. **Bully breeders' jobs are not in jeopardy for hiring bullies.**
   If there's a bully in the house, there's a corporate environment that promotes mediocrity. The numbers don't really matter. Politics

rule. Eighty-one percent of executives, managers, and supervisors agree that obtaining their leadership positions was based more upon politics than competencies.[36]

2. **Bully breeders are at risk if they don't hire bullies to weed out the superstars**.

   If a new bright spark in your department continually presents new financial opportunities for the firm, the bully's boss will look inept for not seeing those opportunities before. That bright spark could replace the bully, and the bully's manager! Mediocre managers need a bully in the bullpen. Newcomers are at high risk. Fifty-eight percent of executives believe that an outsider has a better chance of getting leadership positions.[37] If you ensure that all newcomers fail, you lower the risk that the company will bring in one to replace you!

3. **Bully breeders have low self-esteem.**

   Watching the *Jerry Springer Show, Celebrity Rehab,* or *Flavor of Love* makes us feel good about ourselves. "Boy, those people are really stupid, out of control, and messed up. Compared to them, I've really got it together." On with the show. There are no disadvantages in being Jerry Springer! As long as people keep tuning in, he keeps getting paid. And it pays well.

4. **Bully breeders are conflict avoiders and seesaw managers**.

   Terrified of conflict, they'll go to any length to avoid dealing with the bully. Conflict avoiders, due to anxiety over having to make decisions that might result in confrontations, are shortsighted. Rather than acknowledge the recidivism rate of conflict caused by the bully, they cower, praying each incident (and each target) goes away. The bully breeder can relax again when each talented target quits, because the problem was resolved without the bully's boss making any decisions or taking any action. Refusal to make decisions that aren't universally popular has enhanced bully breeders' status in big companies. Their noncommittal, hands-off, no-support management style carries over to all aspects of their business personas. They let bullies make the decisions. The only exceptions to their hands-off approaches are when bullies have been ineffective at knocking down outstanding top performers or when top performers try to stop the bullying. Threatened by employees who are better liked or better qualified, the bully breeder then encourages the bully to step up the abuse. The bully breeder is always aware of the bully's history and will deny or minimize this when and if confronted.

5. **Bully breeders see bullies as reflections of themselves. Today's corporate bullies were yesterday's school bullies.**

   Bullying is a chronic condition starting at an early age, encouraged by the majority of those in the know who denied, ignored, or supported them. Schoolyard bullies' parents deny their children have behavioral problems and defend the abusive actions. "He's just being a boy; she was just playing." "*Everybody* agrees it was a mistake." "My son/daughter is a *good* child." Despite almost monotonous visits to the principal's office to discuss details about the latest incident with the umpteenth victim, and reports from other adults, parents will parrot back the stack of lies and excuses their antisocial child made about the victim, encouraging their child to continue dysfunctional, escalating behavior. They believe that admitting that their child is a problem or enjoys hurting others would mean that there is something wrong with their parenting skills. The problem with their parenting skills arose the moment they first denied the child's abusive behavior or defended their child. Dysfunctional parents voice criticism of the victims and principals or teachers, particularly in front of their bullying child, recognizing that the child shares their low self-esteem and believing this will improve it.

   Obviously, these actions reward the child for abusing other people. Some parents privately reward their children for hitting others, because they secretly wish they could get away with whacking people themselves. What starts as name-calling becomes lying, stealing, then becomes a slap, pinch, push, punch, or threat. The parents defend each more grievous action more assertively. The child learns that if he attacks, the parents will join in on the attack. There's nothing like a common enemy to bring the weak-minded together. The child learns that imagining or creating an enemy or getting scolded by a teacher reaps parental affection, attention, and support. The child fabricates lies so often that he has trouble distinguishing between reality and fiction. When the lies don't work to draw affection, the abuse escalates. As the parents begin to realize their encouragement has led the child to repeat acts that are more hostile more frequently, they deny the abuse more fervently and give more affection to the "poor" bully child to soothe their own guilt. They desperately seek a label such as ADHD to justify why the child will always be that way. In the next breath, they deny Mary bullies at all, to deny that if they punished Mary early on she wouldn't bully. The incidents never happened. Excuses, excuses. Mary's boss will someday come up with the same excuses. Mothers of serial murderers convicted of multiple crimes from DNA evidence still insist their children "couldn't" or didn't do it. Bullies' bosses will deny their attacking employees ever lied to them or others, even when presented with the voice mail or e-mail evidence.

Antonio Rodriguez was a 69-year-old corn vendor on the Southwest side of Chicago. He couldn't afford to retire and had sold corn in the neighborhood for 10 years. Like most targets, he never had any trouble. One day he scolded an eight-year-old boy who'd tried to flip over his corn cart. The little bully, angry at being confronted, went home, lied, and returned with an adult. Without discussion, the adult beat Rodriguez in the head with a baseball bat and killed him.[38] The valuable lesson the child learned is his innocent targets will be killed.

While it's an extreme example, it does lend itself to comparison. Bully breeders let their bully subordinates know that they will destroy anyone not eliminated by the bully or anyone who confronts the bully.

Remember the Glenbrook North High School hazing incident in spring 2002? That's when a group of juniors who'd been promised they wouldn't be touched by a group of seniors during hazing ended up being bloodied on video. Five juniors were hospitalized after having an ear ripped, being knocked unconscious, choked with pig intestines, bashed in the head requiring 10 stitches, kicked until sustaining a fractured tailbone, having an ankle broken, being punched, threatened with a baseball bat, and having objects slammed on their heads and backs. Parents were later arrested for supplying alcohol to the underage high school students and providing partying quarters to the bullying seniors.

These underage bullies had no fear of retribution, since they openly guzzled beer from kegs and beat the juniors senseless while video cameras were capturing it all on tape. Obviously, their parents minimized, denied, or ignored their violent behavior in the past?

When confronted with videos of their children assaulting and battering other people, the upscale parents attacked the *media* for covering the event and the *school* that had tried to prevent the mêlée. One parent immediately asked for a temporary restraining order against the county because the school district was "denying her right to an education" for her lovely daughter, who had been suspended for brutality.[39] Some blamed the juniors for showing up (probably so they wouldn't get bloodied behind the school the next day after being threatened to "show up or else"). Others blamed it on alcohol (a common excuse for domestic abusers or substance-abusing workplace bullies). Or better yet, parents whispered how other teens caused more injuries than their teen. Most reports talked about how the hazing incident was considered by parents to be no big deal, blown out of proportion, just something that "got out of hand" with "tee hee, teenagers unable to control themselves."

I quit my sorority in my sophomore year because I refused to be a bully bystander. As teenagers, neither I nor my friends lost control to the point of breaking tailbones and ankles, beating and kicking sitting ducks, knocking people unconscious, or splitting someone's head open for fun. (And it's pretty obvious from the video that the attackers were having fun assaulting fellow students.) Yet there were the parents publicly blaming everyone but the person who caused others to be hospitalized—their children.

John Warner, an alumnus of Glenbrook North High School and college professor, lamented that many students are shocked when they realize there are repercussions for negative or neglectful behavior:

> It's hard to even blame students for their initial incredulity in the face of consequences, as the vast majority have been bailed out many times by parents who will lie for them, who will create fake excuses or justifications for bad behavior. Some even threaten and intimidate teachers and schools (read: litigation) that may stand in the way of their child's achievement.[40]

Think about it: Schoolyard bullies are never the brightest students and can only get better grades by cheating or friendships with teachers who lack integrity; workplace bullies are never A-class employees unless they steal credit from others or force out the top employees. Straight-A students are usually schoolyard bully targets; A-class employees are usually workplace bully targets. The bullies haven't changed; they've simply aged.

Bullies are not overachievers; they abuse others to cover their inadequacies. The self-employed usually are overachievers.

The Glenbrook High parents realized long ago that their little darlings were never going to make it on their smarts. Their kids weren't top of the class and never will be. Let's face it—if you're smart, you're not spending your time smearing dog feces in someone else's face, or collecting dog feces for that matter. If the straight-A students aren't stepping in your shit, smearing it in their faces is even better. If your kid can bully the straight-A students out of the school or cause them enough stress to hurt their grades, your dumb kid will look smarter, and you'll feel better. Who cares? If you've been an enabler for your child's emotionally bankrupt behavior, your bankrupt parenting skills put you in the mediocre-at-best category yourself. Since underachievers flock together, no doubt you'll use your political skills to get them a big job in a big company working for a bully breeder friend.

Coming to your company soon: graduate bully.

Perhaps you can recall the story of *The New York Times* journalist Jayson Blair, finally fired for plagiarizing. Even as a student, "he was alienating virtually everyone he worked with on ...the student newspaper." It was clear to everyone working with Blair that he had a "reckless disregard for the truth." Shortly after Howell Raines was appointed executive editor of *The Times,* a flurry of top correspondents left (one went on to win a Pulitzer Prize), and Jayson Blair arrived. Blair "came with a loaded reputation." Former coworkers at *The Boston Globe* staffers called friends, warning them about Blair, whose reputation was "for trafficking in nasty gossip, stealing story ideas and sucking up to superiors." Yet, management denied there was a problem despite repeated instances of plagiarism, and disregarded a "personnel file full of warnings and reprimands."

Higher-ups promoted him and showed favoritism by giving him the juiciest assignments.[41]

Much of management, of course, claimed they were unaware of any issues while watching the revolving door of most-talented employees migrating to their competitors on a regular basis. Raines, the bully breeder, bragged to his staff after Blair's departure: "You view me as inaccessible and arrogant."[42] That, and a lot more, too. "Raines also acknowledged that he had angered some staff members…by the time he 'stepped on a land mine named Jayson Blair.'"[43] Ooopsie. Where was Raines's boss during 25 years of angering staff members? A few years later, Raines wrote an article loaded with excuses in *Atlantic Monthly*, with the narcissistic title "My Times."

The Wall Street Journal explained "Why Jerks Get Ahead":

> …the really big jerks almost never acknowledge their devious behavior. In many ways, that's the secret to their success…. They tend to be narcissistic, arrogant, manipulative and goal-oriented. They trust no one and refuse to collaborate. They lack a capacity for empathy but are skilled at politics. Though they purposely disregard how they're coming off to colleagues or subordinates, they're often very good at sweet-talking bosses, who remain oblivious to their dastardly ways. The result: Good people get fed up and leave companies, while jerks get promoted.
>
> "I have seen entire departments wiped out, and the only ones left standing are the boss and his jerk," says John Hoover, an organizational leadership consultant whose new book is titled *How to Work for an Idiot*.

Writer Jeffrey Zaslow concludes, "And there isn't much you can do about it."[44]

Oh yes there is. Americans are doing something. They are quitting. They are retiring early. They are choosing not to work in places with a jerk in the works.

Good people don't want to work for someone who's known for supporting counterproductive rottweilers. It's time to put down the dirty dogs and stop shooting the messengers. It's shameful that the very people who have the power to retain incredible staff and drive the corporation toward unparalleled success are the ones who send out the message that mistreatment of staff will be rewarded and promoted. Who let the dogs out? It's time to fire the irresponsible gatekeeper too.

The business of the Catholic Church has been irreparably damaged by the negligence of bully breeders in Church leadership (or lack thereof). In this case, the bullies were picking on children. What the Church seems to be oblivious to is that the lay people's anger is not mainly at the pedophiles, but at the bully breeders' apathy, cover-ups, and denials. Instead of removing abusers from the priesthood where they had access to the public, they paid off victims or accused them of lying, transferred dishonest, known pedophiles to new locations providing unfettered access to virgin victims, and encouraged the proliferation of pedophiles by not openly punishing repeat offenders and by quieting victims. One state's attorney general reported: "The widespread abuse of children was due to an institutional acceptance of abuse and a massive and pervasive failure of leadership."[45]

The similarities to corporate America are staggering. The widespread abuse of employees is due to an institutional acceptance of abuse and a massive and pervasive failure of leadership. The leaders are screaming "integrity" while promoting and enabling people who destroy lives. Only 150 people were willing to accuse Father John Geoghan of abusing them. As with the corporate abuser, there was an endless rosary of victims. As one was paid off, another was targeted. The first complaint about Geoghan preying on children was in 1979. He wasn't removed from his parish position until 1992. There were 789 complaints of sexual abuse, but Robert Banks kept his position as bishop and Cardinal Bernard Law continued to preach the good word. Bully breeders encourage bullying: 237 priests in that archdiocese have been accused of sexual crimes against children.

Corporations pay off employees to leave quietly, or tell targets they're to blame or they imagined it. They transfer targets to other departments (often damaging the target's reputation or career), providing bullies with a fresh supply of new, normal, happy people to destroy. They do everything but remove the problem. The complaints pile up against the same few people, but the target who has no history of complaints is pushed out, transferred, dismissed, paid off, permanently damaged.

Rather than fix the problem, the bully breeders will send out, you guessed it, a survey and then set up, you guessed it, a committee. Because when there are incompetent people you don't want to deal with, you create another process role and process department. To deal with the public's outrage but not the problem, the Church's survey included "'thousands of hours' of interviews with experts, priests, victims and prelates" to uncover "possible causes of the abuse crisis."[46] No one wants a survey except for the bully breeders. Everyone else wants all abusers and their knowledgeable superiors removed from the priesthood, immediately.

Naively, corporations believe that the few decent employees remaining who might be wavering about leaving will stay if they claim they're "investigating" the issue with surveys and process pencil pushers. Whenever corporations claim they are investigating issues, they can be certain that the smartest employees are investigating how to get out of the toxic environment as quickly as possible. To stop the brain drain, stop the investigating and start extricating bullies, immediately.

What a coup for Catholicism if the cardinals and bishops had paraded the dysfunctional priests right out of their jobs and right into jail 10 years ago. The reason they didn't is the same reason that corporations support their dysfunctional people managers. They are friends of the abusers, have a history of supporting numerous abusers and their escalating abuse, and the abusers know too much information about them. What a coup for corporate America if managers removed people who hurt people. What a change if corporate America announced a zero-tolerance policy for bullying.

Watch the ones crying, "God bless America," with hands over hearts. While our government is slamming other countries for "crimes against humanity" and "civil rights abuses," we detain foreigners for years who have had no access to legal representation or a fair trail in Guantanamo (in Cuba, a country that U.S. citizens are prohibited from visiting as tourists because America is the land of the free, right?) and sweep Abu Ghraib abuses under the carpet. Our government employees destroy tapes showing torture of foreigners during interrogation. We punish other countries because they won't run their countries our way, because we are smarter about how to run things, as we demonstrated in the aftermath of Katrina. We invade and occupy countries simply because we don't like the guy who runs the place, because he's not democratically elected (although our best oil buddies in Saudi weren't either). Because we believe in free speech, we tag anyone who objects to spending billions to send our citizens to die in a country that has no weapons of mass destruction as unpatriotic and not "supporting our troops" (can you say "Dixie Chicks"?). To win popular support for an unpopular war, our government records and reports the "rescue" of soldier Jessica Lynch, covered for weeks on the news. Years later, her statement that the whole thing was staged lasted about 30 seconds on the same newscasts. Due to the terror embedded in Iraqi civilians after our invasion and occupation, more than 1,000 people are trampled to death on their way to pray, which gets less than 20 seconds of news coverage. Would it be OK for other countries to invade and occupy the U.S. because they don't like our president and because more than half the citizens who could be bothered to vote didn't vote for him? Hell, no. Is it any wonder that we've increased anti-American sentiment abroad? Are we surprised that our image as a people with ethics, innovation, and opportunity is diminishing? Is it any wonder America is getting a reputation for being the Bully Nation?

August 20, 1986, was a turning point for workplace bullies. On that day, Patrick Sherrill killed 14 fellow postal employees in Edmond, Oklahoma, and the term "going postal" was created. What changed is that bullies would officially be viewed as victims, and avenging bullies' targets would be officially labeled as "crazy."

Depending upon which biography of "Crazy Pat" you read, Patrick Sherrill lettered in three sports in high school, served in the Marine Corps, never had a criminal record, scored high on the U.S. Postal Service entrance exam, supported and resided with an ailing mother, and worked for two supervisors who ganged up on him on a regular basis.

According to the press, on August 19, 1986, Bill Bland and Richard Esser, Jr., post office supervisors, lambasted Sherrill. Although Sherrill was considered an "excellent worker," Bland threatened to fire Sherrill. Sherrill called union headquarters to ask for a transfer to the maintenance department. And the answer he got wasn't promising.[47]

We all know the result. At the end of his revengeful r
Sherrill killed himself, whereupon postal employees and the p-
circulated stories about his mental instability. Ironically, supervisor
Bill Bland, who had harpooned Sherrill about tardiness, lived because
he slept in late that morning and wasn't present at the massacre. No
stories were circulated about Bill Bland's mental instability for
continuing to verbally pummel an employee who was obviously
becoming depressed and had begged for a transfer to avoid further
conflict. What the public remembers from the post office massacre is
not how abusive bully *managers* are, but that there are a lot of crazy
workers at the post office. Did Bland remain in his job. Who is
responsible for the deaths? Sherrill, Bland, or both?

If Sherrill had had the resources to buy a franchise of Mail Boxes
Etc. (now the UPS Store) and managed his own business, the tragedy
probably would not have occurred. But then a veritable government
monopoly was hard to compete against, particularly when its
managers were whittling away at workers' self-esteem.

If you're wondering why Sherrill targeted coworkers, perhaps this
is the answer: **When reporting bullying to coworkers, 57 percent
side with the bully!** Twenty-eight percent, like Sherrill's union
according the newspapers, do nothing.[48]

We know that almost all the kids who have massacred teachers
and classmates felt picked on, but the stories are always focused on
the picked on student who finally cracked up and never on the mental
problems of the bullies who did the picking. Who can remember the
name of one bully who was responsible for student Rambos going on
the rampage? Where are they now? Were there *any* repercussions for
them and the role they played in the murder of their classmates and
teachers?

The data shows that most fellow employees are aware of the
bully's dysfunctional behavior and know employees who have
already left because of the bullying. Why would coworkers stay quiet
knowing that the bully has a history of choosing a new target as soon
as one is defeated?

Coworkers support bullies because it makes them feel better about
not getting off their duffs and leaving a company that's bad for their
health. You can justify staying in your go-nowhere "safe" job since
your coworker is unlikely to become a "Crazy Pat." However, if the

abusive postal managers were labeled "Rich the Wacko" and "Bill the Bully," you might see parallels to your own organization. Thus, we go on criticizing the Jerry Springer crazies, able to offer an opinion because we've watched it for ourselves perhaps on documentaries or news reports. It feels OK to be a bully bystander as long as the crazy leaves before he draws a gun on the audience.

The chances of getting shot at work are negligible. The chances of being the target of a bully manager are one in three. The world made Pat the problem so the post office was not a reflection of the dysfunctional environment they worked in. Making Pat the crazy one means we can laugh about "going postal" rather than cry about being surrounded by bullies.

The top reason most coworkers defend bullies is because they believe that they are unlikely to be the bully's next target. Remember that bullies choose the most popular, best educated, most dedicated, and *most competent*. If someone else in your team is always being bullied, it's typically a sign that you're not the cream of the crop, and you know it. Bullies and bullies' bosses do not surround themselves with cream players because comparatively, they would be encouraging their own replacement. (Competent workers train and hire staff who can replace them, because they have the skills and self-esteem to be promoted and hope to have their former position filled by someone who will support the company's growth.) Coworkers are fervent supporters of bullying because it helps them maintain a mirage of competency. When the company standard stays at the lowest common denominator, mediocre coworkers can rise to the top, or at least keep their jobs. If the choice for getting ahead in corporate America is between working your butt off or letting a bully batter a more qualified colleague, it's an easy decision if you don't have the brains or skill to compete. A bully supporter is a hanger-on— someone whose main objective is to stay unnoticed (while sapping salary and benefits) to stay employed. Most large corporations were then happier with the hangers-on than those who would surf out front and hang ten. The best surfers caught the self-employment wave right out of the cesspool.

How do employees feel about working with the hangers-on? In a McKinsey study, individuals who worked with underperformers said it made them want to leave the company (86 percent), stopped them from making larger contributions (82 percent), hurt their career development (81 percent), and prevented them from learning (76 percent). Despite this damage to employee retention and performance, only 7 percent claimed that their "company is actively moving underperformers out of the company or into less critical roles."[49] Coincidentally, that's the same percentage of companies that the former survey stated were taking punitive action against bullies.

Bullies and under-performers are one and the same. The corporate officers who are denying that there are bullies in their ranks are also claiming that they exit underperformers. There's hardly a large corporation out there that isn't grandstanding its "policy" of removing underperformers. Yet, only 7 percent of employees at mid- or large-sized companies say this is true. Considering that even the underperformers in McKinsey's survey agreed their companies were safe havens for losers like them, there's not a lot of reason to stay in a larger company. Since 93 percent of bigger companies are the homes of underperformers, you can deduce that birds of a feather are flocking together. Your chances of succeeding if you open your own business are much greater than your chances of working in a large company that's not a nest of incompetent losers. It's a better bet to spread your wings and fly the coop. Hence, the brain drain.

While these corporations are doing nothing to make their work environments loserfree, hundreds of employees are quitting or being paid off with agreements laced with gag orders. Why aren't these gag orders reciprocal? In other words, if the layoff agreement or dismissal agreement has a clause that the ex-employee can't defame the company or its employees, shouldn't there be a clause regarding the employees' freedom to badmouth the ex-employee? Why would companies incorporate gag orders into their standard dismissal agreements unless they had consistently mismanaged people or situations? If there were nothing bad to say, they wouldn't have to make employees promise to not say bad things about them. When employees have been treated fairly and consistently, they're not angry with the manager or the company if dismissed. You shouldn't need gag orders but it's no wonder they are so prevalent. People being fired and laid off are working for others who are so incompetent, they sparkle in comparison. The Bureau of Labor Statistics listed the national employee turnover rate at 40.7 percent for 2006. It's simple mathematics to calculate the quality of people exiting, either under their own or another's volition. Since 93 percent of bigger companies are not dismissing underperformers, guess who the 40.7 percent are? Gag.

For 21 weeks, the novel *The Devil Wears Prada* remained on *The New York Times* Best-Seller List. It chronicles the workplace goings-on of the assistant of a "highly successful" fashion magazine editor who is the boss from hell. While the demands of the omnipresent boss unravel the assistant's friendships and family relationships, everyone insists that the assistant's position is one "a million girls would die for."[50] The protagonist's final business decision is consistent with the statistics on bullied assistants. Judging by the success of the book, millions of readers were able to recount or relate to the behavior described. Bully bosses are so prevalent that their existence is almost accepted as normal in the business workplace. We read tongue-in-cheek, comical accounts to laugh, lest we cry.

Why do we love bullies? Why are we glued to *The Apprentice* when Omarosa is calling her colleagues "idiots," when Janice Dickinson is berating hopefuls applying for contracts at her modeling agency, or when Tiffany "New York" Pollard is telling every suitor to "Get the f*** out of here" while her bully-breeding mother Sister Patterson confronts the daters with snipes regarding their height or mental acuity? Why is it entertaining to watch Simon Cowell demolishing American idols? What have we become?

Because bullying awards celebrity status, corporate bullies brag to the press about how mean they are. Viacom's COO Mel Karmazin is described by *Fortune* magazine as cultivating a "reputation for being a tough boss" and having a "pugnacious, intimidating style." When the *Fortune* interviewer told Karmazin that Viacom's staff no longer were afraid of him, he said, "I hope you don't print that, because my image is very important to me. The words 'nice guy' and 'Mel Karmazin' better not be written in the same sentence." Since Karmazin's executive colleagues also described him as "funny"[51] (birds of a feather?), hopefully this statement was his attempt at humor. Somebody's got it wrong. Karmazin is either not nice, or not funny, or both.

When I interviewed people who recounted episodes of being bullied at work, none of them thought it was nice or funny. In fact, almost everyone I raised the subject with had either been attacked or had a close friend who had suffered from bullying. Years later they were still angry, not at the bully, but at their companies for allowing and therefore encouraging it. Among them, there was disbelief that the behavior that was so apparent and disturbing to them and their colleagues could be supported by their superiors and colleagues. Almost all had left large corporations or were planning their exit strategies.

There was no problem compiling tales of bullying, because so much of it continues. People who shared stories conveyed common practices. The similar brazen behaviors of their tormenters include:

1. **The bully was a chronic liar, whose lies were accepted and believed without investigation by senior management.**
   When management took punitive action against the victims, all refuted the bully's claims, every time. Yet, management continued to believe that *all* the victims were liars and the bully was honest. They neglected to question or verify the bully's stories before reacting against the victim.

   The lying started with the bully's résumé and fabricated qualifications, so an easy way to dismiss the bully would have been to uncover misinformation given on the application form. A survey by employment screening company HireRight revealed that 20 percent of all resumes had fraudulent degrees, 40 percent had inflated salaries, and 80 percent misled.[52]

   As a former expatriate and avid world traveler, I was fascinated when a job applicant told me about her relevant work experience in Hong Kong. "How did you get a work permit?" I asked, knowing they were hard to come by, particularly for recent graduates. The woman told me she couldn't remember how she got her work permit.

   I told my peer who was managing the group where the woman would be working about the odd answer. He and the other interviewers gave her the thumbs-up. I blackballed her. I told HR, "She's a liar. I doubt she worked in Hong Kong at all. Nobody *forgets* how she got her work permit. If she's brazen enough to lie about a work permit, it'll be easy to find a bigger pack of lies in her application." Lying is a chronic condition. Sure enough, the background check that she'd been warned about before applying indicated that she'd inflated her previous salary by 30 percent. As a result, she was not hired. The HR manager was laid off a month later.

Joni, whose resume listed her Yale degree and extensive experience, was only at her job two months (most of it spent lunching with the top brass) before she started lying to get her boss's job. Joni wept as she told how her boss Bob personally "ripped her to shreds" in front of all her colleagues in meeting. Actually, Joni had stormed out of the meeting after one of the other attendees asked her for a report that was five weeks late. After Joni documented a list of fairy tales about Bob's negative interactions with other staff that she claimed to have witnessed, he was fired.

The first time Bob had heard about the accusations was during the firing. Of course, Bob inquired how the company could have so many make-believe stories. Who would say such things? Had one person made all the accusations? Had the company ever confirmed the accusations with *any* of the alleged victims? Had the company asked anyone else in the meeting what happened?

Because HR's primary responsibility these days is preventing law suits (because employees have so many reasons to sue companies), the company went ahead with the firing and promoted Joni.

Within weeks, Joni's new staff bitterly complained to management and HR that Joni couldn't possibly have the experience she claimed to have. Joni, with a shiny, new title that was way over her head and certainly her capabilities, quickly found another job at a competitive firm, with an even bigger title and salary, and lots of inside information to share. A few weeks later, Joni was fired, apparently for lying about her Yale degree.

Seventy-three percent of the general public believe that CEOs and Fortune 500 executives "cheat often."[53] They didn't mean on their wives, but we know that goes on, too. Forty-three percent of high school students believe "a person has to lie or cheat sometimes to succeed" and 37 percent said they'd be willing to lie "if it would help me get a good job."[54] Corporations are losing honest and moral people because the public has watched the dishonest and immoral rise to the top. The conclusion: It seems that it's imperative to lie to be successful in a large corporation.

ABC Primetime aired a segment entitled "Caught Cheating" in which 74 percent of high school students admitted to cheating on an exam in the past year. Half of the faculty members admitted that they ignored it. About the same percentage "moved up" to cheat in college. Guess which college group had the highest incidence of cheating. No surprises here—the business majors. Said one future CEO, "I think cheating prepares you to be more cut-throat and more successful in business." Students corroborated that grades matter most and integrity matters little to colleges, parents, or hiring companies. Like big business, "everything is about the grade...nobody looks at how you got it."[55] The theme of the cheaters was that they were emulating how they would succeed in the future, based upon how others had made it to the top. The cheaters stated their employment goals. None wanted to have his or her own company. None of them probably could.

The goal of the bully's lies is to get others to gang up on the victim. Bullies are actually cowards and will move on to another victim when outnumbered. Beware believing coworkers' stories. Never repeat a negative story about a coworker.

Liar, Liar, Pants on Fire. The 13 ways to spot a liar were listed in the previous chapter. It's not expected that bully breeders will remember them or use them to decipher who the liar is, because evidence could have been easily uncovered by talking to a few people or reading a few e-mails. The bully breeder is living a lie, and giving the liar a living.

2. **Bullies are experts at deception**.
   That Hong King Kong was a real charmer, saying all the things the interviewers wanted to hear. She almost got in the door. Had she become the new bully on the block, her manager would have backed her up rather than admit he made the wrong decision.

   The second characteristic cited was that **bullies were persuasive, charming, and endearing toward senior management**. They spent all their time managing up. The perception of women bullies as loud and aggressive is far from the truth. They often use baby voices or giggly girl tactics to befriend male managers. They can cry on demand.

Bullies scored significantly higher than average on managing up and management manipulation, and lower than average on managing staff- and job-related skills.

3. **Lunch and après work socializing was top on the list for bullies**.
   While the targets were doing work, the bullies were doing lunch— not with clients, with colleagues. The bullies were cleverly probing into the private lives of senior managers over long lunches and lengthy social sessions. They could be found in the office after hours only when a senior advocate or prospective promoter with power was present. Their home relationships were fraught with discord, so socializing with management was a convenient way to avoid family issues. They charmingly appeared in the haunts of key work and community influencers, including churches and bars.

   Even career advisers are telling job seekers that accepting and supporting the incompetence and social habits of management is the way to become successful in today's corporate environment. Being good at your job or driving corporate success is unlikely to hoist you up the corporate ladder.

   I didn't know what to think when I read this advice from Carol Kleiman, career/job business columnist for the *Chicago Tribune*, concurring that people on the "fast track" to upper management are best at engineering great relationships with upper managers:

   > I have some additional suggestions, some inside tips, on the nitty-gritty of how to partner with your boss...:
   >
   > • Join the same golf or health club as your boss.
   > • Cover up for his/her long lunches.
   > • Do all the work your boss is supposed to do.[56]

   Does she have the same sense of humor as Karmazin? What happened to being the best candidate to do the job? You can't be outraged when you realize that she is simply serving a dose of reality. If you are going to work for someone else in a big company, chances are you will have a manager who does long lunches, at the club, and doesn't do a lot of work. The corporate world is a dog's dinner—a mess. Was this distasteful to me because the state of today's corporations seems hopeless? Or because I knew I could never consider a second helping of corporate America because my golf game is so weak?

4. **Bullies talk about people; workers talk about business.**
   Every opportunity with a senior manager was a chance to talk about what somebody said or did, rather than the products and sales. Typically, they played to the breeders' insecurities, creating fables of how others had criticized the breeders' or CEO's personality, actions, or business plan. The rare product opinions or ideas they offered as their own were stolen from their victims. Gossip and secrets about people are their bargaining chips. When a colleague has more to say about other people than about what he's accomplishing, it's because he's accomplishing nothing but bullying.

4. **The bully has at least one strong advocate in a senior management position.**
   That person is often the person who hired or promoted him or her and can't admit he screwed up. The bullying starts only after the support is established. The bully often jokes with the advocate about the abuse. Once the breeder is aware of the abuse or laughs with the bully about it, the breeder's fate is sealed. Confronting the bully means confronting the breeder's lack of integrity. The breeder has become a bully advocate.

   The bully positions the target as incompetent and dispensable to human resources staff and management. Charmed by the bully, these groups often become pawns in the ruse, interrogating, threatening, and terminating the slow parade of innocent workers.[57] At some stage, the employer knows he or she has been duped, often revealed by the victim. However, most are angered by the *unveiling* of their stupidity rather than by the bully who's used them. They go about eliminating the one who disclosed their naïveté rather than the one who exploited it. After all, they didn't feel stupid while being deceived by the flatterer; they felt stupid when it was explained to them how they were used.

This is why no one wanted to hear how Private Jessica Lynch was brought to a hospital, treated, and cared for by those "terrorist" Arabs and was free to walk out as soon as she was well enough to. We feel stupid knowing we were fooled by the staged rescue where there was obviously no one preventing the soldiers from going in or out of the hospital. The only people who had cause to feel in danger for their lives were the Iraqi doctors, nurses, and patients who stood by while American soldiers waved loaded weapons during the "rescue."

When breeders are no longer useful to the bully, they quickly find that the company is pushing them out. After being laid off, one breeder whined, "The victim was right about everything. I tried to defend her once, but they started giving me a hard time." Boo, hoo. Save your whining. Breeders who refuse to stop attacks by their staff or on their staff are incompetent at managing. The breeder is still unemployed after a year and doesn't possess the job skills to set up his own company. Stupid is as stupid does.

6. In team meetings, **bullies rarely share** what projects they're working on (usually because they're not really working).
   But they rarely resist criticizing, interrupting, or rolling their eyes at what everyone else shares, and insist those who aren't sharing so they won't be skewered are "not team players." The criticizing is done in one on ones, behind closed doors, where the victim can't defend himself.

7. **Obsessed with the victim's competence, bullies practically stalk the victims.**
   One bumbler would review his peers' work on the company intranet, then fly out to the client's office the day before the presentation to pitch the idea as his own. The departmental manager (an incompetent bully breeder) ignored dozens of complaints about the stalker, losing all his top staff. After three years, when he was down to the last group manager who could do his work, the departmental manager demoted the stalker, making him report to a subordinate. The subordinate fired the stalker a few weeks later. Yup, another dirtbag getting someone else to do the dirty work.

8. **Crying "wolf."**

When caught, the bully claims to be the victim. Despite damning e-mails, voice mails, and eye-witnesses (ignored by management), the bully produces another hard luck sympathy-inducing story line that the breeders and HR suck up their noses. The breeders chime in by shearing the victim, saying how they and the other 10 victims all simply "misunderstood" the wolf. The sheep are then told that to demonstrate they are "team players," they should try to "just work it out" with the wolf; in other words, they should stop bleating. If the sheep insist upon not returning to the butchery or that the shepherd protects them from the wolf, the sheep will be labeled as "difficult" and scheduled for slaughter.

To shut up the complainers, management might warn the bullies there would be repercussions if they did "it" again, even though this was the 10th time they had done "it" and had received a similar warning each time. Bullies knew they were idle threats delivered by those with idle hands.

9. I heard this one from so many formerly bullied entrepreneurs, I had to look it up. The majority of cases relayed to me about bullying cited that the **bullies or bully breeders were involved in extramarital or inappropriate affairs with coworkers**.

A May 2002 Gallup poll indicated that more than 90 percent of Americans believe that extramarital affairs are morally wrong. Ironically, onlookers who thought infidelity was immoral believed the immoral adulterer was truthful about his/her behavior in the workplace. Workplace affairs in most cases were open, flaunted, or widely acknowledged, yet it was as if people believed that immorality at lunchtime or in the evening with a coworker had no correlation to other immoral or unethical behavior in the workplace. In other words, management wanted to believe that immoral cheaters were only immoral cheaters during a small portion of the day or night and model employees during the rest of their waking hours. Let's open the doors of our prisons since thieves aren't stealing 24 hours a day. They're wonderful people for 23 hours of the day, so let's let felons work in our midst. It's no coincidence that the cheater is also a liar. "I did not have sex with that..." Follow the leader?

In half of the 6,000 cases reported to *Bully OnLine*, the bully was having an affair with another employee. Says *Bully Online:*

> The affair has little to do with friendship, and a lot to do with strategic alliance in pursuit of power, control, domination and subjugation. In a further quarter of cases, there's often a suspected affair....
>
> If the bully is a female in a junior position, she finds a weak male in a senior position.... Once promotion is gained...he is ditched and another adopted....
>
> If the bully is a male in a senior position, he is often sleeping with a secretary or office administrator, as this is where he gets information and spreads his disinformation.[58]

Whether it's two married (but not to each other) employees involved or the creaky boss making out with the inept 20-something bella in his department who is suddenly promoted to vice president, these improprieties gave other bullies fodder for blackmail. Bullies who were privy to these illicit relationships used the information as power to get away with everything. Fire me, they'd imply, and I'll snitch, to your spouse, to *your* boss, to everybody. Targets claimed that the spouses and bosses appeared to be the only people who *weren't* aware of the inappropriate relationships.

Considered a family man and a nice guy by his superiors, the same type of guy who is cheating with one of his junior staff is violating the company's gift/tax policy by "asking" a vendor for two free tickets to the Super Bowl. He doesn't consider any of these acts unethical. Because he's "special." Yes, he certainly is.

You meet those special people every day. They run red lights, double and illegally park (but only for a short while, which suits their convenience), and hold cell phones or text while driving. That's because laws were made for the little people, not them. They think of themselves as good people—because they're just so special.

10. **The bullies have tenure**.
They've been around, so they have established alliances, and have cemented their relationships with senior advocates. They

also tend to be the least productive. Employees are most productive in the first few years at a job. Gallup research indicates that there is an inverse relationship between the level to which a worker feels satisfied by his or her job, and length of service. Dissatisfied, disengaged employees negatively impact profit and sales and *customer* satisfaction.[59]

11. **Bullying isn't their only psychological problem.**
A no-brainer. No, they're not all psychopaths, but you won't be surprised if you find they also have low self-esteem, drug/alcohol problems, are histrionic ("excessive emotionality and attention-seeking," creating drama because they feel their lives are empty), are depressed, anxious, narcissistic, or exhibit road rage.

There you have it: 11 ways bullies and bully breeders identify themselves. After senior management incompetence, the most prevalent reason why most of the interviewees left is that they were aware of countless formal complaints made about the same few bullies, all of which were met with eyes wide shut by the people who purported to have integrity, to promote and reward the best people, and to care about the future of the corporation.

"In the majority of cases, the bullying that comes to light is only the tip of an iceberg of wrongdoing. From lying on their [sic] [resume] to falsifying the circumstances around the departure from their [sic] previous job, the serial bully is almost always misappropriating budgets, leaking confidential information, breaching rules...whilst making false claims about their [sic] own work and achievements. Indiscretion, maladministration, malpractice and negligence are also common. But often, glib, superficial charm combined with an exceptional verbal facility ensure that the serial bully is able to talk their [sic] way out of every corner."[60]

The final decision for the bullied to leave their companies was made because management was standing in the bully's corner, helping to mop the forehead and put brass knuckles in the gloves of their top fighter for another round.

The existence of bullies is apparent, so let's stop claiming we don't know why the best people are no longer loyal to big business. Dr. Gary Namie, a psychologist who is probably the most respected authority on workplace bullying, asks us to remember that **the bully**

targets the "best and brightest workers: those who are technically competent, independent, possess good social skills and have strong ethics.... Do a cost-benefit analysis of tolerating this person while all the other good, talented people you spent good money to train flee. Is it worth keeping the one when you've lost the 25 in the last three years?"[61]

Stanford's Jeffrey Pfeffer says, "Loyalty isn't dead—but toxic companies are driving people away. There isn't a scarcity of talent— but there is a growing unwillingness to work for toxic organizations."[62]

No one wants to work in an underperforming business. But for the most talented, it's a bigger deal than working for a financially reputable corporation. After September 11, 2001, most Americans put a higher priority on home and health. The people who worked the hardest, the most dedicated, the ones who arrived before 10 a.m. to get an early start on 9/11 were blown to pieces. Is it worth it? Most Americans are deciding it's not. We're no longer willing to work in dangerous companies. It's not worth being in the path of the terrorists. It's not worth getting sick about. America's business leaders need to make it safe to come back to big companies by clearing out the people laying the land mines and by preventing the bomber pilots from entering the building.

I should have gone long ago. On my way to the Phnom Penh airport, I looked out the window of my taxi. My mind flashed back to the doe eyes of the pretty beggar at the border who was missing a leg.

The orange morning haze made me squint. A motorbike passed. In her smart uniform, a tiny student waved at me with her other arm wrapped tightly around her father's waist. Her plastic schoolbag bounced against her back as the motorbike swerved through traffic on the way to school. Her smaller brother was holding the handlebars, cradled in his father's lap where he felt secure. Education. A chance for a better job, a better future?

As the taxi passed through the channel of orderly drivers, I couldn't help thinking about how fine everything appeared on the surface. The motorbike on its way to school pulled alongside the window of my taxi again. The schoolgirl with the smiling eyes waved again, eager for me to return her friendly signal. Again I thought of the girl at the border. Perhaps it wasn't a land mine, but merely a motorcycle accident. Merely. I waved and she smiled. Delighted with the response, she waved harder and faster. A little would never be enough. My eyes wandered lower; the spinning wheels of the motorbike were hypnotic.

The night before, I'd finally felt well enough to venture out after being bedridden for two days. I couldn't leave Cambodia without visiting the famous Foreign Correspondents Club that overlooks the junction of the Tonle Sap, Mekong, and Bassac rivers. I'd been starved and prone for two days. My hotel was only a few blocks from the club, and I was pleased to be walking again. The gentle exercise felt good. The usual crew of moto drivers (motorcycle taxis) were at the gate, soliciting aggressively for my business. There were always a dozen or so standing there beside their vehicles despite the hotel being almost empty. They took turns and the moment I appeared on the hotel steps, I was assigned to the moto driver with the gray T-shirt. "Taxi, taxi?" he asked. "Cheap, really cheap," he pleaded.

"I'm just going around the corner," I replied. "I want to walk."

The gossip machine was well-oiled in Phnom Penh, so I was certain they knew I'd been ill and holed up in the room for days. Not only did I want the exercise, but I didn't want to barf all over Mr. Gray Moto should I feel a sudden urge. Mr. Gray Moto had failed in his chance to get me to hop on the back of his bike. Time was up and the remaining Mr. Motos moved in. "Ma'am, ma'am," they circled, each with a different sales pitch to get me to take their moto two blocks away. "You'll feel better if you take my moto."

"Thank you, no." I managed to be polite despite feeling weak both physically and mentally from being harassed and mobbed by beggars continually since crossing the Thai border (things have changed in Siem Reap now). I was aware there was no work, and no source of income, for a large percentage of the population. The constant badgering and number of beggars here was intense and tiring. I smelled their oozing desperation. A moto ride would have made me feel worse. I passed through the gate.

Mr. Gray Moto lost it. He started screaming at the other moto drivers, twisting his body in agony as the veins bulged in his neck. It was as if someone was stabbing him repeatedly. They were pains of despair. His screams dissolved into sobs as I walked away, melting into the dusk. Mr. Gray Moto had not solicited a single fare in almost a week and as a result had not eaten in two days either. I was going to eat at the Foreign Correspondents Club, and he was going home face his wife and children for whom he'd not provided a meal in days.

The look of fear. At the onset of my illness, I'd wandered the Killing Fields of Choeung Ek then, in reverse order, visited Security Prison S-21 (the Tuol Sleng Musuem) where the brightest and best were remanded and tortured first. Photos of the detainees, certain of their limited future, lined the walls. Stark fear in their eyes. I started to sweat and feel dizzy. I desperately wanted to leave. Dashing to escape the hundreds of bulging monochrome eyes, I clutched a trash can and vomited.

I gingerly climbed the steps to the Foreign Correspondents Club's roof bar and sat by the edge watching the bustle on the street below in the yellow street lights. Oasis. I ordered a pizza. Everything was fine on the surface. I imaged the ancient city of Angkor 1,000 years ago, with its fine, ornate temples. The most desirable place to live, with the greatest artisans and architects. The land of dreams come true and civilization on the cusp of happily ever after. Now just a pile of rubble surrounded by land mines. All because of a minority of mindless bullies—managers of mass destruction—who were determined that everyone live in turmoil and despair rather than allow one person to succeed, and lead everyone to a better life. For years, they deterred countless tourists, the country's greatest potential source of income, and left the masses desperate, begging for business or a way out. At least I could leave. Those who can, do.

CHAPTER

8

Picturing the Future: Teamwork

November 4, 1992. Wherever we went, people pointed and stared. We would never pass this way again—in a British double-decker bus, built in 1958, reconstructed into a camper. The top deck had been converted to bunk beds; the bottom level had a kitchenette among the seats. There was no toilet. The world was our toilet. Under a bridge, behind a bush, behind the bus. Eleven of us were on the overland journey from London to Kathmandu in the diesel double-decker hotel.

On this date, we crossed the border from Turkey into Iran. Ayatollah Khomeini had been dead for three years. Four years earlier, fathers and sons had stopped dying in the Iran-Iraq war. The previous day, Bill Clinton had won the U.S. presidential election.

The fact that the U.S. government publicly sided with and supported Saddam during the eight-year-long Iran-Iraq War left a bad taste in Iranians mouths. Then, and years later, the Iraqis had the same thing for dinner. The Iran-Contra affair indicated that the U.S. government was supplying weapons not only to Saddam, but also to the ayatollah's fighters at the same time. "The enemy of my enemy is my friend." The U.S. had many enemies, errr friends, in this region, and nothing much had changed in a decade. The plan worked, perpetuating geographical instability, while feeding both warriors with weapons. Once Iran backed down (eight years later), the U.S.

stepped in to destroy the victor. Boy, the analogies you could make to corporate infighting here!

While in Iran, I met no other Americans. I have dual citizenship and was traveling on my British passport. So "technically," I was a Brit. There were a Canadian and two other Brits, and the others were Kiwis or Aussies. It didn't matter. Iranian people were warm and welcoming to all nationalities.

I can't remember whether it was the Iranian or American government (not people, government) that was mostly responsible for discouraging Yanks from spreading their greenbacks around. Frankly, there weren't many tourists at all, fewer than 2,000 annually with many of those being spouses of Iranians or overseas Iranians. The lack of tourists was shocking in a country loaded with breathtaking archaeological ruins, a rich history, delicious watermelon smoothies, mountains of cheap pistachios, and delightful people.

The warning from the U.S. Department of State was: "Persons who violate Iranian laws such as those concerning proper dress, may face penalties that are, at times, severe." Iranian law dictated that only a woman's face, hands, and feet could be exposed (atypical in the Middle East). Showing any hair was a no-no. Some women gripped the *chadors* in their teeth to keep them from falling off their heads.

The border guards asked us to exit the bus. We women gathered up our billowing *chadors* and *abayas* in our free hands as we awkwardly descended the curving staircase from the top deck, being careful not to trip. It was our debut in Islamic dress, and while we felt incredibly silly as if going to a Halloween party, being disrespectful of our hosts' way of life was unlikely to speed the processing of our passports. We sat in a waiting room with stale green walls and pictures of a couple of ayatollahs on the wall.

What *were* they doing? There appeared to be no other work for the checkpoint guards to do, yet after an hour, they hadn't begun checking our vehicle. We soon realized that we were the entertainment. Once we left, the day would dissolve into just another humdrum day of the usual Mohammads and Asads driving delivery trucks. It wasn't every day that a double-decker bus full of Westerners landed on this lonely station.

"Passports, passports," called the Persian commander. As we walked to the passport control room, out a sliver of window we saw a group of uniformed officers entering the bus and some looking underneath. They went through our luggage, not really looking for contraband, but simply interested in what we brought with us. Underwear, books or magazines, underwear, toiletries, underwear, whatever.

Our passports were handed in together, and while our visa photos were in Islamic dress, our passport photos obviously were not. The Persian fellow behind the desk lifted a corner of his mouth, and looked up, directly at me. I knew why he was looking for me. I'd made a bad decision.

When I got my British passport in the 1980s, glamour photos were the rage. I'm sure you recall them. A professional makeup artist and hair stylist made you up to look like a movie star. With dangling earrings and more Cover Girl than a high-street hooker, your sultry portrait was taken against a starry backdrop. Not being photogenic, I decided to maximize the opportunity by having passport photos taking during the same sitting. Minus the dangling earrings and fuchsia organza wrap, there I was with the same sultry look. Bad idea. A bad idea I'd have to live with for the next 10 years. Worse was that it was the best photo of me there was.

We must have been boring, as were the contents of our luggage. Within three hours, we were on our merry way. This part of Iran was fairly desolate. Our bus driver, Rowdy (because he wasn't), would drive for hours without seeing a town.

Out of nowhere came the first police patrol car. The police stopped the bus and stepped inside saying, "Passport, passport," with accents straight out of *Saturday Night Live*. We blobs hurriedly adjusted our headgear, while Rowdy handed over the stack of passports. (Our passports were always kept together since they were so often requested.) They asked us to exit the bus, while they filtered through the contents of our luggage. Underwear, books and magazines, underwear, toiletries, underwear, whatever. They stared long and hard at the pictures in the women's passports, hair and all. Soon bored, they got in their car laughing together about who knows what.

A few hours later, we were stopped again. Part of the problem was that all the bunk beds were on the same floor, which meant that unmarried women and men were sleeping in the same quarters. I'm certain they imagined that the promiscuous Westerners were having wild sex parties because we noticed that after nightfall, the double-decker was stopped more frequently. Sometimes Rowdy would drive through the night and sleep during the day when we were touring the sights. We always had to sleep in our blobwear for the periodic onslaught of uniformed visitors.

At 2 a.m. on the way to Esfahan, Rowdy was pulled over again. The blobs were nestled, all snug in their sleeping bags, when out on the doorstep, there arose such a clatter, we prayed they'd be tired and just scatter. No such luck. "Passport, passport." We all pretended not to be awakened by the commotion. We knew not to turn our faces to the window, or they'd wake us to check our identity. So we always tried to stay absolutely still with our eyes shut feigning sleep while they walked inches from us, ensuring the women were properly covered, and wondering what kind of nuts would travel across Asia in a double-decker bus (valid!).

Passports in hand, they climbed the stairs, and I knew one of them was eyeing my glamour photo. I heard the name as it appeared in my passport at the bottom of the steps: "Barbara, Barbara." (Always with an echo.) I was being singled out. Suddenly, images of trying to outrun two Iranian policemen, in my *abaya*, flashed through my mind. At the top of the stairs, one started to check each bunk, trying to match the face with the passport photo. "Barrrbarrra, Barrrrbarrrra," he half whispered. I was quickly learning the advantages of being "under cover." He was so close I could hear him breathe. His face was close. He was definitely in my personal space. "Barrrbarra." My eyelids didn't flutter. I didn't flinch. Neither did my fellow blobs. My glamour photo could have been any of us. Without makeup, covered up, we blended. No one stood out. No one was different. No individuality. Like bits of mercury that collect and soak up debris then blend into a seamless mass, we were indistinguishable. We blobs, we all looked the same. The police, maybe they were all the same too. Not enough to do. Probably looking for excitement by digging through baggage or preventing others from traveling forward. Not knowing what they were looking for, and not finding it. "Team players," going with the flow to maintain an aura of power, while actually having none. Protected by similar cookie-cutter cutouts under cover. He strolled away, accomplishing nothing, defeated.

"He's just not a team player," Desmond's coworker told the boss.

We hear a lot these days about team playing and how that's a good thing in corporate America. To stop the corporate brain drain, the concept of "team" must be abandoned, and individualism, entrepreneurship should be reinstated within each organization.

In school, did you hear the valedictorian complaining about lack of teamwork? How often do you hear the top contributor complaining about team playing at work? Is the sole-proprietor multimillionaire moaning and stomping his feet because the other guys aren't being "team players"?

The only players who are advocating "one for all and all for one" are those who make the smallest contribution and need others. Team playing requires that the exceptional contributors dumb down to become average. It's time to raise the bar.

Summary: The advocates of teamwork are those who want to steal the credit or share the blame, because they're incapable of going it alone.

Relative to large corporations, entrepreneurs and small-business owners work and play better with vendors, customers, employees, and other entrepreneurs. They aren't talking the talk about teamwork, diversity, meritocracy. They just do it. Each person in their tiny organizations has a job to do. If the job is done well, they continue the business relationship. If the person stinks, they find another who will do it right. The average small business has three employees. There's no room for a slacker. Each person must deliver competently, or the entire business will fail. An SBO cannot afford to spend resources on a nonperformer. Small-business owners will ditch the weak link rather than let the business fail. This isn't the culture in large companies. Small-business owners got tired of picking up the slack for the "team players" in their former jobs. In a small business, if three people work a total of 150 hours, that's 150 hours of production. In large corporations, if three people work 150 hours, generally:

Thing One works about 20 hours playing politics, going to meetings, and sending provocative e-mails;

Thing Two is a project or process manager working 50 hours doing work that the other people should be incorporating into part of their jobs, so it's mostly duplication of effort;

Thing Three is working 80 hours a week trying to get anything done, cajoling people to do their own jobs so the product will operate, and writing CYA (cover your ass) memos to ward off the people attacking him because he might get promoted for being better and working harder than they did. Thing Three (also known as Bachelor Number Three because his entire life is work) is the one who's going to leave and start his own business. He's good at math, too. If he puts his energy into having his own company, he can reduce his hours by 25 percent, have a personal life again, and actually create something he is proud of, instead of CYA memos.

For Thing Three, it's worth leaving just to leave behind the pile of "it's not my job" memos from people who can't seem to find anything that *is* their job but still get the corner office and receive promotions, awards, bonuses, and trading cards. Is it any wonder there's a brain drain? Start your own company and you can have all four corners and not have to look at stupid memos from inept people. What a bargain!

"In a study by William M. Mercer, Inc., 25 percent of workers said they were capable of doing 50 percent more work."[1] So much for "team players." Your own experience will tell you that the people with the fewest good ideas are also doing the least work. No wonder they want to be part of a team. Is it any wonder that team players rarely become entrepreneurs?

Entrepreneurs don't hire process managers, project managers, or quality managers. They are in charge of the process, project, and quality—and succeed or fail by their performance. If you started a new company, would a process, project, and quality manager be your second, third, or fourth employee? Of course not. Would you spend valuable sales revenue or venture capital to put those people on your limited payroll or hire an outside firm to do those "tasks"? Isn't it time we held all individuals accountable for the quality of the projects they manage?

You've seen the numbers indicating that a growing number of corporate workers (particularly women) have been leaving to start new businesses or are planning to start new businesses in the near future, and a growing number of teenagers and college students plan to avoid corporate life all together. America's corporations are convincing no one that they are willing to change, or allow change.

America's corporate brain drain will intensify as the valedictorians reject corporate offers, 60-somethings retire early from deaf employers to start hobby jobs or consulting, and anyone else who can find a way out does. No one is thrilled about staying in staid, dying corporations where creative accounting props up stock prices that are no longer driven by creative products.

"An Army of One" was the U.S. Army's brilliant recruitment slogan that sang the praises of the individual, until they blew it up in 2005. Said its Army Reserve ad: "You can spend the rest of your days telling the same old stories. Or you can go get some new ones." The message: "The Army empowers individuals to succeed by strengthening them mentally, physically, and emotionally to ultimately master any challenge—equipping them to do things they never thought they could do." Empowers. Individuals. Succeed. Master. Equipping.

There is no malarkey about teamwork. **When you have all the best and brightest individuals, you have the best "team."** When **every** person is an outstanding innovator, manager, strategist, tactician, *and* implementer, you have the best company. When you hire people who have only one or two of these skills, you fill in the blanks with process roles, project managers, quality managers, strategy managers, customer relationship managers, etc., but you still end up with half a brain. The resultant brainstorming, or blamestorming, will never make up for having an entire company of smarts, people with brains that are firing on all cylinders, no matter what the conditions. The company with the brightest sparks, the highest-grade fuel, those recently tuned to the latest industry specs, the most experience, the best design, and the impeccably maintained will win the race. The brain drain continues because those who want to use all their minds, all their capabilities, are tired of pretending they have half a brain, usually the same half that the half-witted have.

In companies where everyone is competent, nobody's whining about the person who's not the "team player," because she doesn't need him. She is complete. She is whole. Each person is capable of creating the next big thing and putting it into the market with success. In a company of three, there are three times the ideas. Who cares about the team player who's dependent upon others to make it, to look good, to parse the blame, to get promoted. Instead of equipping individuals with what they need to "master any challenge," corporate America has encouraged those who want to contribute most to leave and fight on the opposite side, creating products and services that directly compete.

As long as the sandbox is crowded with idle hands, the minority of builders are going to keep leaving to create their own sandbox. It's time to stop believing that we can train, mentor, or incentivize current VIPs to design or build anything new. Let's kick out people who have been kicking down the sand castles and kicking sand in the faces of the builders. It's time for the people who have proven that they can build sand castles on their own to be crowned.

Buying an entrepreneur's bigger sand castle will not save the old kingdom. Once the sand castle is managed by the big old kingdom, it will start to crumble for the same reasons the old kingdom was unable to design its own new construction. And the entrepreneur can quickly build another castle that is even better, that he can keep for himself or sell to another rival kingdom.

In *Good to Great: Why Some Companies Make the Leap...And Others Don't,* author Jim Collins says, "The purpose of bureaucracy is to compensate for incompetence and lack of discipline—a problem that largely goes away if you have the right people in the first place. Most companies build their bureaucratic rules to manage the small percentage of wrong people on the bus, which in turn drives away the right people on the bus, which then increases the percentage of wrong people on the bus, which increases the need for more bureaucracy to compensate for incompetence and lack of discipline, which then further drives the right people away, and so forth."[2]

The three most political environments are probably government, large corporations, and Hollywood. Stephen H. Zades, founder of Odyssey Network, a strategy and brand consulting company, interviewed actor/director/entrepreneur Robert Redford.

"The innovation right now in business—as far as I can tell—is coming out of paper and air," said Redford. "The signs are everywhere. The collapsing of certain corporate structures, the mergers, the consolidation that was supposed to beef up profit are clearly, by and large, not working.... If you create an atmosphere of freedom, where people aren't afraid someone will steal their ideas, they engage with each other, they help one another."[3]

Are entrepreneurs leaving because their freedom and ideas are threatened, or because the corporate hangers-on are threatened by entrepreneurs?

The Bureau of Labor Statistics reports that almost seven out of 10 American workers don't like their jobs. Medical records show that more heart attacks happen on Monday morning. Domestic abuse is highest on Sunday night when workers are doped with anxiety about tomorrow's work routine.

Numerous studies show that entrepreneurs are happier, and that workers who hate their jobs are more likely to be in large companies. Misery loves big companies. Entrepreneurs have chosen to leave the company of miserable people.

Let's review the numbers for small businesses. Small businesses:

- Encompass 99 percent of employers
- Employ 52 percent of private-sector workers, and 38 percent of workers in high tech companies
- Provide about 75 percent of the net new jobs
- Are 96 percent of goods exporters[4]

The pool of great talent, corporations will agree, is limited. For those who have decided that sole proprietorship is not for them, small businesses have the best opportunity to hire the innovative, creative, hardest working who don't want to be the "team players" at the bottom of the totem pole. International work is in small businesses. The majority of *new* jobs next year will be in small businesses. The ability to innovate, to do multiple jobs, to use your whole brain is more likely to exist at a small company—or your own company.

"Start-ups and small companies will continue to absorb a fair amount of talent. The supply of managerial talent is limited. Although the size of the total workforce in the United States will grow a total of 12 percent over the 10 years from 1998 to 2008, the number of 25- to 44-year-olds—the demographic segment that will supply companies with their future leaders—will actually *decline* six percent during the same period."[5]

It's going to get tougher for the large companies as more workers decide they just don't want to be part of their teams. The best and brightest are no longer willing to work for the team when they can work for themselves and their families—in entrepreneurships where they're finally teeming with pride.

I wandered through Imam Khomeini Square in my blobwear, wishing I'd bought an extra head scarf. Dust was in my hair, everywhere. The square was deserted. I looked at the sunstone in the square that said that prayer time had passed and the crowd had gone back to their stalls at the nearby souk, their restaurants, their arts. It was a country of small businesses, and grand mosques. Previously called The *Masjid-i-Shah* (King's Mosque), the Imam Mosque was a beautiful Goliath. The intricate tile designs in a myriad of blue and gold hues that covered the facade changed shades according to the changes in light, with no two tiles the same. In awe, I was reminded that change is inevitable and constant, and that long-standing, grand structures are made up of unique parts. The more special each piece is, the more magnificent is the whole.

The domed ceiling is majestic and you feel quite small, the way you often feel in a large company where the organization overpowers you. There's a spot where you stand and speak upward in the tiniest whisper, and everyone can hear you clearly.

I pictured the future in corporate America if the brain drain continued. The best and the brightest had lost their voices in the huge maze of halls and hierarchies, now deserted. The relative whispers of small businesses will be heard loud and clear by consumers. They'll gather round to see the changes.

The picture of the future is that individuals will decide their own destiny, rather than letting corporate America paint their path. I looked at a billboard that said, "The best way to predict the future...is to create it." Picture perfect.

CHAPTER

9

It's a Small World

November 22, 2003. I was wandering in the museum gift shop at the Art Institute of Chicago, waiting to meet a former staff member who had decided to leave corporate America and work for a small business in Cincinnati. I rummaged through a bin full of colorful papier-mâché lacquered boxes that I instantly recognized.

November 22, 1992. "Macaroons. Macaroooooooons. Macaroons."

Another *shikara-wallah* or gondolier was announcing his arrival. It had been quiet, too quiet, and the arrival of a merchant coming to sell his wares was welcome. I forced myself off the intricately carved chaise lounge and walked onto the verandah of the gingerbread-trimmed houseboat. The wooden lattice carvings on the deck rivaled the metalwork on the famed houses of New Orleans. The air was brisk. Dal Lake looked cold. The mountainous backdrop was snowcapped. Breathtaking. My brochure said, "Truly a glimpse of heaven with its soaring peaks, winding rivers and canals, misty lakes, and green flower-filled meadows." Accurate.

The uproar over jobs going to India isn't about the lion's share of jobs being lost; it's about the *type* of jobs. Nobody said "boo" when Radio Flyer announced its little red wagons would be manufactured by blue-collar workers in China. But when Ph.D.s in India covet our programming, software troubleshooting, and customer contact positions, there's a rumble—not of change, but of complaint. Jobs for the best and brightest are going abroad because the best and brightest aren't in America's corporations anymore, although they can still be found in India's. Our companies are overflowing with checklist checkers in process roles at the expense (and demise) of highly skilled labor. Our best and brightest have left our corporations for entrepreneurship. The best and brightest *Indians* are still willing to work for America's corporations—as a stepping-stone. Isn't it funny how the people complaining the loudest about the *best jobs* being done in India for a fraction of the cost are the same people who drove the *best people* who used to do those jobs in the U.S. out of their companies!

Sanjiv, a former executive in a large American software corporation, was reminiscing about his family vacation in Kashmir. "It was the first time we had seen snow," he recalled, as his eyes twinkled with childhood memories of sibling snowball fights and catching snowflakes on tongues. For the corporation, he set up a satellite business in India for the software development. More than half of the Fortune 500 have since outsourced to India.

With his success cutting programming costs in the American headquarters by 80 percent while increasing innovation and productivity by 30 percent (I guess the Indian workers were working instead of politicking), Sanjiv worked steadfastly to develop a new software application for social networking, probably the largest global trend for the next decade. The sales managers, who had hung many a diversity poster, weren't going to let some "iconoclast" (particularly one who had proven abilities) sell something to their clients. They blocked the new software from their clients' ears while engaging ferociously in the number one bully behavior—lying about someone behind his back—with the top brass. Even that wasn't enough; they had to crush Sanjiv. After all, if Sanjiv's social networking software was more profitable than the current offering, they'd no longer be the experts. They really didn't understand social networking, thinking it was just some Facebook and MySpace thing for kids. They whispered about how hiring Indians at the expense of American jobs would create dissention throughout the company, while in reality, they were creating dissention. And think about all the jobs that would be eliminated if the new software was successful. Why, all the employees (like themselves) on the old dog product might be out of work! They neglected to mention the new jobs created by the increased demand for new software which had hundreds of applications, not only with existing social networks, but with DSL and cable companies e-mail platforms and financial services companies. They didn't currently have clients in those industries. They were afraid, so they set out on a mission to instill fear into others. "If Sanjiv is successful, you'll be out of work," they cried.

Sanjiv ignored the riffraff and concentrated on generating income for the corporation. Software sales remained stagnant because the sales force refused to present the new product to clients. The head of the division didn't press his sales buddies.

Sanjiv did **what the best and brightest do before they leave corporate America. They think of ways to create an autonomous small business within the corporation**, to prove the product sells. Sanjiv asked if he could have 20 employees to sell the software application direct to businesses, instead of through the sales intermediaries. He knew staff who had contacts at prospect companies. Convinced that Sanjiv would fail without their united support, and delighted that this would spell his demise, the sales force agreed with the division leader that Sanjiv could test his proposal.

Not surprising, Sanjiv's new business venture was a huge success, quickly, without the bureaucracy. He had hired 20 innovators—20 brilliant businesspeople, to whom he gave the credit where credit was due. They collaborated fantastically with their Indian counterparts. Each had bigger and better ideas, which were tested. And the bigger and better his separate division got, the more angry and abusive the sales force became.

The beginning of the end was when Sanjiv started receiving awards and accolades from the CEO of the overall corporation. Sales spread rumors of mistakes and failings. There were two minor bugs, which were quickly corrected. But the sales team spent all their time on the phone (which was inverse to the amount of time servicing their clients) talking up a blamestorm about the two bugs. Kill, kill, kill. It was like a scene from *Psycho*.

The sales directors managed to create internal confusion, politicking, and alarm—just what they wanted—because they could never create anything clients or customers wanted. The leaders of the division and corporation decided that the politicking and dissention were too disruptive to the business. The warmongers were a team— real team players. None of them had a range of job skills enabling them to get better jobs elsewhere. They didn't understand social networking or the new platforms, so they had to stick together. Besides, they all did exactly the same thing, and lacked all of the same skills, so none were a threat to the others.

The final episode: Instead of letting go of the warmongers (who had been friends for a long time and had been in his office gossiping day and night), the CEO sent Sanjiv packing, with a great package.

Sanjiv, armed with valuable experience from the corporation, started his own successful company in, of course, social-networking software development. He was inspiring for his professionalism and love of invention—the type of guy corporations should fight over to hire, not fight with.

Sanjiv's abandoned division was dismembered. Two years later, after massive turnover and layoffs (due to lost clients) ensuring that no one could remember Sanjiv's idea and division, the sales managers relaunched Sanjiv's product, marketed it to their clients, and claimed credit for the idea. By then, of course, most of the clients were sick of waiting and already were using a competitor's product. The product failed.

The directors' slicing and dicing had no lasting effect on the resilient Sanjiv, nor on a few dozen other brighter and better employees who left to work with him. It had a lasting impact on the 5,000 remaining employees at the big company who watched it, and their children who listened at the dinner table to horror stories of a-day-in-the-life in corporate America. They thought the bullying of the A students would stop when they reached adulthood. Lost clients, lost business, lost profits eliminated many of the 5,000's jobs, but not their memories.

The tragedy is that the place that should be filled with glorious memories of catching snowflakes, climbing mountains, and building unique snow castles for all the world to see has become the place known for its destructiveness, infighting, and decay. It had all the makings of paradise. Those blinded by brainstorms and blizzards think everyone else is wearing the same blinders. But the visionaries see what they're doing. Live there? They don't even want to visit.

Mary Lou Quinlan, the former CEO of advertising agency N.W. Ayer, where I worked as a consultant, says, "The reason a lot of women aren't shooting for the corner office is that they've seen it up close, and it's not a pretty scene. It's not about talent, dedication, experience, or the ability to take the heat. Women simply say, 'I just don't like that kitchen.'"[1] Quinlan left to start her own consultancy, Just Ask a Woman. She also became a judge on the TV show *American Inventor*.

You don't need to ask women. You can see they're voting with their feet as many men already have. The number of self-employed women in the United States has increased 77 percent since 1983 compared to 6 percent for men. Those who can leave, do.

Americans hate working for big companies, and they're doing something about it. They're leaving.

If you're unhappy, you should, too. Start a business. Find a small business that needs your talent. The best and brightest are going fast, and if you're staying, well...

The fear of jumping ship has been beaten out of the future leaders of America's businesses. What will the future hold for large corporations? The talent shortage will be staggering, recession or no recession, if they don't change, and change now.

States *Fortune* magazine:

> "Today's entrepreneur isn't as much focused on money and power as he or she is 'wildly excited' about an idea and utterly convinced of its success and its ability to change the industry, the world and how people live."[2]

Give entrepreneurs the ability to change the industry, change the world, and change how people live, and they will stay in big companies. They will return! In other words, give entrepreneurs the ability to do what they are doing now—running a business!

So how do we stop or reverse America's corporate brain drain? The solution is obvious and easy. **America's corporate brain drain will cease when:**

- corporations offer people jobs better than those they enjoy when running their own companies
- successful entrepreneurs *replace* those in the leading positions in large corporations

Entrepreneurs and innovators already enjoy these things:

1. Company structured by P&L rather than by process or functional roles
2. Total hiring/firing authority
3. Company run by an innovator and filled with innovators. Innovators who are the majority and in all key roles
4. Company run by a business owner and manager
5. No process roles, working with outside businesses that provide process services
6. Employees causing excessive employee turnover fired
7. Employees causing multiple staff to leave fired
8. Incompetent staff replaced instead of just adding staff
9. Not working with blockers or saboteurs
10. Having the authority and ability to make decisions about products and people, and are accountable for those decisions
11. An environment where inventors and innovation are prized
12. Product development, quality, strategy, and managing projects an integral part of each employee's job

Since entrepreneurs have these things now, they will not return to corporate America until the environment mimics this environment that's making them a lot happier. Give them active ownership of innovation and implementation, rather than just stock ownership, which hasn't kept the best and brightest locked up.

They'd better hurry up because some companies are already starting to woo entrepreneurs back. David Parker, founder of executive-search firm D.P. Parker & Associates in Wellesley, Mass., says, "We see demand for people with proven records of accomplishment in new-product development and commercialization as companies attempt to grow organically rather than by acquisition."[3]

People who can innovate and run a business successfully will increasingly be targeted for employment by big companies, and small.

When large companies have lost their best people, they do the strangest thing. They hire them back, or people just like them, on a temporary basis. And since corporations have lost so many of the best and brightest, it's becoming a common occurrence. The hirers will tell you it's because they're trying to control full-time staff levels. The truth is that the people the big companies encouraged to stay aren't getting the job done right. The free agents they're hiring are the ones with the exceptional business talent who quit.

> Are big companies becoming obsolete?...We see it in the emergence of virtual companies, in the rise of outsourcing and telecommuting, and in the proliferation of freelance and temporary workers. All these trends point to the devolution of large, permanent corporations into flexible, temporary networks of individuals...judging from current signs, it is not inconceivable that it could define work in the 21st century as the industrial organization defined it in the twentieth. If it does, business and society will be changed forever.[4]

Free agents, freelancers, and consultants often receive job offers when on assignment. If they accept, the tenure is short-lived. The reason the company has a freelancer is that it couldn't keep anybody who has those job skills or didn't see the value of hiring a well-rounded specialist before. The manager making the job offer might be the best boss on the planet, but if you worked in a big company, you know the chance of the same person being your manager in a year is slim. The fact that the company didn't think the freelancer's job skill was important enough to fill on a full-time basis instead is a danger sign.

Unable to keep those freelancers and get them to take full-time jobs, large corporations are heading for the last resort. They're begging those who left to come back. The *Chicago Tribune* reported, "The old view of corporate execs—employees who leave for other jobs—was that they were deserters and traitors who must never be spoken of again. The new view: They're a fantastic network.... Particularly in fields where the labor pool is tight, today's ex-employee is seen as tomorrow's current employee." In 2006, EDS said that 7.5 percent of its new hires were former employees.[5]

Used to be that you were warned by your friends not to burn your bridges when you quit. Now companies are the ones worried about their britches burning. Alumni networks of former employees used to be where you went to bitch and snitch. Now companies are treating their alumni to wine and appetizers.[6]

So many deserters claimed that corporate America stinks? "Who cut the cheese?" Now they're ready to go back for another whiff.

The world is changing (thank you, God). It used to be when you said you were a freelancer or consultant, folks felt sort of sorry for you. They thought you were between jobs, praying for a position back in corporate America with them. Now, they envy you. "Must be hard," joked a client. "Going on vacations whenever you want, being your own boss, picking and choosing whom you want to work with." In a word, freedom.

That envy turns into action for many. In fact, 15 percent of the working population are free agents.[7] Workers are queuing up by the thousands to join the army of ones as consultants, temporary staff, and freelancers. The not-so-few, the brave, the proud.

The army is growing. The number of part-time entrepreneurs has increased 500 percent in recent years. One's former colleagues see a happier worker in the person who left the fold to go it alone. The organization men who are hiring the freelancers are usually the ones who are right behind them. Their futures in companies are as fleeting as the freelancers they've contracted. They know that the company they work for doesn't have the talent it needs, and can't or won't get it. They also want to be free—free agents.

> Today's best talent see themselves as free agents, willing and able to move quickly to another company, country, or hemisphere for the right opportunity. Knowing their market value, they welcome new challenges, new adventures, and new experiences (hold on the word "experience"—it is important).[8]

Do most sole proprietors return? Not the best ones. Not the brightest ones. Especially not the ones who spent years getting mauled by bulldogs in big companies. You can't make them an offer they can't refuse. They don't want to come back to the corporate world. They're smart and they know it. But they are willing to do a project or create a solution for corporations on their terms. So you can rent their minds, a piece of their brains, because it makes the big company man believe that the continuing brain drain's not that bad.

They say, "'We want to stay independent. We're having too much fun....' In the end, these entrepreneurs-slash-inventors get to do what they love—dream up ideas all day long and turn some of them into gold. They're having such a good time, they don't want it to end."[9]

Hiring freelancer agents and consultants seems like a great way to "get smart." Remember that the people who still make the final decisions on freelancers' work and what is done with it are the same people who created the brain drain.

Hiring freelancers and contractors, no matter how many, isn't going to stop the brain drain. Putting a few cups of water in a bucket that still has holes doesn't stop the leaking. The best and brightest still leave at the same rate no matter how much water you add. True, water will last longer, but it costs more to keep running for water than to repair the holes. And the newer water never stays in the bucket either. Uncontaminated water is no longer clean when poured into the same pail as sewage. First, empty the bucket. Repair the holes. Then pour. The agents must change for corporations in America to grow.

The elimination of process roles, the hiring of terrific people, better products and services, a happier work environment, the division of the business into a plethora of small companies—all that would happen organically with the replacement of people who can't innovate with people who can.

What we have to know is why our leaders are so unwilling to flush out the people—yes, people (not processes or products)—who *are* the gaps in America's corporate brain drain. Remember, corporations have hired exceptional talent, but they haven't stayed. **It's not whom you *hire*. It's whom you *fire* that stops the brain drain.**

Peter Drucker, in his book *Innovation and Entrepreneurship*, reminds us that his purpose is to tell corporate America that "...innovation and entrepreneurship have to become an *integral* life-sustaining activity in our organizations, our economy, our society. This requires of executives in all institutions that they make innovation and entrepreneurship a normal, ongoing, everyday activity, a practice in their own work and in that of their organization."[10] To stop the best and brightest from leaving, it's necessary to take "integral" to the extreme. To stop the brain drain, we not only have to make innovation integral, but innovators integral.

As soon as I tell HR managers to get rid of the managers in *every* department who do not have a history of innovation, they cry, "But it's impossible to find people who do!" Those HR managers are precisely the ones who should be exited first and prove my point about process roles. "But it's impossible to program the VCR and DVD!" That's why simple instructions are included. But no matter how simple you make it, they're never going to open the instructions at all or ask for directions. Instructions: Finding innovators who own companies is as simple as logging on to the Internet. The U.S. Patent and Trademark Web site at http://www.uspto.gov provides a search engine to find mountains of innovations by industry, by category, by customer segment, etc. The addresses of the inventors are there. You don't have to be Einstein to find innovators who also run companies! Or just google to find small companies that do what you do and provide a *better* work environment than they do. See that wasn't so hard.

Instead of having a bunch of meetings or brainstorming sessions to find the inventor/business owners, corporations better start acting instead of meeting. According to McKinsey's yearlong study, over the next 20 years, talent will be the most important and scarcest corporate resource. Start now and you can get the goodies. Wait a day or two, have a meeting or two, and *adiós*. AlliedSignal gets the picture. It says, "We are competing with start-ups, not [large corporations].[11]

So that's it. All big companies have to do to stop the brain drain is be like small businesses. They need to divide to become a plethora of small entrepreneurships led by empowered innovators—the best and brightest. "The best large companies have learned how to mimic small companies. They create smaller, more autonomous units."[12]

A few large companies such as Asea Brown Boveri and British Petroleum are divided into independent units that transact business and behave as independent companies. In investment banking and consulting, businesses are often structured like "confederations of entrepreneurs, united only by a common brand name."[13] This is the business model of the future. Tomorrow's business landscape will be a nation of confederations of entrepreneurs and small-business operators within the corporation—a state of independence. This is the structure that's attractive to the drivers of today's economy and GDP. It's a small world, after all.

We're not talking about setting up autonomous units that are additional. You need to *replace* all existing core business with separate business units, headed by innovators. Setting up separate satellites or separate worlds for innovation is reassurance to the anti-innovators in the main headquarters that their behavior is sanctioned, and innovators are outsiders. Many entrepreneurs only sell their businesses to big companies when they have something bigger and better they want to do. It's a shame big companies with big resources aren't selling their businesses off because they're doing something bigger and better. Corporate America is usually selling its divisions when it's cash poor or getting slammed by Wall Street for not having a strategy—that is, not having significant new ways to compete. If you believe that success can be achieved by buying innovation or setting up satellite product development divisions, you will soon come crashing back to earth.

Rather than push one old snowball back up the hill and make it more cumbersome, it's better to start over with several new snowballs at the top of the hill. The best and brightest will accumulate where the core is solid.

So, do you think corporations will fire lackluster "leaders," eliminate process roles, disengage bullies, reward individual contribution in lieu of teamwork, and replace managers with proven innovators? Do you believe entrepreneurs ever return to large companies? Do you imagine America's corporate brain drain will end?

It's pretty clear why we hate big business. The good news is that the innovators and entrepreneurs believe it can change. *We* have the power to stop America's corporate brain drain. And we should.

"Macaroons. Macarooooooons." I saw the vendor arriving on his floating candy store. He was barefoot despite chilly temperatures in the low 40s. In Kashmir, on Dal Lake, the stores came to you on *shikaras*, a combination of covered canoes and punts. Earlier the pharmacy had floated by, with shampoo, Band-Aids, batteries—

everything you'd expect to find at Walgreens. You simply waved for the store and they'd row to your gangway.

"Helloooo, I am Mr. Macarooooon," said the sun-scorched candyman with a toothless smile. Mmmmmm. Macaroons, fudge, chocolates. The houseboat owner's son, a six-year-old with green eyes as big as saucers, quietly smiled, hoping I'd buy some goodies, and share. I decided to try the fudge and negotiated a fixed rupee amount, whereupon Mr. Macaroon lifted his silver scales in one hand while he slipped chunks of fudge into a bag with tongs with the other. My little friend, who really wanted the famous macaroons, tried to hide his disappointment.

Throughout the day, there was a host of other visiting vendors who should have been called Mr. Kashmiri Carpet, Mr. Fruit-n-Veg, Mr. Woodcarvings, Mr. Toys R Me, and Mr. Marijuana, to provide a continual source of entertainment, or potential entertainment.

I had just flown in from Amritsar, the center of Sikhism. Americans instantly recognize Sikhs for their turbans, hiding their uncut hair (a characteristic of their religion). Sikhs are known for being courageous (OK, it's a generalization, with probably some truth behind it) and all have the surname "Singh," which means "lion." I would soon find out that it wasn't going to be easy to get back to Amritsar.

Everyone in the neighborhood knew when a tourist had arrived. Before 1989, each year 60,000 foreign tourists and over half a million Indian tourists clamored for reservations on the lake. Now it was deserted with barely 100,000 each year, mostly Indians. The economy was devastated. So were the people.

Kashmir has been fought over for as long as anyone can remember. The Mongols, Afghans, Persians, Sikhs, Pakistanis, and Indians have all laid claim to Kashmir at different points in history. And, oh yes, the British.

The Brits built (or rather, commissioned the building of) these cedar houseboats in their image and likeness. During the British Raj, British officers and their families wanted to escape the intense un-English heat during the Delhi and Bombay summers in this scenic paradise. The local maharaja wouldn't allow them to own property. So they designed and had constructed these Victorian palaces on water, complete with wood paneling, chandeliers, floral-patterned damask draperies, fringed lampshades, and exquisite carpets. Just like home.

Along came Mr. Mâché...Mr. Papier-Mâché, on his *shikara*. He asked to come aboard and ascended the gangplank looking very much like Santa with his big bursting cloth bag over his shoulder. There they were, the lacquered boxes, bowls, cups, and coasters, painted in Arabesque designs with gold and metallic blues, greens, and reds. Mr. Mâché must have sold half his stock to the Art Institute.

Depending upon who's counting, between 40,000 and 100,000 people have died in the past few decades in the daily gun battles over who owns Kashmir—the Kashmiris, the Indians, or the Pakistanis. Sometimes one wonders if the fighters are thinking that if they kill all the Kashmiris, that'll solve one problem.

Sure enough, on Day Two in paradise, another ugly gunfight broke out that the Indian "security" forces lost. So they closed the airport, again. Tourists were quarantined. I saw little of Kashmir except the view from the houseboat—phenomenal, but limiting. My return to Amritsar was a memorable 170-mile (274 kilometers) bumpy ride through the hills, waiting for multiple landslides to be cleared—a 14-hour journey. The politicking had little chance of abating. I thought of Dal Lake's shore outlined by formerly majestic cedar houseboats, some dilapidated and half sunk from lack of funds, lack of tourists. My first trip outside the U.S. had been to Mexico. Would this be a future Teotihuacan—like the most populous Aztec city of pyramids that was slowly abandoned...deserted?

At the museum gift shop, I ran my fingers over the smooth lacquer box while scanning other ornaments and artworks—the African mask, rainbow glass fish from Italy, the Syrian inlaid mother-of-pearl backgammon set, a Russian scarf, a green money Buddha from Vietnam, the Indonesian mobile, and the voodoo doll from Bolivia. The walk through the museum and its gift shop was life's journey— like a career. For future adventurers, would it be filled with treasures or with ruins? Would the former intrepid travelers ever come back?

Would the corporate empires of today continue to crumble like Teotihuacan? Or will they change? Can they produce products and services that are like art—exciting, refreshing, invigorating, dynamic? Will they welcome the talent who can do that and eliminate the barriers to seeing things a different way? Can they allow newer artists to paint a different canvas, sculpt a unique future? Can we create an environment where talent and innovation are prized? Will we stop America's corporate brain drain?

Notes

CHAPTER ONE

1. David Lazarus, "Workers Unhappy All Over," *San Francisco Chronicle*, 13 June 2007, retrieved 11 January 2008 from http://www.sfgate.com/cgi-bin/article.cgi?file=/chronicle/archive/2007/06/13/BUG77QE51R1.DTL&type=business.

2. Carol Kleiman, "Job Hatred Called a Crisis for Corporate America," *Chicago Tribune*, 17 March 2005, Section 3, 2.

3. Anne Fisher, "How to Battle the Coming Brain Drain," *Fortune*, 21 March 2005, retrieved 11 January 2008 from http://money.cnn.com/magazines/fortune/fortune_archive/2005/03/21/8254854/index.htm.

4. Lynn Taylor Rick, "Concept of Retirement Changing," *Rapid City Journal*, 17 December 2007, retrieved 11 January 2008 from http://www.rapidcityjournal.com/articles/2007/12/17/news/features/doc473dfc631aa2f168295961.txt.

5. "Yahoo Poll: Most Americans Dream of Starting Business," *Silicon Valley/San Jose Business Journal*, 12 April 2006, retrieved 11 January 2008 fromhttp://bananamarketing.com/blogging/Yahoopoll_Americansdreamofstartingbusiness.pdf.

6. Jeff Cornwall, "Does It Feel Crowded Out There?" *The Entrepreneurial Mind*, Belmont University, retrieved 10 January 2008 from http://forum.belmont.edu/cornwall/archives/003486.html.

7. Jim Hopkins, "Fewer Entrepreneurs Set Up Shop Last Year," *USA Today*, 30 May 2002, retrieved 11 January 2008 from http://www.usatoday.com/educate/entre1.pdf.

8. AARP Working in Retirement Study, AARP Knowledge Management, 2003, retrieved 11 January 2008 from http://www.nasra.org/resources/aarpexecsumm.pdf.

9. Paul Kaihla, "The Next Job Boom," *Business 2.0*, 3 May 2006, 89-90. "College Students Favor Smaller Employers."

10. *Recruiting Trends*, February 2006, retrieved 11 January 2008 from http://www.recruitingtrends.com/issues/43_4/research_corner/154-1.html.

11. "Presenting: The Class of 2001," Harris Interactive, 18 May 2001, retrieved 11 January 2008 from http://www.harrisinteractive.com/news/allnewsbydate.asp?NewsID=292.

12. Stacy A. Teicher, "White-collar Jobs Moving Abroad," *Christian Science Monitor*, 23 July 2003, retrieved 11 January 2008 from http://www.csmonitor.com/2003/0729/p01s03-usgn.html.

13. John C. McCarthy, "3.3 Million US Services Jobs To Go Offshore," Forrester Research, 11 November 2002, retrieved 11 January 2008 from http://www.forrester.com/ER/Research/Brief/Excerpt/0,1317,15900,00.html.

14. Alf Nucifora, "Life's Predictability Keeps Boredom Factor High," *BizJournals.com*, 14 August 2000, retrieved 4 June 2003 from http://seattle.bizJournals.com/extraedge/consultants/shoestring_marketing/2000/08/14/column111.html.

15. Rebecca Theim, "Gearing Up for Activity Ahead," *Employment Management Today, Society for Human Resource Management*, Spring 2002, retrieved 11 January 2008 from http://www.shrm.org/ema/emt/articles/02springtheim.asp.

16. "U.S.: The Heroic Consumer: Down, but Not Out," *BusinessWeek Online*, 27 January 2003, retrieved 4 June 2003 from http://www.businessweek.com/magazine/content/03_04/b3817051.htm.

17. Yuki Noguchi and Amy Joyce, "Bad Job! Done with Tech Careers, New Entrepreneurs Say It's Better to Go Solo," *Washington Post*, 20 July 2002, E01, retrieved 4 June 2003 from http://www.washingtonpost.com/ac2/wp-dyn?pagename=article&node=&contentId=A34733-2002Jul19&notFound=true.

18. Jay A. Conger, "Leading in the New Century: Storm Clouds and Silver Linings on the Horizon," *Leaders Talk Leadership: Top Executives Speak Their Minds* (New York: Oxford University Press, September 2002).

CHAPTER TWO

1. "Careers in Management and the Effects of Restructuring," DBM Australia, 16 March 1998, retrieved 4 June 2003 from http://careers.aol-seek.com.au/editorial/0-6-2_managers_careers.htm.

2. Harley Shaiken, Steven Lopez, and Issac Mankita, "Experienced Workers and New Ways of Organizing Work: Case Study of Saturn and Chrysler Jefferson North," Institute of Industrial Relations, University of California, Berkeley, retrieved 4 June 2003 from http://www.iir.berkeley.edu/ncw/shaiken/page3.html.

3. "People Are and Will Remain the Greatest Asset of Any Business," Dickey, Rush, Duncan, Ansell & Co., P.C., retrieved 4 June 2003 from http://www.drdacpa.com/human.htm.

4. Alex Taylor III, "Honda Goes Its Own Way," *Fortune*, 8 July 2002, retrieved 4 June 2003 from http://www.fortune.com/fortune/print/0,15935,371390,00.html?

5. "The History of Voice Mail," *The 800 Voice Mail Store*, retrieved 4 June 2003 from http://www.800voicemailstore.com/voice-mail-history.htm.

6. Lee Clifford, "Why You Can Safely Ignore Six Sigma," *Fortune*, January 22, 2001, retrieved 4 June 2003 from http://www.fortune.com/fortune/print/0,15935,367825,00.html?

7. "Nonsense, Go Study Quality History," posted by: Jim Parnella, 1 November 2000, Six Sigma Bulletin Board, retrieved on 25 February 2003 from http://www.isixsigma.com/library/content/c020815a.asp.

CHAPTER THREE

1. "Dubai Has 30,000 Construction Cranes," *Gulfnews.com*, 18 June 2006, retrieved 12 January 2008 from http://archive.gulfnews.com/articles/06/06/18/10047703.html.

CHAPTER FOUR

1. Dr. John Sullivan, "Retention—Why Employees Leave," *Chicago Job Resource*, retrieved 12 January 2008 from http://www.chicagojobresource.com/recruiter_retention8.htm.

2. Mark Chediak, "Walmart.Com CEO's Outlook Cheery after Holiday Sales," *San Francisco Business Times*, January 10, 2003, retrieved 12 January 2008 from http://sanfrancisco.bizjournals.com/sanfrancisco/stories/2003/01/13/news column6.html.

3. Lewis Lazare, "Draft-FCB Merger a Dark Day," *Chicago Sun-Times*, 2 June 2006, retrieved 12 January 2008 from http://64.233.167.104/search?q= cache:Lq18vTXdtHQJ:findarticles.com/p/articles/mi_qn4155/is_20060602/ain 164274+draft+fcb+merge&hl=en&ct=clnk&cd=1&gl=us.

4. Wayne Friedman, "P&G Takes $2.4 Million Super Bowl Spot," *AdAge.com*, 1 July 2003, retrieved 29 July 2003 from http://www.adage.com/news.cms? newsId=38206.

CHAPTER FIVE

1. Alan Deutschman, "Change or Die," *Fast Company*, May 2005, Issue 94, page 53, retrieved 13 January 2008 from http://www.fastcompany.com/magazine/94/open_change-or-die.html.

2. Peter F. Drucker, *Innovation and Entrepreneurship* (New York: HarperBusiness, 1985), 151-169.

3. Ibid., 151.

4. Christine Canabou, "Fast Talk: Mother (and Fathers) of Invention," *Fast Company*, February 2004, 46.

5. Elaine Appleton Grant, "Creation Nation," *Inc. Magazine*, October 2002, retrieved 28 January 2004 from http://www.inc.com/magazine/20021001/24701.html.

6. Daryl R. Connor, *Leading at the Edge of Chaos* (New York: John Wiley & Sons, Inc., 1998).

7. Caren Berlin, "How's It Integrating?" *Reveries.com*, retrieved 4 June 2003 from http://www.reveries.com/reverb/research/integrated_marketing/.

8. "Attracting and Keeping Top Employees is Still Difficult," *Human Resource Management Guide USA*, 15 September 2002, retrieved 16 June 2003 from http://www.hrmguide.net/usa/recruitment/attracting_keeping.htm. Source: "Sustaining the Talent Quest: Getting and Keeping the Best People in Volatile Times," Report #1318-02-RR, The Conference Board.

CHAPTER SIX

1. Christopher Oster, "The Customer Service Hall of Shame," *MSN Money*, 26 April 2007, retrieved 16 January 2008 from http://articles.moneycentral.msn.com/SavingandDebt/Advice/TheCustomerServiceHallOfShame.aspx.

2. Cora Daniels, "Mr. Coffee: The Man Behind the $4.75 Frappuccino Makes the 500," *Fortune,* 14 April 2003, retrieved 14 January 2008 from http://money.cnn.com/magazines/fortune/fortune_archive/2003/04/14/340892/index.htm.

3. Barry Petchesky, "Get More Perks From Your Plastic," SmartMoney.com, 1 January 2008, retrieved 14 January 2008 from http://finance.yahoo.com/banking-budgeting/article/104143/Get-More-Perks-From-Your-Plastic.

4. "Shopping as if the Union Mattered," Northwest Labor Press, retrieved 14 January 2008 from http://www.nwlaborpress.org/2005/11-18-05Label.html.

5. Keith H. Hammonds, "Retail's Challenge: The Overstuffed Consumer," *Fast Company*, December 2001, retrieved 17 June 2004 from http://pf.fastcompany.com/articles/2001/12/liebmann.html.

6. Fred Hoyne, "Yoshiaki Shiraishi: Inventor of Satellite Sushi," *Goodbye!*, July 2001, retrieved 10 December 2003 from http://www.goodbyemag.com/jul01/shiraishi.html.

7. Charles Fishman, "The War for Talent," *Fast Company*, August 1998, Issue 16, 104, retrieved 8 January 2004 from http://www.fastcompany.com/online/16/mckinsey.html.

8. Norman Scarborough and Thomas Zimmerer, *Effective Small Business Management: An Entrepreneurial Approach* (Upper Saddle River, N.J.: Prentice Hall, A Pearson Education Company, 2002), 7th edition, Chapter 1.

9. Dale Dauten, "In Corporate America, Some Nice Guys Finish First," *Chicago Tribune*, 2 February 2003, Section 5, 6.

10. *The Keirsey Temperament Sorter II*, Prometheus Nemesis Book Company, 1996-2003, retrieved 12 January 2004 from http://keirsey.com/personality/.

11. Avery Comarow, "Lone Inventors," *U.S. News and World Report*, American Ingenuity Special Report 2003, 58.

12. Joanne Gordon, "My Job, Myself, My Problem?" *Forbes.com*, 24 January 2003, retrieved 8 January 2004 from http://www.forbes.com/2003/01/24/cz_jg_0124work.html.

13. "Leadership IQ Study: Nobody Likes Low Performers," *Leadership IQ News*, 20 June 2006, retrieved 14 January 2008 from http://www.leadershipiq.com/news_lowperformers.html.

14. Robert D. Shelton, "Developing an Internal Marketplace for Innovation," *Prism*, Arthur D. Little, Issue 1-2001, 16-17.

15. Brooke R. Envick and Margaret Langford, "The Five Factor Model of Personality: Assessing Entrepreneurs and Managers," *Academy of Entrepreneurship Journal*, Volume 6, Number 1, 2002, 9, retrieved 8 January 2004 from http://www.alliedacademies.org/entrepreneurship/aej6-1.pdf.

16. Fishman, "The War for Talent," 11.

17. "Rainforest Café in Burlington, MA," *Pricetool.com*, 3 November 2003, retrieved 17 June 2004 from http://www.pricetool.com/content_91482721924.

18. "Brand Impact of Experiential Marketing," Net Results Strategic Partners LLC, November 1999, 13, retrieved 17 June 2004 from www.netresultsllc.com/interviewcopy.PDF.

19. Chris Hansen, "America's Highest Paid Women," *Insight*, Medusa Scientific Corporation, The Home Based Business Council, Inc., 24 September 2003, retrieved 29 December 2003 from http://www.medusaonline.com/hbbc/insight_0009.htm.

20. "Brand Impact of Experiential Marketing," 12.

21. Hammonds, "Retail's Challenge: The Overstuffed Consumer."

22. William F. Gloede, "Diet, Inc.," *American Demographics*, December 2003/January 2004, Volume 25, Number 10, 33.

23. Ibid.

24. "Sam's Club is Making Business Its Business," *NACS Online*, News and Media Center, 29 May 2003, retrieved 19 December 2003 from http://www.nacsonline.com/NACS/News/Daily_News_Archives/May2003/nd0529037.htm.

25. Laurie Wertz, "What's Your Body Language Style," *Third Age*, retrieved 17 December 2003 from http://www.thirdage.com/romance/dating/quiz/body language/.

26. *Dr. Phil*, NBC, Harpo Productions, aired 31 December 2003.

27. Gary Hamel, "Innovation Now: It's the Only Way to Win Today," *Fast Company*, December 2002, 121-122.

28. Ibid, 120-121.

29. Matt Shea, "Deep in the Subway, Nobody Can Hear You Scream," *The Japan Times*, 16 May 2002, 13.

30. Ibid.

31. Alan Solomon, "Why not Japan?" *Chicago Tribune*, 25 January 2004, Section 8, 10.

32. Sheila Riley, "Rise in Foreign Patent Filings in the U.S. Noted," *EE Times Asia*, 16 October 2007, retrieved 16 January 2008 from http://www.eetasia.com/ART_8800483744_480100_NT_10bba180.HTM.

33. Scarborough, *Effective Small Business Management*.

34. CHI Research, Inc., "Small Serial Innovators: The Small Firm Contribution to Technical Change," SBA Office of Advocacy, 27 February 2003.

35. Paul Judge, "Is the U.S. Slipping as an Innovator? New Evidence Says, 'Definitely.'" *BusinessWeek Online*, 16 March 1998, retrieved 31 June 2004 from http://www.businessweek.com/bwdaily/dnflash/mar1998/nf80316e.htm.

36. Inc. Staff, "Reasons for Starting a Business," *Inc. Magazine*, July 1993, retrieved 5 January 2004 from http://www.inc.com/magazine/19930701/3636.html.

37. Tracey Drury, "New Challenges Motivate Female business Owners," *Buffalo Business First*, 16 March 1998, retrieved 5 January 2004 from http://buffalo.bizjournals.com/buffalo/stories/1998/03/16/story6.html.

38. Sumaria Mohan-Neill, "Work Satisfaction and Entrepreneurial Dreams," *Academy of Entrepreneurship Journal*, Volume 6, Number 1, 2002, 19, retrieved 5 January 2004 from http://www.alliedacademies.org/entrepreneurship/aej6-1.pdf.

39. "Paths to Entrepreneurship," Catalyst and NFWBO, 28 February 1998, chart 3, retrieved 5 January 2004 from http://www.nfwbo.org/Research/2-24-1998/2-24-1998_chart3.htm.

40. "Where's the Big Idea?" *reveries.com*, Surveys, 30 June 2003, retrieved 30 June 2003 from http://www.reveries.com/reverb/research/bigideas.

41. Susan Kelly, "Executive Upheaval Rises With Economy," *Chicago Tribune*, 26 December 2003, Section 3, 3.

42. Deutschman, "Change or Die."

43. Diane Downey and Tom March, "Comfortable Fit: Assimilating New Leaders" (New York: Downey Kates Associates, 2003), retrieved 19 January 2004 from http://www.ddassoc.com/executive_talent_article_assimilating_new_leaders.htm.

44. Ibid.

45. F. Nietzsche, "Absolut Innovation," retrieved 22 January 2004 from http://ourworld.compuserve.com/homepages/ESanchez/cr-inno.htm.

46. "Innovative Ways to Unorganize for New Product Success," Fox and Company, Inc., Avon, Conn., 2000.

47. "William J. Bratton - Police Executive of the 20th Century," *Policetalk.com*, 2002, retrieved 26 January 2004 from http://www.policetalk.com/bratton.html.

48. Jeffrey S. Reed, "The Turnaround: How America's Top Cop Reversed the Crime Epidemic," *Amazon.com*, Book Review, 8 July 2002, retrieved 23 January 2004 from http://www.amazon.com/exec/obidos/tg/cm/member-reviews/-/ANLOQJQU5472N/1/ref=cm_cr_auth/002-7790182-7373627.

49. Donna Tappelini, "Digital Crime Fighter," *CIO Insight Page*, 1 June 2001, retrieved 18 June 2004 from http://www.cioinsight.com/article2/0,3959,9827,00.asp.

50. F. Nietzsche, "Absolut Innovation."

51. "Vacuum Cleaner," The Great Idea Finder, retrieved 16 January 2008 from http://www.ideafinder.com/history/inventions/vacleaner.htm.

52. Del Jones, "Xerox CEO: Customers, Employees Come First," *USA Today*, 15 December 2003, 3B.

53. Kelly, "Executive Upheaval Rises With Economy," 1.

54. Shawn Taylor, "Being One's Own Boss the Right Fit For Many," *Chicago Tribune*, 23 November 2003, Section 5, 5.

55. Julie Appleby, "43.6 Million Don't Have Health Insurance," *USA Today*, Money Section, 9 September 2003.

56. Kim Norris, "Number of Uninsured is Rising in Big Firms," *Chicago Tribune*, 26 October 2003, Section 5, 5.

57. "Americans Not Afraid of Loneliness at the Top," *PR Newswire*, Looksmart, 5 August 2002, retrieved 4 January 2004 from http://www.findarticles.com/cf_dls/m4PRN/2002_Augsut_5/90128904/p1/article.jhtml.

58. Ibid.

59. Mohan-Neill, "Work Satisfaction, Entrepreneurial Dreams."

60. Scarborough, *Effective Small Business Management.*

61. "Entrepreneurship," California State University, Los Angeles, College of Business and Economics, 7 January 2004, retrieved 23 June 2003 from http://cbe.calstatela.edu/mkt/entrepre.htm.

62. Lyric Wallwork Winik, "What You May Not Know about Workers in America Today," *Parade* magazine, Intelligence Report, 26 October 2003.

63. Kimberly Palmer, "Putting a Price on Rewards," *U.S. News & World Report*, 24 June 2007, retrieved 16 January 2008 from http://www.usnews.com/usnews/biztech/articles/070624/2credit.htm.

64. Traci Purdum, "Executive Word—Experience Breeds Innovation," *IndustryWeek.com*, 1 March 2003, retrieved 20 June 2004 from http://www.industryweek.com/CurrentArticles/asp/articles.asp?ArticleId=1397.

65. Nicholas Bornoff, *The National Geographic Traveler: Japan*, National Geographic Society, Washington, D.C., 1999, 22, 200.

66. Ibid., 23.

67. Michael A. Lev, "Japan: Economy Has Been Slumping for Thirteen Years," *Chicago Tribune*, 20 July 2003, Section 1, 10.

68. F. Nietzsche, "Absolut Innovation."

69. Ibid.

70. Scarborough, *Effective Small Business Management.*

CHAPTER SEVEN

1. Alan Solomon, "Angkor Wat: A Million Visitors Expected Here by Year's End," *Chicago Tribune*, 12 January 2003, Section B, 11.

2. "Angkor: Introduction," *Go.cambodia.com*, 9, retrieved 13 June 2003 from http://www.gocamdodia.com/angkor/introduction.asp.

3. Frédéric Amat & Rathavary Duong, "Looting," *The Free Angkor Complete Guide*, 3D Printing House, Cambodia, Volume 6, July-December 2002, 24.

4. Manus Brinkman, "Illicit Traffic, Fighting an Uphill Battle," ICOM, Museum Document Association, Volume 5, Number 3: Delivering Diversity; Promoting Participation Conference Proceedings, p. 2, retrieved 13 June 2003 from http://www.mda.org.uk/info5313.htm.

5. Debra Mandel, Ph.D., "Your Boss is Not Your Mother: Nine Steps to Eliminating Office Drama and Creating Positive Relationships at Work," synopsis retrieved 17 January 2008 from http://search.barnesandnoble.com/booksearch/isbnInquiry.asp?ISBN=1932841164.

6.   Teresa J. Rothausen-Vange, Ph.D., "Retention 2010: How to Keep Good employees in a Tight Labor Market," *Minnpost.com*, 10 January 2008, retrieved 17 January 2008 from http://www.minnpost.com/community_voices/2008/01/10/541/retention_2010_how_to_keep_good_employees_in_a_tight_labor_market.

7.   "Attracting and Keeping Top Employees is Still Difficult," *Human Resource Management Guide USA*, 15 September 2002, retrieved 20 February 2003 from http://www.hrmguide.net/usa/recruitment/attracting_keeping.htm,   Source: "Sustaining the Talent Quest: Getting and Keeping the Best People in Volatile Times," Report #1318-02-RR, The Conference Board.

8.   Renee Diehl and Kathy Bote, "Companies Combat Workplace Violence through Online Training," *Houston Business Journal*, 15 March 2002.

9.   Gary Namie, Ph.D., "U.S. Hostile Workplace Survey 2000," Workplace Bullying and Trauma Institute, Bellingham, Washington, retrieved 20 June 2004 from http://bullyinginstitute.org/home/twd/bb/res/surv2000.html.

10.   "In the News—Use These Alarming Statistics in Your Fight against Management Malpractice," *Management Malpractice*, 2005, retrieved 17 January 2008 from http://www.managementmalpractice.com/in_the_news.php.

11.   Lynne McClure, Ph.D., "Violence and Harassment in the Workplace: Top Security Threats and Management Issues," Pinkerton Consulting & Investigations, 2002, retrieved 16 June 2003 from http://www.mcclure assoicates.com/info/threats.html.

12.   Susan Vaughn, "There's a Menace in the Workplace," *Chicago Tribune*, 26 August 2001, Section 6, 7.

13.   Patsie Krakoff, Psy.D., "Bullies in the Workplace," *Advantage,* HR Contents, November 2000, retrieved 20 June 2004 from http://www.pcnorthwest.com/advantage/adva1100.cfm.

14.   Marsha McVicker, "Making Employees Happy, Healthy and Productive—While Reducing Costs: A Challenge Worth Pursuing," a white paper by Errand Solutions, retrieved 17 January 2008 from http://www.errandsolutions.com/dell/docs/whitepapers/WhitepaperMcVicker.pdf.

15.   Namie, "U.S. Hostile Workplace Survey 2000."

16.   Ibid.

17.   Richard Miniter, "Generation X Does Business," *The American Enterprise*, July/August 1997, 38, retrieved 16 June 2003 from http://www.americanenterprise.org/taeja97b.htm.

18.   "Generation 2001—Wave II," Northwestern Mutual Financial Network Survey conducted by Harris Interactive, Study Number 13336, 20 March 2001.

19.   Namie, "U.S. Hostile Workplace Survey 2000."

20.   "Entrepreneurial Ideas Motivate Women to Start Businesses," Center for Women's Business Research, press release, 24 February 1998, retrieved 20 June 2003 from http//www.nfwbo.orb/Research/2-24-1998/2-24-1998.htm.

21.   Namie, "U.S. Hostile Workplace Survey 2000."

22. Lorna Lynch, "Battle Workplace Bullies," *Profitguide.com*, 2001, retrieved 20 June 2004 from http://www.profitguide.com/greatplace/article.jsp?content =653.

23. *Probation Project* Newsletter, California Institute for Human Services, Sonoma State University, Volume 1, Winter 1999, 4, http://www.sonoma.edu/ cihs/html/Probation/PROBnewsletterWi00.pdf.

24. Namie, "U.S. Hostile Workplace Survey 2000."

25. Vaughn, "There's a Menace in the Workplace.," 1.

26. Krakoff, "Bullies in the Workplace."

27. Peter Freiberg, "Bullying in the Workplace is a Violence Warning Sign," *APA Monitor*, American Psychological Association, Volume 29, Number 7, July 1998, retrieved 16 June 2003 from http://www.apa.org/monitor/jul98/ bully.html.

28. Namie, "U.S. Hostile Workplace Survey 2000."

29. Keith H. Hammonds, "Why We Hate HR," *Fast Company*, August 2005, Issue 97, p. 40.

30. Lisa Skolnik, "Up Against It," *Chicago Tribune*, 21 May 2003, Section 6, 1.

31. Namie, "U.S. Hostile Workplace Survey 2000."

32. "Those Who Can, Do. Those Who Can't, Bully," *Bully OnLine*, UK National Workplace Bullying Advice Line, retrieved 20 June 2004 from http://www.bullyonline.org/workbully/serial.htm.

33. Namie, "U.S. Hostile Workplace Survey 2000."

34. Greg Burns, "Brands: A Rose by any Other Name Would Smell Sweeter," *Chicago Tribune*, 23 February 2003, Section 2, 1.

35. "Roamin' Numerals," *Chicago Tribune Magazine*, 19 November 2006, 8.

36. Terri Kabachnick and Ken Banks, "How Do You Live Up to Your Brand Strategy in the Store?" Retailing Smarter 2002, presentation at the University of Florida, 11 June 2002, Data source: TKG Research 2000-2001, survey of 450 executives, managers and supervisors, retrieved 21 June 2004 from http://www.cba.ufl.edu/CRER/ExecEducation/Symposium/Presentations/total rand.pdf.

37. Ibid., survey of 4,000 retail executives and associates from large and mid-size companies.

38. Simone M. Sebastian, "Street Vendor Dies After Attack," *Chicago Tribune*, 22 June 2003, Section 4, 3.

39. John Warner, "Mess with the Bull, You'll Get the Horns," *The Morning News* (online), 15 May 2003, retrieved 26 June 2003 from http://www.themorning news.org/archives/editorial/mess_with_the_bull_youll_get_the_horns.shtml.

40. Ibid.

41. Seth Mnookin, "The Times Bomb," *Newsweek*, 26 May 2003, Volume 121, No. 21, 430-451.

42. Ibid.

43. Associated Press, "Ex-Times Editor Reflects on 'Land Mine,'" *Chicago Tribune*, 24 July 2003, section 1, 2.

44. Jeffrey Zaslow, "Why Jerks Get Ahead," *The Wall Street Journal*, 29 March 2004, R6.

45. Steve Chapman, "The Real Perpetrators of Priestly Sex Abuse," *Chicago Tribune*, 27 July 2003, Section 2, 9.

46. James Janega, "Bishops Applaud Pace of Abuse Plan," *Chicago Tribune*, 22 June 2003, Section 1, 6.

47. Fred Dungan, "Mass Murder and the Postal Purges—An American Tragedy," retrieved 25 August 2003 from http://www.fdungan.com/usps1.htm.

48. Namie, "U.S. Hostile Workplace Survey 2000."

49. Nicolaus Henke and Bernd Uhe, "Talent Strategies: Why Are Companies Ill Prepared?" McKinsey & Company, December 2001, presentation at AESC Conference, retrieved 21 June 2004 from http://www.fia.com.br/PortalMBA/menu/seminarios/pdf/mckinseytalent.pdf.

50. Lauren Weisberger, *The Devil Wears Prada*, (New York: Doubleday, 2003), book jacket.

51. Marc Gunther, "The Kid Stays in the Picture," *Fortune*, 14 April 2003, 136.

52. John Jurgensen, "Psyche! In the Workplace, What Makes a Fake?" *Chicago Tribune*, 25 May 2003, Section 13, 8.

53. "Leaders: Losing the Vote of Confidence," *Brandweek*, 14 July 2003, 19, Source: *U.S. News & World Report*.

54. "The Young and the Truthless," Source: Report Card 2002: The Ethics of American Youth; Josephson Institute of Ethics, *Brandweek*, 14 July 2003, 19.

55. "Caught Cheating," *ABC Primetime Special,* ABC, Inc., aired 29 April 2004.

56. Carol Kleiman, "Don't Work for Your Boss—Work with Him," *Chicago Tribune*, 9 March 2003, Section 5, 1.

57. Tim Field, "The Hidden Cost of a Bully on the Balance Sheet," *Accounting and Business*, 1 February 2002, retrieved 30 June 2003 from http://www.accaglobal.com/publications/accountingandbusiness/315685.

58. "Those Who Can, Do. Those Who Can't, Bully," *Bully OnLine*.

59. "Performance Management and Employee Retention —a Fund Management Approach," Serious Consulting Pty Ltd, 2002, retrieved 30 June 2003 from http://www.seriousconsulting.com.au/download/employee_retention.pdf.

60. Field, "The Hidden Cost of a Bully."

61. Jay McDonald, "Bullying Employees Can Cost Your Company," *Bankrate.com*, 19 October 2001, retrieved 20 June 2003 from http://www.bankrate.com/brm/news/biz/Biz_ops/20011019a.asp

62. Alan M. Webber, "Danger: Toxic Company," *Fast Company*, November 1998, Issue 19, 152.

CHAPTER EIGHT

1. Chris Mullins, "How to Retain Employees in a Boom Economy," *e-NUGGETS*, Above & Beyond, Mullins Media Group, retrieved 21 June 2004 from http://www.abovebeyond.net/v1/employees.htm.

2. Jim Collins, *Good to Great: Why Some Companies Make the Leap...And Others Don't* (New York: Harper Business, 2001), 121.

3. Stephen H. Zades, "Creativity Regained," *Inc. Magazine*, September 2003, 61-68.

4. "Fascinating Facts About Small Business," *Small Business Opportunities Online*, 14 January 2003, retrieved 1 February 2004 from http://www.sbomag.com/hottips.html.

5. Ed Michaels, Helen Handfield-Jones, and Beth Axelrod, *The War for Talent* (Boston: Harvard Business School Press, 2001), 6.

CHAPTER NINE

1. Linda Tischler, "Where are the Women," *Fast Company*, February 2004, 60.

2. "A New Generation of Ambitious, Optimistic Entrepreneurs," America's Young Entrepreneurs Trend Data at-a-Glance, National Association for the Self-Employed, retrieved 21 June 2004 from http://www.nase.org/fey/youngentrepreneurs_stats.htm, original source: *Fortune*, 7 June 1999.

3. "Hiring Outlook '03," *BusinessWeek Online*, 2 January 2003, retrieved 24 June 2004 from http://www.businessweek.com/bwdaily/dnflash/jan2003/nf2003012_8336.htm.

4. Thomas W Malone and Robert J Laubacher, "The Dawn of the E-Lance Economy," *Harvard Business Review*, September/October 1998, 76.5, 144-152, retrieved 24 June 2004 from http://modeling.cstp.umkc.edu/~place/Sections/Organization/org11.txt.

5. Ellen Simon, "Companies Courting Former Employees," *Chicago Tribune*, 24 December 2006, Section 5, 4.

6. Ibid.

7. Jim Harris, Ph.D., "Retention@Netspeed: How to Retain Top Talent in an Internet-Speed Work World," Executive Forum, 18 October 2000, retrieved 25 June 2004 from http://www.executiveforum.net/pdfs/harris.pdf.

8. Jim Harris, Ph.D., "Top Trends Impacting Employee Retention," The Jim Harris Group, Inc., 2000, retrieved 8 January 2004 from http://jamesharrisgroup.com/Article-TenTrendsImpactingEmplRetention.htm.

9. Elaine Appleton Grant, "Creation Nation," *Inc. Magazine*, October, 2002 retrieved 28 January 2004 from http://www.inc.com/magazine/20021001/24701.html.

10. Drucker, *Innovation and Entrepreneurship*, 253.

11. Fishman, "The War for Talent."

12. Ibid.

13. Malone, "The Dawn of the E-Lance Economy.

Index